Let Us Die Like Brave Men

ALSO BY DANIEL W. BAREFOOT

General Robert F. Hoke: Lee's Modest Warrior
Haunted Halls of Ivy
North Carolina's Haunted Hundred: Haints of the Hills
North Carolina's Haunted Hundred: Piedmont Phantoms
North Carolina's Haunted Hundred: Seaside Spectres
Touring South Carolina's Revolutionary War Sites
Touring North Carolina's Revolutionary War Sites
Touring the Backroads of North Carolina's Lower Coast
Touring the Backroads of North Carolina's Upper Coast

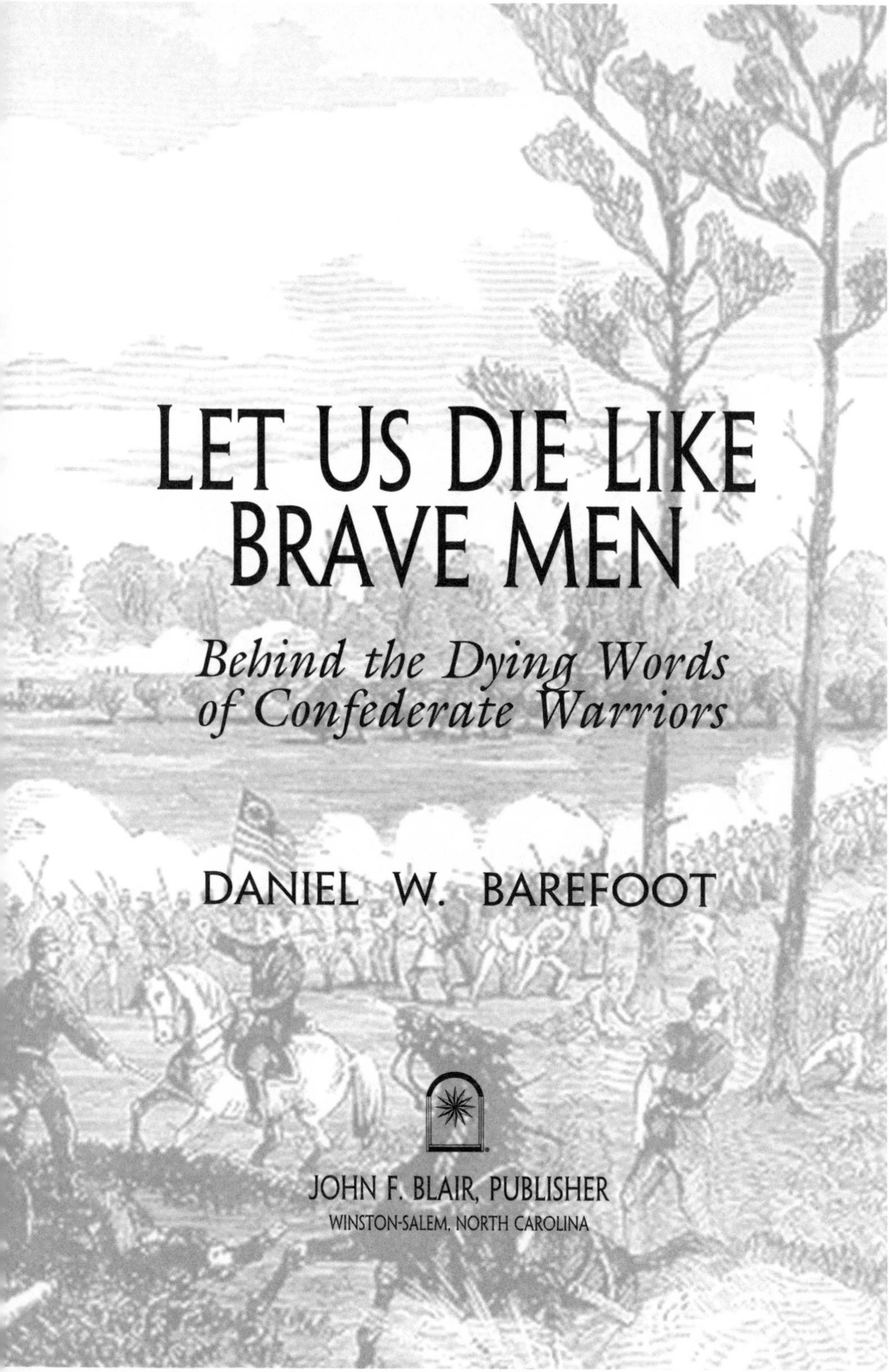

LET US DIE LIKE BRAVE MEN

Behind the Dying Words of Confederate Warriors

DANIEL W. BAREFOOT

JOHN F. BLAIR, PUBLISHER
WINSTON-SALEM, NORTH CAROLINA

The paper in this book meets the guidelines for permanence and durability of the Committee on Production Guidelines for Book Longevity of the Council on Library Resources.

Cover Image
Painting by Don Troiani, www.historicalprints.com
The Boy Colonel *shows Colonel Henry "Harry" King Burgwyn, Jr., at the Battle of Gettysburg.*

Library of Congress Cataloging-in-Publication Data
Barefoot, Daniel W., 1951–
Let us die like brave men : behind the dying words of Confederate warriors / by Daniel W. Barefoot.
p. cm.
Includes bibliographical references and index.
ISBN 13: 978-0-89587-311-8
ISBN 10: 0-89587-311-7 (alk. paper)
1. Soldiers—Confederate States of America—Death. 2. Death—Social aspects—Confederate States of America. 3. United States—History—Civil War, 1861–1865—Social aspects. I. Title.
E545.B37 2005
973.7'42'0922—dc22 2005007429

DESIGN BY DEBRA LONG HAMPTON

Contents

Preface

"The tongues of dying men enforce attention like deep harmony."

William Shakespeare, *Richard II*

This is a book about courage in the face of death. In the pages that follow, you will read the dramatic, often bittersweet stories of fifty-two Confederate soldiers who went to their deaths with almost limitless courage, fortitude, and defiance. These gallant individuals came from every state of the Confederacy, and they ranged in rank from general to private. Some of their names—Stonewall Jackson and Jeb Stuart, for example—are familiar throughout much of the world, while others are virtually unknown.

In every time and in every place in the military history of the United States, Americans have been willing to fight, bleed, and die for causes they perceived to be just and right. The words uttered in their last moments allow us to understand what was foremost in their minds as death called. Indeed, a book could be written about the dying words of American soldiers in every war in which this nation has fought. Why, then, the Civil War, and more particularly the soldiers of the South?

No war cost more American lives than the Civil War. From the terrible bloodshed of that titanic conflict came myriad accounts of soldiers, both from the South and the North, who courageously marched into the face of the enemy and willingly paid the ultimate price for their respective causes. In a speech on Memorial Day in 1884, Oliver Wendell Holmes, Jr., justice of the United States Supreme Court and a hero of the Civil War, stated ever so eloquently, "We believed that it was most desirable that the North should win. . . . But we equally believed that those who stood against us held just as sacred convictions that were the opposite of ours, and we respected them as every man must respect those who give all for their belief. . . . The soldiers of the war need no explanations; they can join in commemorating a soldier's death with feeling not different in kind, whether he fell toward them or by their side."

Despite the debate that continues to rage over why the South fought a devastating war from 1861 to 1865, the Confederate soldier holds an honored place in the annals of American history. His bravery under fire, attention to duty, and determination to fight against overwhelming odds are legendary. His willingness to stand until the bitter end against an enemy superior in both manpower and materiel harks back to the three hundred Spartans of old. His dying words are still celebrated as a manifestation of the qualities of character for which the Confederate soldier has achieved enduring fame and glory.

My interest in the stories behind the dying words of Confederate warriors began almost twenty years ago. At the time, I was working on a sermon to be delivered at my church, First Presbyterian in Lincolnton, North Carolina. One of the stories included in my sermon highlighted the life and death of Major General Stephen Dodson Ramseur, a lifelong member of the same church. The account of the last words of the twenty-seven-year-old Confederate hero, spoken from his deathbed at Cedar Creek, Virginia, in 1864, just a week before his first wedding anniversary and only days after the birth of his only child, brought wet eyes to many in the congregation.

Several years later, I was invited to speak at the rededication of the Confederate monument on the old courthouse grounds in historic Morganton, North Carolina. There, I related to the crowd the dying words of Colonel Isaac E. Avery after he fell in the Confederate assault up Cemetery Hill at Gettysburg on the evening of July 2, 1863. Then, after delivering a speech at the North Carolina Department of Archives and History in 2001, I was afforded the opportunity to view the original bloodstained, handwritten note bearing Avery's dying words.

The stories of Avery and Ramseur are in this book. It was their dying words and those of other Confederate warriors that led me to wonder about my great-great-great grandfathers, one of whom died in action at Gaines Mill, Virginia, in 1862 and another of whom died as a prisoner of war at Elmira, New York, after being captured at Fort Fisher in January 1865. As it is with the descendants of many other fallen Confederate soldiers, I shall probably never know their last words. But thanks to the recollections of the attendants, both friend and foe, who were present in the final moments of the gallant soldiers documented in this volume, we know the utterances that came from the lips of these fifty-two brave men and boys.

Be forewarned: The stories in this anthology may evoke a tear or two. And that prompts the question, Why write a book in which all the main characters die? Granted, each of the accounts herein is tinged with sadness. Yet they manage to celebrate life and offer hope. Though these soldiers fell tragically and prematurely, their voices continue to speak from beyond the grave. Their last words serve as an uplifting example to all Americans who cherish the time-honored ideals of bravery, self-sacrifice, and duty. Truly, their dying words embody the triumph of the American spirit.

Acknowledgments

This book is one that I long dreamed of writing. It represents the culmination of many years of research on the Civil War and the soldiers who took part in that great conflict. Without the assistance and kindness of countless people, *Let Us Die Like Brave Men* would never have become reality.

In the course of my research at university libraries and other repositories located in many of the states where the Civil War was fought, staff members courteously answered my questions and directed me to materials related to my work.

Several individuals merit special mention for their willingness to aid in the creation of this book. Steve Massengill, the very able photographic archivist at the North Carolina Department of Archives and History, was particularly helpful in my quest to locate images. Don Troiani, eminent artist of the Civil War, graciously granted permission for the use of his magnificent work *The Boy Colonel* for the front cover.

Let Us Die Like Brave Men is released as John F. Blair, Publisher, embarks upon its second half-century of producing quality literature. I am indebted to Carolyn Sakowski, the president of Blair, who took a special interest in this book. From personally reading the initial proposal to obtaining permission from Don Troiani for the jacket image, she has carefully guided this project from its inception. Steve Kirk, an extremely talented writer, edited this book as he has all of my others—with great skill, patience, and good humor. His keen mind and sharp eye have smoothed the rough edges of my prose. Debbie Hampton produced a beautiful jacket and designed an appealing layout. Anne Waters, Kim Byerly, Ed Southern, and all of the other staff members at Blair have worked hard to ensure that this volume maintains the tradition of fine books established by Mr. John F. Blair some fifty-one years ago.

This is my tenth book in a ten-year period. All the while, I have practiced law. I also served a five-year stint in the North Carolina House of Representatives. Managing such a hectic lifestyle has required the patience, encouragement, affection, aid, and forbearance of my family.

My mother has continued to express the love and unwavering support that she and my late father extended to me in my every endeavor.

Since the release of my first book in 1995, my daughter, Kristie, has matured from a young teenager into a high-school English teacher. All along the way, she has taken great interest in my literary career.

For this book and the nine others that have preceded it, my dear wife, Kay, deserves limitless praise, gratitude, and credit. When I first proposed writing *Let Us Die Like Brave Men*, Kay greeted the idea with great enthusiasm. And during the course of my work, she meticulously read every word of the manuscript, caught many of my mistakes, and shed genuine tears for the men and boys about whom I wrote.

Kay is my best friend, my soul mate, and my all: she has kept the home fires burning while I was on the road; she has rejoiced in my triumphs and successes and comforted me in my frustrations and disappointments; she has always believed in me, in my abilities, and in my dreams; and her special love and beautiful smile have always been there in the bad times as well as the good.

This book is the realization of a dream. And Kay, most assuredly, is a dream come true.

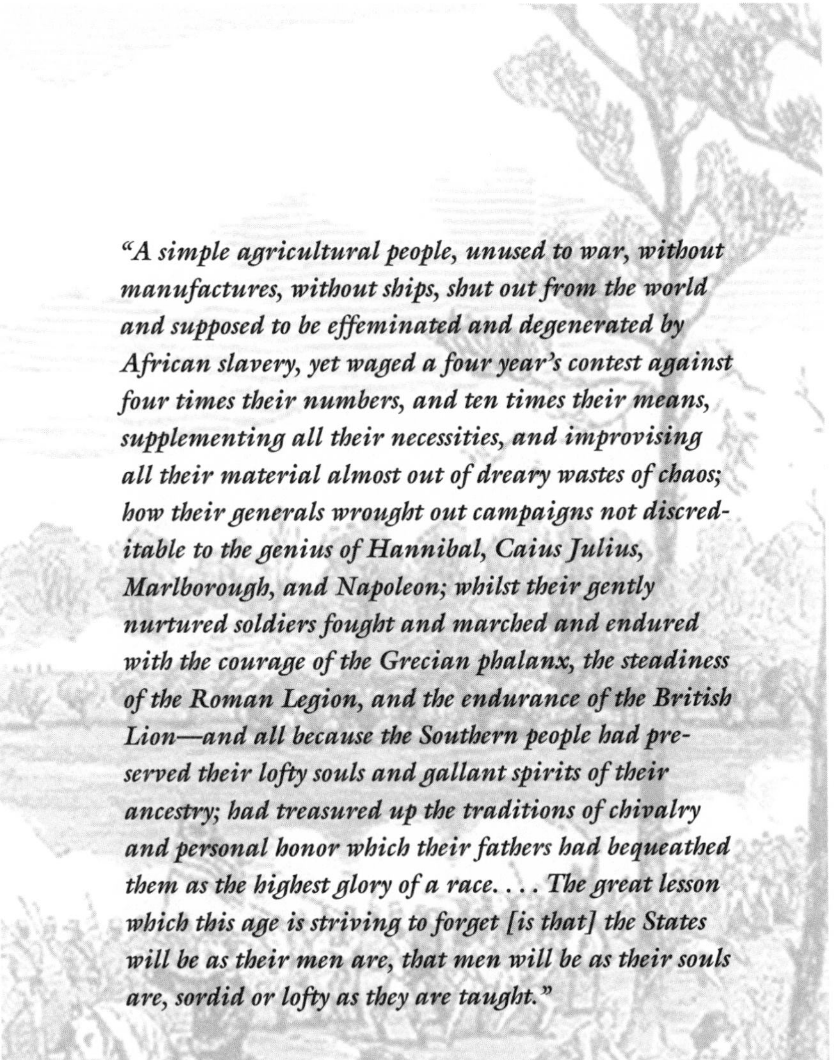

"A simple agricultural people, unused to war, without manufactures, without ships, shut out from the world and supposed to be effeminated and degenerated by African slavery, yet waged a four year's contest against four times their numbers, and ten times their means, supplementing all their necessities, and improvising all their material almost out of dreary wastes of chaos; how their generals wrought out campaigns not discreditable to the genius of Hannibal, Caius Julius, Marlborough, and Napoleon; whilst their gently nurtured soldiers fought and marched and endured with the courage of the Grecian phalanx, the steadiness of the Roman Legion, and the endurance of the British Lion—and all because the Southern people had preserved their lofty souls and gallant spirits of their ancestry; had treasured up the traditions of chivalry and personal honor which their fathers had bequeathed them as the highest glory of a race. . . . The great lesson which this age is striving to forget [is that] the States will be as their men are, that men will be as their souls are, sordid or lofty as they are taught."

Zebulon Baird Vance, United States senator,
North Carolina governor, and
colonel of the Twenty-sixth North Carolina

James F. Jackson, Innkeeper

One Flag, Two Martyrs

Alexandria, Virginia
May 24, 1861

"The flag will come down over my dead body."

In modern America, no issue related to the Civil War has generated more debate than flying or posting the Confederate battle flag, the most widely recognized symbol of the Southern fight for independence. Less familiar to the general populace are the Confederate national flags, a series of three official banners adopted by the Confederate Congress between 1861 and 1865. Affectionately known as "the Stars and Bars," the first national flag of the Confederate States of America had three broad horizontal stripes for the bars—the middle one white and those on the top and bottom red. In the upper left corner of the flag, a blue union with a circle of seven white stars represented the original states of the Confederacy. In Alexandria, Virginia, on May 24, 1861, a deadly confrontation over that flag yielded martyrs for both the South and the North and set the stage for the great war soon to come.

Only bitter sectional differences could have caused the paths of James F. Jackson, a civilian innkeeper and former member of the Virginia state militia, and Colonel Elmer E. Ellsworth, the commander of the Eleventh New York Zouave Regiment, to cross on that spring day in 1861 just across the Potomac River from Washington, D.C.

In the years preceding the war, Jackson had settled in Alexandria to operate an inn and tavern known as the Marshall House. A respected boxer, he sported a striking physique; he was lean, muscular, and six feet tall. His outspoken political beliefs quickly became known throughout the city. One citizen observed of Jackson that "grim, stern, obstinate determination was stamped emphatically on every feature." To the patrons of the Marshall House, he expressed his disdain for Republicans. When Abraham Lincoln was elected president, Jackson openly advocated the secession of the Southern states.

On the other hand, Ellsworth, a handsome New Yorker in his early twenties, was one of the darlings of Lincoln's presidential campaign. Following the election, the new president took Ellsworth with him to Washington as his adviser and bodyguard. So closely associated was Ellsworth with the first family that he shared the measles with the president's young sons, Tad and Willie. President Lincoln openly proclaimed Ellsworth to be "the greatest little man I ever met." Despite his youth, Ellsworth came to the Lincoln administration as an accomplished military leader. His brightly attired Zouave regiment, comprised primarily of volunteers from the New York City Fire Department, arrived in Washington on April 29, 1861, twelve days after the Virginia Secession Convention had voted to secede.

Across the river at Alexandria, the first national flag of the Confederacy was already a fixture atop the Marshall House. James Jackson had not waited for his native state to join the Confederacy to hoist the flag. Rather, as soon as one was fashioned after the flag was officially adopted, the Stars and Bars fluttered above the expansive three-story brick building at the corner of King and Pitt Streets. Jackson boasted that he was the first person to publicly fly the Confederate banner in the state.

As April gave way to May, regiment after regiment followed Colonel Ellsworth's soldiers to Washington. Day by day, the citizens of Alexandria, just seven miles distant, grew increasingly apprehensive about a potential Federal invasion of their city. Jackson's friends, cognizant of the danger to which the hotel owner would be exposed upon the arrival of enemy troops, begged him to leave the city or at least to take down the Southern flag. Jackson thanked them for their concern and then declared, "No, I mean to stay where I am and protect that ensign of liberty even at the risk of my life."

The Marshall House was located at King and Pitt Streets in Alexandria, Virginia. The inn was owned by James F. Jackson, who died there.
Courtesy of Library of Congress

On May 23, when the citizens of Virginia voted three to one to ratify secession, the threat of invasion by Union troops increased dramatically. Through his influence with President Lincoln, Colonel Ellsworth was assured that he and his men would be the first Federal soldiers to set foot on Virginia soil.

At first light the next morning, Ellsworth's Zouaves disembarked from a Federal transport at a wharf on the Alexandria waterfront. Facing only light resistance from a meager force of Virginia militiamen, the New York soldiers, dressed in their distinctive baggy trousers, poured into the center of the city. Colonel Ellsworth, dressed with flair for the big day, wore a magnificent new uniform adorned with a gold medal bearing Latin words meaning, "Not for ourselves alone but for country."

As he made his way up King Street, the Zouave commander became irate when he caught sight of the Confederate flag atop the Marshall House. To Ellsworth, there was but one course of action: The flag must come down.

Minutes later, Federal soldiers surrounded the inn as Ellsworth and several other men scrambled up the winding staircase to the roof.

Meanwhile, James Jackson, alerted to the intentions of his unwelcome guests, grabbed his loaded double-barreled shotgun. As the incensed Virginian stormed up the steps, he was heard to say, "The flag will come down over my dead body."

Once Ellsworth cut down the flag, he began his descent with the prize in his hands. Leading the Yankees down the stairs was Corporal Francis E. Brownell. Then came Ellsworth, followed by Edward House, a reporter for the *New York Tribune*. Ellsworth was jubilantly exclaiming "Behold my trophy!" when the Northerners came face to face with the thirty-eight-year-old Jackson, who was standing on the third-floor landing, his gun aimed at them. Jackson, nodding at his weapon, greeted Ellsworth with but two words: "Behold mine." Corporal Brownell used his musket to push the shotgun away, but Jackson managed to pull the trigger. According to House, Ellsworth "dropped forward with heavy, horrible headlong weight which always comes with sudden death." Jackson fired again, almost simultaneously with Brownell. The second shotgun blast missed its mark, but the proprietor of the Marshall House was hit flush in the face. Though Jackson was clearly dying, Brownell was determined to finish the job quickly and brutally. He repeatedly thrust his bayonet into the body, then sent the corpse cascading down the steps. Turning to Colonel Ellsworth, Brownell and House found his lifeless body crumpled on the Confederate flag he had hauled down. His gold medal had been driven into his chest by the shotgun blast.

News that the Union had lost its first officer in the war quickly spread across the river. President Lincoln, stricken with grief, ordered that an honor guard escort the body of his young friend to the White House, where it lay in state on May 25. Looking down over the corpse, the president cried out, "My boy! My boy! Was it necessary that this sacrifice be made?"

Throughout the North, the name Ellsworth resounded as Yankees rallied to avenge the death. One Northern minister told his parishioners, "We needed just such a sacrifice. Let the War go on."

Back in Alexandria, the coroner noted this in his report about James Jackson: "He was killed in defense of his home and private rights." One Southern newspaper decried, "Jackson perished amid the pack of wolves."

As word spread about his sacrifice in defense of the Confederate flag, the innkeeper achieved martyrdom.

Ironically, a modern hotel stands at the site of the old Marshall House. A plaque on its wall recalls the moment played out by Jackson in 1861: "Not in the excitement of battle but coolly and for a great principle he laid down his life, an example to all, in defence of his home and the sacred honor of his state VIRGINIA."

Pieces of the Confederate flag over which Jackson and Ellsworth fought and died are held by the Smithsonian Institution, located just across the river from the building where the banner rose and fell.

Colonel Francis Stebbins Bartow

The Martyr of First Manassas

Manassas, Virginia
July 21, 1861

"They have killed me; but boys, the day is ours. Never give up the field!"

As the states of Dixie seceded one by one during the first third of 1861, some of the best and brightest men of the South were forced to choose the way they would serve their homeland during the coming war. Would they remain at home in the political arena, or would they take up arms and travel to distant battlefields to fight against the North? By and large, most such men chose to be soldier rather than politician, and a significant number of them gave their lives in the four-year conflict. Francis Stebbins Bartow was one of the first to lay his life on the altar.

Born on September 6, 1816, into a Savannah family of great prestige and affluence, Bartow was educated at Franklin College (now the University of Georgia) and the Yale University School of Law. On the eve of the Civil War, he was an avowed secessionist whose forceful speeches propelled him into the forefront of the effort to convince Georgia to leave the Union. A seventeen-man committee was appointed to draft Georgia's ordinance of secession, and Bartow's name was on the select list.

Georgia joined the Confederacy on January 19. Several weeks later,

Colonel Francis Stebbins Bartow
Courtesy of *Confederate Military History*

Bartow was elected to represent his state at the Provisional Congress of the Confederate States of America, which convened in Montgomery, Alabama. There, he chaired the Committee on Military Affairs. In the course of his work, he offered his own military unit, the Oglethorpe Light Infantry, to President Jefferson Davis for service in the army of the new Southern nation. Tradition maintains that the Savannah company captained by Bartow was the first such combat force tendered to the Confederate cause.

When the constitution of the Confederacy took full effect in April, it contained a provision that proved quite troublesome for Bartow: National government officials, including members of the Confederate Congress, could not serve in military positions as well. After several weeks of deliberation about the matter, Bartow resigned his congressional seat and resumed command of the Oglethorpe Light Infantry, which he promptly took to Virginia, over the vehement objections of Georgia governor Joseph E. Brown.

While stationed in the Shenandoah Valley, Captain Bartow made every effort to prepare himself and his command for combat. In a letter to his family, he noted, "I sleep about five hours in the 24 and very seldom take off my clothes or even my shoes." For his hard work, Bartow was promoted to colonel of the Eighth Georgia on June 21. In that capacity, he served as commander of the Second Brigade of the Army of the Shenandoah.

Just a month after his promotion, Colonel Bartow was ordered to rush a portion of his command, together with the remainder of General Joseph E. Johnston's army, to the aid of General Pierre Beauregard at Manassas. Joel S. Yarborough, one of Bartow's soldiers in the Eighth Georgia, documented the difficult journey to the site where the first major battle of the war was to take place: "We . . . marched all night in order to get there. We waded the Shenandoah River by moonlight, and the scene, which was very beautiful, I recall distinctly. There was a good deal of amusement caused by boys slipping on the rocks when the river was shoally. We had our luggage tied on the ends of our fixed bayonets, and when we slipped and fell into the water everything got wet. We struggled across, however, and went to Piedmont, where we took cars for Manassas, and arriving there, we marched out a few miles and bivouacked. We were put on picket and stayed all night."

At sunrise the next day, July 21, the echo of fire from a signal cannon reverberated up and down the Confederate lines. Yarborough noted, "It struck through us that we were going to have a battle that day." Soon, he and his comrades were on the march again, double-quicking for eight miles until they came within sight of the Henry House, soon to become an important landmark in the battle.

Suddenly, Colonel Bartow, who had been checking on the remainder of the brigade, rode up. Bartow was very nearsighted and did not readily recognize the soldiers. He called out, "Boys, what regiment is this?"

"The Eighth Georgia," the men proudly responded.

The beaming Bartow then exclaimed, "My God, boys, I am mighty glad to see you!"

Yarborough described the reaction of the regiment: "Of course, we were glad to see him, and cheered him long and vigorously, for we all loved him like a father."

Bartow ordered the soldiers to lie down in a corn row running diagonally from the Union lines. In a few minutes, artillery shells began crashing about the Confederate position.

Around nine-thirty that morning, the colonel received an order to deploy the brigade to reinforce Beauregard's threatened left. For several hours, Bartow's men and two other brigades made a determined stand against repeated attacks by two Union divisions. By early afternoon, overwhelming numbers of Federals were able to make their way around the Confederate left. Bartow and his surviving soldiers retreated to the crest of the hill on which stood the Henry House. Just as it appeared the day was lost for the South, Thomas Jonathan Jackson arrived to form his famous wall of soldiers behind the crest of the hill. Inspired by the reinforcements, Bartow grabbed a regimental flag and galloped up and down his lines in a desperate attempt to regroup his battered brigade.

The ferocious combat raged for several hours, neither side gaining the upper hand. In the thick of the fight, Bartow shook off a wound to his leg and survived a nasty fall when his horse was shot from under him. With the outcome of the battle hanging in the balance, the injured colonel limped to another horse, struggled to climb into the saddle, and rode out front alongside the color sergeant bearing the flag of the Seventh Georgia. Then came his order to charge the enemy.

In the midst of the furious Confederate charge down the hill, a Yankee bullet plowed into Bartow's chest near the heart. As life ebbed from his body, the colonel looked up at the devoted soldiers gathered about him. To them, he offered his last words: "They have killed me; but boys, the day is ours. Never give up the field!"

Bartow was right. He was indeed dying, but the day belonged to the Confederate States of America. His Georgians and their fellow Southerners completed the rout of the Federal forces and sent them fleeing to Washington, D.C. The example of Colonel Francis S. Bartow drew widespread attention throughout the South. His death made him one of the first—if not *the* first—martyr for the Confederate cause.

Second Lieutenant William Preston Mangum, Jr.

Earning a Regiment Its Famed Nickname

Manassas, Virginia
July 29, 1861

"As I only had my sword instead of a musket, I fear I did but little in the fight."

With the chasm between the North and the South growing wider and wider in May 1861, thousands of North Carolinians volunteered to aid in the defense of their state as secession became inevitable. From the red-clay soil of the Piedmont region, a hearty group of men comprised primarily of farmers and railroad workers formed the Sixth North Carolina. This well-trained infantry regiment was destined to earn distinction on numerous battlefields from the early moments of the war until the surrender of General Lee at Appomattox.

Among the regiment's best and brightest young soldiers was William Preston Mangum, Jr., a junior officer of Company B. Prior to his military duty, Mangum had attended the state university at Chapel Hill in his native Orange County. On July 11, 1861, two months after his enlistment, the private was promoted to second lieutenant. As the fortunes of war were soon to decree, Mangum would have little time to serve as a Confederate soldier, but his character, example, and sacrifice inspired his regiment to earn its respected nickname, "the Bloody Sixth."

Second Lieutenant William Preston Mangum, Jr.
Courtesy of the North Carolina State Archives

Before Willie Mangum and his comrades had an opportunity to fight the enemy, a pall of gloom—perhaps a precursor of the deaths soon to come—fell over the Sixth North Carolina. On July 10, Willie and his fellow soldiers in Companies B and C served as an honor escort when the body of Governor John W. Ellis arrived by train in Raleigh. Ellis had died unexpectedly in Red Sulphur Springs, Virginia, three days earlier. Less than three months before his death, he had inspired the young Mangum and countless other Tar Heels with his bold refusal to provide the troops requested by Abraham Lincoln to put down the "Southern insurrection." Ellis's fiery words in a telegraph to Lincoln's secretary of war, Simon Cameron, served as a battle cry for Willie and the men of the Sixth North Carolina: "I can be no party to this wicked violation of the laws of the country and to this war upon the liberties of a free people. You can get no troops from North Carolina."

On July 11, the day Willie received his promotion, there was little time to celebrate, for the regiment entrained in Raleigh for an all-night journey to Richmond. A week later, he and his comrades were stationed in the Shenandoah Valley when General Joseph Johnston ordered his army to attention on the night of July 18. Johnston notified the soldiers that large numbers of Union troops were poised to attack General Pierre Beauregard at Manassas. Reinforcements were badly needed to repel the expected assault.

Willie soon found himself engaged in the thirty-mile forced march that took the Sixth North Carolina across the Blue Ridge Mountains to Piedmont Station on the Manassas Gap Railroad. After enduring the hot, grueling trek, the soldiers arrived at the train station only to learn that the train had derailed, thus preventing further movement to Manassas.

In an instant, Colonel Charles Fisher, the commander of the Sixth North Carolina, informed the railroad officials that he was the president of the North Carolina Railroad Company, and that many of his soldiers were railroad men. Through a herculean effort, Willie Mangum and his fellow Tar Heels put the train back on the track. He and the other officers then hurried the men into the boxcars. Their miserable twelve-hour journey came to an end when the regiment arrived at Manassas Junction at eight o'clock on the morning of Sunday, July 21. As the train pulled to a halt, Willie discerned the opening sounds of the Battle of Manassas. While Colonel Fisher was receiving his orders at headquarters, the members of the Sixth North Carolina enjoyed a brief but much-needed rest.

In the early stages of the battle, Federal forces took control of the gently rolling plateau where the Robinson and Henry Houses were located. To protect that strategic position, General Irvin McDowell, the Union commander, positioned Captain James B. Ricketts's battery of six field guns—acclaimed "the pride of the Federalists"—in a field on the far right of his lines. Nearby, Captain Charles Griffin's battery also began to perform deadly work on the Confederates. Both batteries operated from a point just southwest of the Henry House, where most of the action was focused.

Back with his men, Colonel Fisher readied the North Carolinians for their first combat of the war. Concern grew as other Southern troops retreated in confusion. Believing that the day would be lost unless the big guns of Ricketts and Griffin could be silenced, Fisher ordered the Sixth North Carolina to charge the deadly artillery line.

Sword in hand, Willie Mangum led his men into battle as shot and shell rained all about. During the gallant assault by the Tar Heel regiment, every cannoneer in Griffin's battery was killed or wounded. Captain Ricketts was killed in the attack. When the order to retreat sounded, the Union batteries could move only three field pieces to safety.

Once the Sixth North Carolina secured the strategic position, Willie and some of his fellow officers surveyed the carnage. One of their number described what they observed: "The enemy lay piled in heaps, and horses strewn all along. I counted forty horses in a distance of fifty yards. . . . All over the battle-field were strewed the dead and dying."

Amid the jubilation of the triumph, Willie and Major Robert F. Webb stood near a captured cannon. Their excitement was tempered because of the severe losses suffered by the regiment in taking the enemy batteries. Colonel Fisher had been mortally wounded in the charge he had ordered and led.

More tragedy was soon to follow. In the course of his discussion with Major Webb, Willie proved to be an inviting target for a retreating Union sharpshooter. When attendants examined the wounded lieutenant, they believed he would survive, since the ball had struck a Bible in Willie's left coat pocket, which had diverted its direction and blunted some of its force. However, the severe flesh wound under his left arm proved to be worse than first thought.

Willie lingered in great pain for eight days. When he realized he was going to die, he "spoke sentences whose echoes would awake the melody of thanksgiving and gladness in the harps of earth and the harps of glory," according to a friend.

Second Lieutenant William Preston Mangum, Jr., had fought and won his first and only Civil War battle. He died wishing he could have done more. As life ebbed from his body, he looked up at the friends at his bedside and muttered feebly, "Do you think I have accomplished anything for my country? As I only had my sword instead of a musket, I fear I did but little in the fight."

Captain Dabney Carr Harrison
In His Brother's Footsteps

Fort Donelson, Tennessee
February 16, 1862

"Company K, you have no captain now, but never give up! Never Surrender!"

Not every young man of the South stepped forward to volunteer for military service as, one by one, the states of Dixie joined the Confederacy. Some able-bodied Southerners genuinely disagreed with the war, some shirked their duty, and some were occupied in other necessary callings. When his native Virginia went to war in 1861, Dabney Carr Harrison expressed sympathy for the Southern cause and a desire to aid in the war effort as a soldier, but he felt compelled to continue his work as a Presbyterian minister. Nonetheless, after four family members fell in battle in the early days of the war, the Reverend Harrison could no longer restrain himself. He promptly removed his frock and donned the Confederate gray.

Born in Albemarle County, Virginia, in 1830, Harrison was reared in a family that had already etched its name on the honor roll of American history. Two of his ancestors were signers of the Declaration of Independence. After he graduated from Princeton University, he pursued the study of law at the University of Virginia. His tenure as an attorney was extremely brief. Overcome by the desire to enter the ministry, he enrolled at Union

Captain Dabney Carr Harrison
COURTESY OF *CONFEDERATE VETERAN*

Theological Seminary in Richmond. Upon his ordination, the University of Virginia appointed the twenty-seven-year-old Presbyterian minister as its chaplain.

The Reverend Harrison's friends and family members had been away at war but a short time when devastating news made its way home. In just three days in July 1861, four of his close kinsmen fell on the plains of Manassas. First, a cousin, Major Carter Harrison, died in action. Then his mother's only nephews, Holmes and Tucker Conrad, fell on the battlefield side by side, almost in each other's arms. The younger of the two had recently completed his seminary studies and was ready for ordination. But no loss was as great for the Reverend Harrison as that of his brother, Lieutenant Peyton Randolph Harrison.

Dr. William J. Hoge, a friend and fellow minister, noted, "The noble deaths of these young men stirred the soul of Dabney Harrison to its lowest depths. From the beginning of the war he had longed to share the hardships and dangers of his compatriots. Nothing but his sacred office held him back for a moment. But now he hesitated no longer."

When notified of Lieutenant Harrison's death, the minister said calmly and resolutely, "I must take my brother's place." He then directed his attention to raising a full company of infantry. Those soldiers were mustered into service and assigned to the Fifty-sixth Virginia. The Reverend Harrison agreed to an appointment as captain only after being assured by Confederate officials that he could also serve as minister to his troops. "He would not have become a captain, if he could not have remained a minister," Dr. Hoge noted. "He entered the army believing that his usefulness, even as a preacher of God's word, would be increased in that new and hazardous field."

Over the six months that Captain Harrison commanded Company K, he willingly suffered the same privations as his men. His steadfast faith quickly won the respect of his peers. Thomas D. Jeffries, a fellow captain in the Fifty-sixth Virginia, observed, "His pleasing address, classic features, serene and contemplative countenance, frank and cordial nature soon attracted attention and endeared him to all the officers. . . . His example for good permeated the entire regiment."

Early in 1862, Captain Harrison and his men were deployed at Fort Donelson, Tennessee, as part of the brigade of General John B. Floyd. As the Virginians prepared to defend the vital fort during the second week of February, weather conditions on the Cumberland River were miserable. Torrential rain changed to driving snow and sleet when temperatures plummeted.

On Monday night, February 10, just two days before the battle that would determine the fate of Nashville, Captain Harrison expressed his devotion to duty and his faith in a letter to his father: "Oh, how all these adventures, with their perils and deliverances, their privations and blessings, do drive us to our God! . . . I think of my precious wife and little ones, and long for their society and caresses; but I am satisfied that it is right that I should be here, and I await development of His will."

A Federal flotilla opened the battle against the fort with a murderous fire on February 13. During a lull in the fighting, one of Captain Harrison's fellow officers remarked to him, "You ought to be braver than the rest of us."

"Why so?" Harrison asked.

"Because," said the officer, "you have nothing to fear after death."

Following a moment of circumspection, Harrison said, "You are right. Everything is settled, I trust, for eternity, and I have nothing to fear."

On Friday night, February 14, uniforms were freezing on the bodies of the Confederate soldiers when Captain Harrison fell victim to exposure. He was reluctantly taken to the fort hospital.

His men were shocked and delighted when their sickly leader stood before them in the early-morning darkness the next day, eager to lead them into battle. Gradually, the precipitation ended, but the bitter cold remained. In the predawn hours of Saturday, February 15, Harrison led his men in prayer. As the sun cast its first light over the hills on the eastern horizon, the captain's voice offered the words of David, the great Hebrew warrior, in Psalm 27: "'The Lord is my light and my salvation; who shall I fear? The Lord is the strength of my life; of whom shall I be afraid?'"

Once there was sufficient light, the enemy began its approach. Captain Harrison paced up and down his lines, calming his men by saying, "Wait on the Lord; be of good courage, and He shall strengthen thine heart; wait, I say, on the Lord!" When the order came down the line, Captain Harrison led his men in a charge against the Federals. Sword in hand, he exclaimed, "Follow me!"

Moments later, he fell. Three balls had harmlessly pierced his hat, but a fourth had cut his temple, and a fifth had plowed through his lung. For more than an hour, the mortally wounded officer lay helplessly on the battleground while combat continued.

Finally rescued by Confederate soldiers, Captain Harrison was placed on a steamer bound for Nashville. During the voyage, he feebly penned a final note to his father: "I die content and happy; trusting in the merits of my Saviour Jesus; committing my wife and children to their Father and mine."

As the steamer neared the landing at Nashville on Sunday afternoon, Captain Dabney Carr Harrison awoke from an uneasy sleep. With the aid of a staff member, he sat up, then said, "Company K, you have no captain now, but never give up! Never surrender!"

He then closed his eyes, slumped into the arms of his attendant, and followed in his brother's footsteps.

Private Charlie Jackson
His Father's Son

Memphis, Tennessee
April 1862

"Tell them to fight the Yankees as long as there is one left in the country, and never give up! Whenever you fill up the company with new men, let them know that besides their country there's a little boy in heaven who will watch them and pray for them as they go into battle!"

Many fathers and sons took part in the Civil War. Some even fought on opposing sides. But most often, the patriarch and his male offspring donned the uniform of the same army. And it was not unusual for a son to serve under the command of his father. What pride these fathers must have felt as they watched their sons' courage on the battlefield, and what despair they must have experienced as they watched them die. And thus it was with Private Charlie Jackson and his father.

In the early stages of the war, Charlie's father raised a company of soldiers in Memphis and assumed command as its captain. Charlie, a teenager, was allowed to drill with the volunteers. In short order, he mastered the manual of arms, and his father appointed him drill master in the training camp.

When marching orders arrived, Charlie was dismayed that his parents

A drawing of the Battle of Shiloh, where Private Charlie Jackson received his fatal wound
COURTESY OF *FRANK LESLIE'S ILLUSTRATED NEWSPAPER*

insisted he was too young to go off to war with the company. Unwilling to accede to their wishes, he informed his mother and father that he would join another company if he could not march with the soldiers he had trained. Reluctantly, Captain Jackson agreed that his son could serve in his command.

For a time, the company was deployed just across the Tennessee line near the important Confederate rail hub at Corinth in northeastern Mississippi. On Friday, April 4, 1862, came an urgent request for troops as the great showdown at Shiloh, twenty miles distant, grew imminent. When Captain Jackson struck camp, Charlie was asleep. Cognizant of the danger the company was soon to face, he could not bear to wake his son.

Several hours after the march was under way, Charlie awoke, only to discover that the camp had been abandoned. In a flash, he gathered his belongings, grabbed the miniature rifle crafted for him by his father, and set out to catch up with his fellow soldiers. He walked and ran mile after mile until he finally came upon his father and the company just as the men were preparing to take the field at Shiloh. Captain Jackson expressed his displeasure to his son, but he could not mask his admiration and pride.

When the company rushed forward into battle, Captain Jackson was at its head. At his father's side was Charlie. As the fierce fighting neared its zenith, a bullet ripped into Charlie's body. Disregarding his pain and severe loss of blood, he struggled forward, offering fire to the enemy and inspiration to his comrades. Following Charlie's example, the Tennesseans rallied. Then, as twilight shadowed the field, Charlie was wounded a second time. This time, the bullet struck him in the leg below the hip. Unable to walk, the boy soldier was cheering his compatriots from the spot where he had fallen when his father stooped down to care for him. Charlie protested, "Father, don't mind me, but keep on. I'll lie here till you come back." But Captain Jackson would have none of it. He gently gathered his son into his arms and carried him to the nearest field hospital.

At the close of the battle, Charlie was transported back to his home in Memphis. Dr. Keller was called in to treat the wounds and was granted permission to amputate the leg, if necessary. But upon examining Charlie, the physician grew somber. He left the room to disclose the grim tidings to the parents: Charlie would not lose his leg, he would lose his life. Nothing could be done other than to provide medication to lessen his pain in the final hours.

When Dr. Keller returned to Charlie's bedside, the patient posed a question: "Doctor, will you answer me a straightforward question, and tell me the truth?"

The physician hesitated, then replied, "Yes, Charlie, I will; but you must prepare for bad news."

"Can I live?" Charlie asked.

Dr. Keller answered, "No! Nothing can save you now but a miracle from heaven."

Resigned to his fate, Charlie said, "Well, I have thought so myself. I have felt as if I was going to die. Do father and mother know this?"

"Yes. I have just told them," the doctor said.

Charlie directed the physician to send his parents into the room. When the grieving father and mother took seats at either side of his bed, he extended a hand to each of them and began to speak: "Dear Father and Mother, Dr. Keller says I can't live. And now I want to ask your forgiveness for all wrong I have done. I have tried to be a good boy in every way but one, and that was when I disobeyed you both and joined the army. I couldn't help that for I felt as if I ought to be right where you were, Father, and to fight as long as I was able. I'm sorry that I can't fight through the war. If I have said anything wrong or done anything wrong, won't you forgive me?"

His parents could only nod their heads.

Mustering his parting words, Charlie Jackson, ever the soldier, said, "Now, Father, one more thing. Don't stay here with me, but go back to camp. Mother will take care of me, and your services are more necessary in your company than they are at home. I am not afraid to die, and I wish I had a thousand lives to lose in the same way. And Father, tell the boys when you get back how I died—just as a soldier ought to! Tell them to fight the Yankees as long as there is one left in the country, and never give up! Whenever you fill up the company with new men, let them know that besides their country there's a little boy in heaven who will watch them and pray for them as they go into battle!"

Brigadier General Robert Hopkins Hatton

A Grand Final Review

Near Fair Oaks Station, Virginia
May 31, 1862

"Forward, my brave boys! Forward!"

It was the dream of most brigade commanders on the battlefields of Virginia to have their troops reviewed by either the commander of the Army of Northern Virginia or the president of the Confederate States of America. Imagine the thrill of Brigadier General Robert Hopkins Hatton when on May 31, 1862, his brigade received reviews, albeit short ones, from General Joseph E. Johnston—then in command of the Army of Northern Virginia—General Robert E. Lee, and President Jefferson Davis. Unfortunately, Hatton had little time to enjoy the glory of the moment, for he soon led his men into the battle that cost him his life.

Few Confederate generals offered greater verbal inspiration to their soldiers than Robert H. Hatton. He may have learned his magnificent oratorical skills from his father, a Methodist minister. Born in Youngstown, Ohio, in 1836 and reared in middle Tennessee, Hatton began his rise to prominence soon after standing first in his law class at Cumberland University in Lebanon, Tennessee. The brilliant young attorney entered politics and was elected to the Tennessee legislature. In 1857, he lost a race for governor. But two years later, Tennessee voters sent him to the United States House

Brigadier General Robert Hopkins Hatton
COURTESY OF LIBRARY OF CONGRESS

of Representatives, where he spoke eloquently for the preservation of the Union.

As the Southern states seceded one by one in 1861, Hatton came home to Tennessee and continued to espouse his pro-Union stance until it became evident that his adopted state was destined to join the Confederacy. Unwilling to turn his back on Tennessee, he promptly volunteered for military duty and was appointed colonel of the Seventh Tennessee on May 26, 1861. Thus began the tragically short army career of the man described by H. T. Childs, one of his charges, as Tennessee's "grandest, noblest, purest patriot, statesman, and soldier."

After a brief stint of duty at home, the Seventh Tennessee was dispatched to western Virginia. There, in anticipation of his regiment's first major engagement, Hatton delivered an impassioned address wherein he told his troops, according to one observer, "that he would rather that his bones should bleach upon the mountain sides at whose base he stood than ever return to his home with the slightest blemish upon his escutcheon."

During that campaign in the mountains, Hatton developed a warm friendship with General Robert E. Lee. George A. Howard, adjutant of the Seventh Tennessee, noted, "Wherever he was placed Hatton was known to his leaders, and wherever courage, energy, and celerity of movement were requisite Hatton was called for."

In late 1861 and early 1862, Hatton led his men through the harsh rigors of Stonewall Jackson's expedition to Romney, a tiny Virginia mountain town along the southern branch of the Potomac River. By the spring of 1862, he was operating on the Virginia peninsula. His exemplarary leadership over the first year of the war resulted in his promotion to brigadier general on May 23. In a letter written to his wife just five days later, the new general tempered his boundless confidence with words that evoked ominous overtones: "My brigade will move in an hour from its encampment, en route for Meadow Bridge, on the Chickahominy. We go to attack the enemy on tomorrow beyond the river. A general engagement between our forces and the enemy's all along our entire line is expected to ensue. May the God of right and justice smile upon us in the hour of conflict! The struggle will no doubt be bloody. That we shall triumph, and that gloriously, I am confident. Would that I might bind to my heart before the battle my wife and children! That pleasure may never again be granted me."

Two days later, on the eve of the Battle of Seven Pines, Hatton formed his brigade in a close column along the road leading to where the two armies would clash. Darkness was beginning to fall as he rode out in front of the amassed flags blowing in a gentle breeze. Over the course of a rousing five minutes, he delivered what one soldier termed "the most eloquent, soul-stirring speech I ever heard." In closing, Hatton exclaimed, "Just in our rear is our capital city, invested by a vandal horde. Should it be sacked and plundered?" Responding to their beloved general, the soldiers thrust their hats in the air and screamed in unison, "No, never! No, never!"

Superstitious men would have considered the weather at daybreak on May 31 an ominous portent. Dark clouds hid the sun, and torrential rains gorged the Chickahominy, causing its waters to spill into the adjacent fields and forest. Throughout the long, miserable day, Hatton's brigade was held in reserve as the battle raged. Late in the afternoon, the Confederate fortunes were sagging when a courier delivered an order from General Johnston that either the Tennessee brigade or the Hampton Legion should be rushed forward. In an instant, General Hatton was in the saddle. "I'll beat Hampton!" he proclaimed. "Forward, double-quick!" As Hatton hurried the brigade toward the battlefield, the soldiers passed President Davis. In unison, they saluted their admiring commander in chief with a boisterous Rebel yell.

Upon reaching the site of the battle, the brigade met up with Joseph Johnston and Robert E. Lee. Turning to General Hatton, Johnston inquired, "What command is this?"

Hatton responded with pride: "Tennessee Brigade."

"Well, put them right in," Johnston ordered.

Without hesitation, the new brigadier formed his line and enunciated a simple order: "Load!"

As the men prepared their guns for battle, a well-directed Union artillery shell exploded near General Johnston, throwing him from his horse and causing him serious injury. Cognizant that many of his men had observed Johnston fall, and sensing the effect the incident might have on his troops as they were about to stare into the face of death, Hatton galloped to the front of the brigade. D. C. Kelly, one of his soldiers, described the scene: "Mounted upon a splendid horse, which seemed almost inspired with the spirit of the rider, he passed along his line, encouraging the weak and securing the confidence of the most intrepid."

Satisfied that his warriors were ready for the task before them, Hatton sounded the order: "Fix bayonets! Forward, guide center!" Wave after wave of Tennesseans stepped forward. Kelly observed, "I have always thought this was the grandest, sublimest sight I ever witnessed. On we moved in perfect line, our arms gleaming in the sunset glow."

Riding just behind the center colorbearers, General Hatton waved his hat to urge the men forward. Then he pulled forth his sword. Adjutant Howard recollected the moment: "In the uncertain light of that closing day and smoking field his gray gabardine and gleaming sword marked the way for the line which followed him."

After crossing a field, the brigade struggled through a marsh filled with fallen trees and high grass. "Forward, my brave boys! Forward!" Hatton called. He said no more before his horse was shot from under him. Struggling to his feet, Hatton moved forward a few steps until a Minié ball plowed into his head. He died instantly. As his soldiers retreated, they bore with them the body of their fallen leader, who fell at the front of his brigade just eight short days after gaining his general's wreath.

Brigadier General Turner Ashby
COURTESY OF *CONFEDERATE VETERAN*

Brigadier General Turner Ashby
To Kill the Yankee-Killer

Near Harrisonburg, Virginia
June 6, 1862

"Charge men; for God's sake, charge!"

Few officers of the Confederacy received more criticism and praise from Stonewall Jackson, a man of few words, than Turner Ashby. Jackson denounced his fellow Virginian for his lack of discipline and opposed his promotion to general. But Ashby, who commanded much of Jackson's cavalry during the first year of the war, proved to be an outstanding warrior, leading Stonewall to remark, "The Confederacy had no truer or braver soldier, nor Virginia any nobler gentleman."

Ashby's success in the field was attributed to his intense dislike of the enemy. One of his soldiers boasted, "He will quit a meal . . . for a chance at a Yankee. . . . [He] perhaps killed more of them with his own hand than any one man in the state. He is the bravest man I ever saw." His well-deserved reputation as a Yankee-killer made Ashby a marked man and forced Union officers in Virginia's Shenandoah Valley to hunt him down.

Born in Fauquier County on October 23, 1828, Ashby, like many of his fellow officers from Virginia, inherited a legacy of military service. His grandfather had served as an officer in the Revolutionary War and his father as an officer in the War of 1812. But unlike many other Confederate leaders from the Old Dominion, Ashby was not a member of the landed gentry. His widowed mother obtained as good an education as possible for her son from private tutors on the family farm. Fascinated by the outdoors, Ashby grew into an accomplished horseman and chose to become a farmer himself.

In the years leading up to the Civil War, many of his neighbors began to advocate secession. But Ashby, owing to his deep reverence for the role his forefathers had played in the establishment of the United States, advocated the preservation for the Union. At the same time, he organized a cavalry company known as the Mountain Rangers. Composed primarily of Ashby's friends, the paramilitary group protected the area from the rogues who followed the construction crews of the Manassas Gap Railroad. Ashby served as the group's commander.

After abolitionist John Brown raided Harpers Ferry in 1859, Ashby's command was mustered into the Virginia militia and dispatched to the site of the controversy. From there, Captain Ashby went to Charles Town, where he met Stonewall Jackson for the first time and witnessed John Brown's execution.

As a militia officer, Ashby was extremely popular with the men in his command. At the close of 1859, his soldiers presented their captain with a ceremonial sword and a silver service as tokens of their admiration.

Once national division became inevitable, Ashby noted, "If war ensues, we will have the consolation that we have done all in our power to avert it."

When Virginia voted to secede on April 17, 1861, Federal forces promptly put the torch to the massive arsenal at Harpers Ferry. Turner Ashby rallied to the cause of his state and the Confederacy. He convinced Virginia governor John Letcher to send the state militia to Harpers Ferry. Although the arsenal was in ruins when Ashby and his men arrived, they were able to salvage and protect the armory buildings.

While Ashby was stationed there in the spring of 1861, he was assigned to the Seventh Virginia Cavalry under Stonewall Jackson. Well into the summer, Ashby and his raiders enjoyed success as they aided pro-Confederate Marylanders across the Potomac and harassed Federal traffic on the Chesapeake and Ohio Canal and the Baltimore and Ohio Railroad.

On July 21, 1861, Ashby was elevated to lieutenant colonel of the Seventh Virginia Cavalry. For all intents and purposes, he served as the commander of the regiment as it grew in size and operated as an independent part of Jackson's army. General John Imboden, a close friend of Ashby's, recalled, "The career of Ashby was a romance from that time until he fell."

Over the next eight months, Ashby and his horse soldiers raided and scouted the enemy with great success in western Virginia. In the course of operations there, the clever lieutenant colonel sometimes impersonated an itinerant horse doctor to gain vital intelligence.

Stories of Ashby's daring exploits were told around blazing fires in Union camps. Soldiers sat spellbound as they heard about a dashing Confederate officer who covered the countryside on a swift white horse. On ridge or hill, horse and rider would stand alone, almost inviting capture or death. But as soon as Federal soldiers neared their prey, man and animal were gone. As the bewildered soldiers looked about for the phantoms, Ashby and his steed would appear on a distant crest. Yankee officers and men who had never encountered Ashby in the flesh discounted his existence. Surely, they reasoned, he was a Southern myth.

But Ashby was indeed real. One of his soldiers offered a vivid portrait: "I'll describe him. Imagine a man with thick coal black hair, heavy black beard, dark skin, large black eyes, sleepy looking except when the Yankees are in sight. Then they do flash fire. . . . His person is small and slight. Say five feet 8, weight about 130, shape elegant—the best and most graceful rider in the Confederacy."

On March 12, 1862, Ashby shed his title as de facto commander of his regiment and assumed complete, official command when he was promoted to colonel. By the time the first anniversary of Virginia's secession approached a month later, the Seventh Virginia Cavalry had mushroomed to twenty-seven companies under the leadership of its charismatic leader. Triple the size of a normal cavalry regiment, it had reached the numbers of a small brigade.

Painfully aware of Ashby's lax code of discipline and his lack of training in drill techniques, Stonewall Jackson decided to assign a large portion of the regiment to other commands. Outraged by the proposal, Ashby threatened to resign his commission and recruit an independent cavalry. Realizing he could not afford to lose the fiery, energetic colonel, Jackson relented. He explained his decision in correspondence to Robert E. Lee: "If I persisted in my attempt to increase the efficiency of the cavalry it would produce the contrary effect. . . . Colonel Ashby's influence . . . would be thrown against me."

At the height of Jackson's famous Shenandoah Valley Campaign in May 1862, rumors circulated that Ashby was to be promoted to brigadier general. Throughout the campaign, the cavalry colonel had excelled in screening Jackson's main army from attack. Likewise, his scouting operations were legendary. Nonetheless, Jackson vehemently opposed Ashby's promotion: "He has such bad discipline and attaches so little importance to drill, that I would regard it as a calamity to see him promoted." Once again, Stonewall relented, and Ashby became a general on May 23.

Less than two weeks after his promotion, a Union expeditionary force was sent to rid the valley of Ashby. On June 6, as the main body of Jackson's army retreated south and east from Harrisonburg, Ashby's brigade served as its rear guard. At the same time, the First New Jersey cavalry moved out of Harrisonburg with orders to "bag" Ashby. Commanded by Sir Percy Wyndham, a veteran British soldier of fortune, the Federals attempted to take their prey at Chestnut Ridge. Upon catching sight of Wyndham's attack force, General Ashby spurred his horse and galloped forward. After the horse leaped a pair of fences, its rider guided the animal to the center of the Confederate lines. Following their general, the cavalrymen charged the Yankees. In but a few minutes, the skirmish was over. General Ashby emerged with his prize—Colonel Wyndham and numerous other prisoners from the New Jersey detail.

As the captured British colonel was paraded past Ashby's victorious soldiers, they marveled at his appearance. One Confederate soldier recalled of Wyndham, "He was very tall, elegantly dressed, wearing every ornament possible under regulations. His low-topped boots had gold tassels hanging in the front." One of his excited troopers pointed at Wyndham and exclaimed, "Look yonder boys! There is a Yankee colonel!" Wyndham, indignant and embarrassed, scowled at the poorly dressed soldier and screamed, "I am not a Yankee, you damn Rebel fool!" His retort brought an uproar of laughter from the Confederates. Unnerved by the lack of respect, the English nobleman began to curse the crowd. An eyewitness noted, "He swore, O how he swore! The louder he swore, the louder the Rebels laughed."

But on that day, the Yankees had the last laugh. In the evening, a larger Federal force attacked Jackson's rear. Recognizing the seriousness of the assault, Ashby called on the infantry to support his cavalry. Rain and fog hampered visibility as the general, attired in a black slicker, led the foot soldiers into action with a booming voice: "Forward, my brave men!"

In the desperate combat that followed, both sides suffered significant casualties. Ashby's horse was shot from under him, but the general quickly regained his wits. Waving his sword, he yelled, "Charge, men; for God's sake, charge!" Just then, a bullet from the rifle of a Pennsylvania soldier smashed into his heart.

Four of the general's cavalry covered his lifeless body with a gun blanket and carried the corpse to the rear. Their tears revealed the identity of the casualty to their comrades. One of Ashby's men cried out, "We shall miss you mightily, General, we shall miss you in camp, we shall miss you when we go out on scout. But we shall miss you most of all when we go out . . ." Overcome with emotion, he could not continue.

Without question, the most glorious eulogy offered for Turner Ashby came from the great Stonewall Jackson, who had so often criticized the cavalry officer. In his official report on the engagement that cost Ashby his life, Jackson wrote, "An official report is not an appropriate place for more than a passing notice of the distinguished dead, but the close relation which Gen. Ashby bore to my command for most of the previous twelve months will justify me in saying that as a partisan officer I never knew his superior. His daring was proverbial, his powers of endurance almost incredible, his tone of character heroic, and his sagacity almost intuitive in divining the purposes and movements of the enemy."

William Bruce Mumford, Disabled Soldier
Treason or Patriotism?

New Orleans, Louisiana
June 7, 1862

"Do your duty in any position you may hold."

As a consequence of the four years of bloodshed and sectional acrimony that gripped America from 1861 to 1865, the United States acquired many inglorious "firsts." For example, the man said to be the first American citizen tried, convicted, and executed for treason against the United States met his fate during the Civil War. John Brown of Harpers Ferry was not that man. When Brown died on the gallows in 1859, he was executed for treason against the state of Virginia. Rather, William Bruce Mumford, a loyal Confederate, gained the infamous distinction in 1862 when he defiantly accepted the noose in New Orleans rather than pledge allegiance to the United States flag.

Born in 1820 in coastal North Carolina, Mumford received his early education in his native state. As a teenager, he attended college in Mobile, Alabama, and served as a volunteer in the Seminole War. When the United States went to war against Mexico, he resumed his military career, serving across the border as a sergeant in the Third Louisiana Volunteers. A leg injury in 1846 ended Sergeant Mumford's service in the United States Army.

Mumford was among the many Louisianians who rallied to the aid of

William Bruce Mumford
COURTESY OF *CONFEDERATE VETERAN*

their state when it joined the Confederacy. Due to his age and lingering problems with his leg, he was deemed unfit for field duty. Instead, Confederate officials assigned him to an administrative post in New Orleans, where he made his home with his wife and three children.

On April 26, 1862, the Union warship *Pensacola* dropped anchor in New Orleans Harbor. Though the Crescent City was yet technically held by the Confederates, the last of its defenders in gray had already abandoned the port. As the day wore on, a small boat bearing a lieutenant and a contingent of marines was launched from the *Pensacola*. It came ashore at the foot of Esplanade Avenue in the French Quarter.

Acting without orders from Admiral David G. Farragut, the Union landing party quickly proceeded to the old United States Mint, a massive Greek Revival structure in the 400 block of Esplanade. There, they ascended to the roof, removed the Confederate flag, and replaced it with the colors of the United States of America.

An angry crowd gathered in the streets of the French Quarter and watched in disbelief. Among the mob were William Mumford and three of his friends. Unwilling to abide by the change of colors, the four men stormed to the roof and brought the Stars and Stripes down by breaking the mast that held it. When Farragut's fleet observed this, it opened fire on the men, but they made a safe exit from the building with their prize. Throngs of citizens cheered as Mumford dragged the flag through the muddy streets of the city. When the grand parade was over, there was but a scrap of banner left.

Three days later, on April 29, New Orleans officials surrendered to Farragut, and General Benjamin Butler assumed military control of the city. He wasted no time in antagonizing the local citizenry. His demands were onerous: All citizens were to swear allegiance to the government of the United States or depart Federal-held territory with no more than their clothes and fifty dollars.

There would be no such escape for William Mumford, however. On his first day in New Orleans, Butler issued another edict: "I find the city under the dominion of a mob. They have insulted our flag—torn it down with indignity. This outrage will be punished in such manner as in my judgment will caution both the perpetrators and abettors of the act, so that they will fear the stripes, if they do not reverence the stars of our banner."

The four friends were hunted, but only Mumford was captured and brought to "justice" before Butler's hand-picked military commission. On June 5, 1862, Special Order No. 70 was issued, thereby directing that William B. Mumford be executed on Saturday, June 7.

Butler imprisoned Mumford in the custom house while he awaited execution. The prisoner's son, William Jr., was allowed to sleep with his father in the last days. The younger Mumford remembered, "He talked to me much, and I recall vividly his conversations. He told my mother that the little corporal with the buttons up the front of his jacket told him that they intended to offer him the oath of allegiance to the United States, but that he could not take it. I can see my mother now when she put her hands on his arms and said, 'Well, William, if you feel that you must not, then do not take it.' My father simply folded her to his heart and kissed her."

As days melted into hours, William Mumford displayed sterling qualities of character. When his son brought meals, the father directed the boy to take a portion to a sick marine in an adjacent room. That made a lasting impression on the child. "When I asked him why he wanted to give that Yankee anything to eat, he said, 'Why, son, you must always be kind to your enemies; and another thing, that poor fellow is sick and needs it,'" William Jr. recalled.

In the meantime, preparations for the execution were under way. Butler directed that the gibbet project from the peristyle of the United States Mint, just feet below the staff bearing the United States flag.

As the end drew near, Mumford offered words of parting to his son: "You must always be brave and never be afraid to die. You must always be truthful and never lie; none but cowards lie. Do your duty in any position you may hold, but remember that you must be no man's slave."

Federal cavalry and infantry were assigned to control the gigantic crowd that assembled to witness what most locals considered murder. Louisiana governor Thomas O. Moore described the execution: "After condemnation he was brought in full view of the scaffold, his murderers hoping to pall his heroic soul. They offered him life on the condition that he would adjure his country and swear allegiance to her flag, but he spurned the offer. He met his fate courageously and transmitted to his countrymen a fresh example of what men will do and dare when under the inspiration of fervid patriotism."

Benjamin Butler, seemingly unaware that he had made Mumford a Confederate martyr, continued to boast of the affair. After reviewing the matter, President Jefferson Davis issued a proclamation three days before Christmas 1862: "Now, therefor, I, Jefferson Davis, President of the Confederate States of America, in their name do pronounce and declare the said Benjamin F. Butler to be a felon deserving capital punishment. I do order that he be no longer considered or treated simply as a public enemy of the Confederate States, but as an outlaw and a common enemy of mankind."

Fortunately for Ben Butler, he was never forced to face his own brand of justice meted out to William Mumford—or that awaiting him from the Confederacy.

Color Sergeant James Hunt Taylor

The Stained Banner

Cold Harbor, Virginia
June 27, 1862

"I can't carry it any further, Colonel."

Among the bravest Confederate soldiers were the colorbearers. As they stepped forward into battle, those young men and boys were bound by duty and honor to keep the Confederate and regimental flags flying at all costs. Virtually defenseless as they marched into the face of death, they proved to be inviting, and often easy, targets for enemy marksmen. No position in the Confederate army was more revered or honored than the color sergeant. Consequently, despite the extreme dangers, soldiers willingly dropped their weapons to carry forward a flag after it had fallen in battle. Of the many colorbearers who fell at their posts of duty, no name ranks higher on the Confederate roll of honor than James Hunt Taylor.

Like a number of his compatriots in the Southern army, James Taylor descended from a family that had long distinguished itself in state and national affairs. His ancestors were legend in his native South Carolina. His great-grandfather Thomas Taylor was a hero of the Revolutionary War. His grandfather served as the first mayor of Columbia, as governor, and as a United States congressman. And his father was a noted physician in Columbia.

A drawing of the Battle at Cold Harbor, Virginia, on June 27, 1862. This is the battlefield where Color Sergeant James Hunt Taylor was killed.
COURTESY OF *FRANK LESLIE'S ILLUSTRATED NEWSPAPER*

The importance of duty having been instilled in him at an early age, James Taylor stepped forward when the call went out for South Carolina to send volunteers to Virginia at the onset of the war. Soon thereafter, the First South Carolina Volunteers departed the Palmetto State under the command of Colonel (later General) Maxey Gregg. Included in their number was the fifteen-year-old Taylor. On their journey to Virginia, the soldiers carried with them a freshly made South Carolina flag. Today, that banner, preserved by the state of South Carolina, bears the damage of shot and shell and the blood of young James Taylor.

Following several months of fighting on the Virginia battlefields, Colonel Gregg entrusted the proud banner to Taylor's hands. According to Gregg, he appointed the boy as first color sergeant of the regiment "as a reward for meritorious conduct as a soldier." Taylor proudly and confidently carried the large blue-and-white banner into battle after battle. His captain, Dan Miller, described the teenager as "bold, free, and dashing."

In the crucial fight to keep the Federal army away from Richmond, the First South Carolina took to the battlefield at Cold Harbor on June 27, 1862. As the South Carolinians surged forward, they were greeted by heavy artillery fire. Taylor was soon hit. Ignoring his loss of blood and terrible pain, he continued to hurry forward, waving the flag to encourage the regiment to follow. Then he suffered a second wound, this one even more serious. Knocked to the ground by the blast, Taylor mustered enough energy to keep the flag flying from his prone position.

Upon seeing the color sergeant fall, Shubrick Hayne dropped his weapon and took the South Carolina banner from the hands of his fallen friend. Despite his injuries, Taylor managed to stand up and stagger behind Hayne, who took but a few steps before he was mortally wounded. As the flag dropped from Hayne's hands, Taylor took hold of it and attempted to inspire the men as he stumbled in the direction of heavy enemy fire. For a third time, he was wounded, a projectile smashing into his chest. The flag fell from his grasp, and he collapsed upon it, blood streaming from his body.

Lieutenant Colonel Daniel H. Hamilton bent down to attend to his dying warrior. All James Hunt Taylor could manage to say was, "I can't carry it any further, Colonel."

A day or so later, as the victorious Confederates scoured the battlefield to tend to the wounded and bury the dead, a South Carolina second lieutenant was shocked when he came upon the lifeless body of the young colorbearer with his arms folded across his breast. That second lieutenant was James's older brother, William Jesse Taylor. He buried James on the battlefield at the very spot where he had proudly carried the South Carolina banner for the last time.

Private John Frederick Krenson

Just One of the "Beardless Boys"

Mechanicsville, Virginia
June 28, 1862

"Then I cannot leave now."

As deadly attrition diminished the ranks of the Confederate army during the last year of conflict, old men and young boys once held in reserve were pressed into active military service to bolster the sagging fortunes of the Southern war effort. For example, the North Carolina Junior Reserves, a command comprised of twelve hundred soldiers under the age of eighteen, participated in the gallant stand at Bentonville against William T. Sherman's sixty-thousand-man army just after it invaded North Carolina in 1865. But from the outset of the war, teenagers, either in small groups or as individuals, made up the rosters of active combat units of the regular Confederate army. During the first several months of the war, Colonel Francis S. Bartow (see pages 8-11) commanded one of the most famous details of young soldiers. Known as "Bartow's Beardless Boys," they were part of the Eighth Georgia when it was organized in the first quarter of 1861. One boy who had never touched a razor to his face when he marched off to war was Private John Frederick Krenson of Company B. This is his story.

When the call for troops to defend Georgia went out in the early spring of 1861, John Krenson was not yet eighteen. Nonetheless, he was among

A drawing of the Battle of Mechanicsville, Virginia, where Private John Frederick Krenson was fatally wounded
COURTESY OF *HARPER'S PICTORIAL HISTORY OF THE CIVIL WAR*

the first to volunteer for duty in the Oglethorpe Light Infantry in his hometown of Savannah. Not long after he was mustered in for duty, he found himself en route to Virginia, where bloodshed loomed.

Attired in the dashing blue-black uniform with buff trim worn by the Oglethorpes, John marched with pride in dress parades before large crowds in the streets of downtown Richmond. But the glory of those fleeting days in the Confederate capital soon gave way to the grim realities of war. The Eighth Georgia was rushed to Manassas for the first major confrontation between the two armies.

John and the other members of the regiment arrived on the morning of Saturday, July 20. Not long thereafter, General Pierre Beauregard rode up to discuss tactics in the impending battle. Colonel Bartow greeted the Creole commander by saying, "General, I am here with the boys, the Eighth Georgia Regiment, I have promised them they shall be in the opening of the fight." Beauregard responded, "They shall be gratified."

A three-mile march led to the small patch of woods where John and his mates bivouacked for the evening. As darkness descended, Colonel Bartow stood before his young soldiers and addressed them in a fatherly tone, proudly telling John and the others that he had secured them the honor of participating in the opening of the battle and expressing confidence that they would acquit themselves well. Then his voice took on a more somber tone when he said, "But remember, boys, that battle and fighting mean death, and probably before sunrise some of us will be killed."

When the great battle unfolded on Sunday, the Eighth Georgia played a conspicuous role in securing the victory for the Confederacy. But the colonel and his boys paid a heavy price. Bartow was killed, and Private John Krenson was among the critically wounded, having been shot through the lungs.

Battlefield surgeons somehow managed to stabilize the young private. As soon as he could be moved, he was transported to a hospital. After an extended stay there, it appeared he would survive, perhaps owing to his youth. But the physicians felt he would never again be fit for combat, given the serious nature of his wound. To make matters worse, John developed tuberculosis. Over his protests, he was mustered out of service. As soon as he was physically able to travel, he was put on a train bound for home.

On the streets of Savannah, local folks were shocked to see what war had done to the once strapping young man. In physical terms, John was a shell of his former self. For months, the pale, gaunt youngster was observed about town coughing, wheezing, and gasping for breath. But despite his frail condition, he tried unsuccessfully on more than one occasion to rejoin the Confederate army.

News that the Union forces of General George McClellan was preparing to move on Richmond reached Savannah in the late spring of 1862. Unwilling to remain far away from the fight, John started out on foot for Virginia. In the course of the long trek, he subsisted on food that he scavenged or begged. It was just a month short of the first anniversary of the Battle of Manassas when John showed up at the camp of the Eighth Georgia at Price's Farm, five miles from Richmond. Only three hundred yards separated the Confederate line from Union pickets when he arrived.

Over the next few days, while the opposing forces made final preparations for battle, John attempted to assume the role of a soldier. But try as he might, he finally had to accept that the doctors were right—his body could not tolerate the rigors of combat duty. Nevertheless, he would not leave camp. When his friends and former comrades in arms asked why he lingered, he responded with a question: "Do you think the battle will begin soon?" When they answered in the affirmative, John said, "Then I cannot leave now."

During the last week of June, the famous Seven Days' Campaign began in earnest. On Saturday, June 28, 1862, Companies A and B of the Eighth Georgia were ordered forward as skirmishers at Nine Mile Road in Mechanicsville. Without a weapon, John Krenson joined the other soldiers as they swept to the front to do their deadly work. Soon, bullets were flying, and the Georgians began to fall. Amid the terrible firestorm of lead, John grabbed the gun of a downed soldier and rushed to the front ranks. Almost immediately, a half-spent Minié ball struck him. Though the end came in but a few hours, the words of John Krenson echoed up and down the Confederate lines: "Then I cannot leave now."

John's corpse was transported to Savannah for burial with honors. Among his personal effects was a folded, bloodstained paper that he had carried in his breast pocket when he fought his final battle. It was his honorable discharge from the army of the Confederate States of America.

A drawing of the Battle of Malvern Hill, where Corporal James Cal Jones sustained his fatal wound
COURTESY OF *HARPER'S PICTORIAL HISTORY OF THE CIVIL WAR*

Corporal James Cal Jones

The Final Farewell

Richmond, Virginia
July 4, 1862

"Why Father, I would have taken up the flag if I had known that I would be killed on the spot!"

Throughout the Civil War, countless young soldiers unwittingly bade a final farewell to their parents and other family members when they said good-bye and marched off to meet the enemy. Many families never again saw their sons alive. For some, there was never closure because their loved ones either died without being identified on some distant, unknown battlefield or simply disappeared. Others received the dreaded news. Whether the grim tidings came from the daily casualty lists posted in towns throughout the South, from a letter or visit by a surviving friend or comrade, or from a telegraph, parents anguished over not having been with their boys in the last moments of their lives. There were, however, a "fortunate" few who were able to be with their sons as they succumbed. The father of Cal Jones was one such parent.

Less than two weeks after North Carolina joined the Confederacy, eighteen-year-old Cal Jones took leave of his parents and his home in the Cape Fear to volunteer for military duty. His enlistment was for the duration of the war. On June 11, 1861, he was mustered into service as corporal of Company C of the First North Carolina. Although his regiment saw little battle action in North Carolina and Virginia over the ensuing twelve months, Cal was proud to hold the post of colorbearer for his company.

In the last week of June 1862, Robert E. Lee successfully defended Richmond during the Seven Days' Campaign. Assigned to the brigade of Rowell S. Ripley and the division of Daniel Harvey Hill, the First North Carolina took to the field in the first major battle of the campaign at Mechanicsville on June 26. Cal Jones gallantly carried the regimental flag as the Confederates won the day. And he did likewise in the horrific fighting over the next six days.

On July 1, the Confederate offensive came to an end at Malvern Hill, where Cal Jones fought his last battle. Late that afternoon, Major General Hill had all but concluded that his division would be spared from combat when he suddenly heard cheering from the charging Confederates on his right. Recognizing the sound as his signal to spring into action, Hill, manning the center of the Confederate line, promptly ordered his five brigades to attack the Union forces located eight hundred yards away.

Carrying the colors in the vanguard of the charge was Corporal Jones. He and his fellow soldiers were forced to scramble up a gradual incline without cover. Their advance was in the direct path of heavy Federal artillery that belched forth an unrelenting rain of shot and shell. Body parts, rifles, knapsacks, boots, and hats exploded into the air as the big guns blew gaping holes in the Confederate lines. General Hill later remarked, "It was not war. It was murder."

But on that day, Cal Jones and the other Rebel warriors quickly closed ranks and continued up the hill. As they drew closer, the Federal gunners changed to case and canister. The resulting shotgun effect mowed down the onrushing Southerners in piles. Recalling the bloody scene unfolding before him as he watched from the Union lines, General George B. McClellan remarked, "I doubt whether, in the annals of war, there was ever a more persistent and gallant attack, or a more cool and effective resistance."

Only darkness ended the slaughter. Among the fifty-six hundred Confederates who fell in the assault was Cal Jones. Upon learning that the colorbearer had been critically wounded, Marcus D. Herring, one of Jones's fellow soldiers from New Hanover County, North Carolina, hurried to the field hospital. According to Herring, "The hospital was simply a level space of ground, no bunks no seats." With his friend at his side, Cal was clinging to life when a Confederate soldier from Maryland rode up with his clarinet in hand. He looked in the direction of his native state, put the instrument to his lips, and played the melancholy notes of "Maryland, My Maryland." In an instant, the thoughts of each soldier present turned to home.

Litter bearers soon removed Cal Jones to a hospital in the nearby Confederate capital. Meanwhile, the news that he had sustained grave battle wounds was telegraphed to his father in southeastern North Carolina. As quickly as he could, the elder Jones boarded a Richmond-bound train on the Wilmington and Weldon Railroad.

On July 4, the birthday of the divided nation, father came face to face with son at the Richmond hospital. Nothing more could be done for the nineteen-year-old, his father's youngest child. Sensing the end was near, the father looked into Cal's weak eyes and asked, "Son, why did you take up those colors?"

Just before he closed his eyes for the final time, Cal whispered, "Why, Father, I would have taken up the flag if I had known that I would be killed on the spot!"

Captain Hugh Augustus White

Exerting a Wider Influence for Good

Manassas, Virginia
August 30, 1862

"Come on! Come on!"

As war between North and South became inevitable during the spring of 1861, many of the brightest and most talented young men in Dixie heard the call to duty. For the majority, the question was not whether or not they would answer that call but how they would serve the South in its hour of need. When Virginia joined the Confederacy in May, one of its most promising sons, Hugh A. White, donned the gray uniform and took up the sword as a soldier in the famed Stonewall Brigade, against his father's wishes. Though his military career and life came to a tragic end at Second Manassas, he never regretted his decision because, for him, it was the way to exert "a wider influence for good."

Twenty-year-old Hugh White came home to Lexington, Virginia, in May 1861 after completing his second year of study at Union Theological Seminary in Richmond. His hometown was already a beehive of wartime activity. A local military company comprised of professors and students from Hugh's alma mater, Washington College (now Washington and Lee University), was being organized. At its head was his older brother,

A drawing of the Battle of Second Manassas,
on August 30, 1862, in which Captain Hugh Augustus White was killed
SKETCHED BY EDWIN FORBES FOR *FRANK LESLIE'S ILLUSTRATED NEWSPAPER*

James J. White, professor of Greek at the college. Noticeably absent from the local military activity was a noted citizen with whom Hugh had worked to establish a Sunday school for black residents. Thomas Jonathan Jackson, an eccentric professor at Virginia Military Institute—the town's other college—had departed for Richmond a month earlier to prepare the state for war.

Hugh's father, Dr. W. S. White, was the minister of Lexington Presbyterian Church, the church attended by Jackson and many other influential citizens. Dr. White was deeply concerned by Hugh's frail condition. As the young man pondered what course he should follow, his learned father weighed in. Dr. White argued that, owing to his son's education, spirituality, and tastes, he should spend the summer as a colporteur, then return to seminary to complete his third and final year of theological study. Thereafter, he could be licensed as a minister and serve the Confederacy as a chaplain. His father feared Hugh could not survive the privations of active military service.

After listening to Dr. White, Hugh responded, "Father, what you say has much force. But this is to be no ordinary war, and for young men like me to hold back will have a very bad moral effect. The superior numbers and resources of the North will make it necessary for every man in the South, not disabled by age or infirmity, to take part in the work of resistance. I have thought and prayed much over this question . . . and the result is as firm a conviction that I ought once to take part in the defense of my native state, and especially of you and mother, as I ever felt that I ought to preach the Gospel."

Won over by Hugh's maturity and sincerity, Dr. White relented with these words: "Go, my son, and the blessing of God go with you."

On June 8, 1861, Captain James J. White stood in front of the courthouse in downtown Lexington and drew to attention the Liberty Hall Volunteers, his fellow professors, graduates, and students of Washington College. Standing in the ranks as a private was Hugh A. White. In a matter of weeks, some of these soldiers would make the ultimate sacrifice for the South.

As Hugh waited for his baptism under fire, he penned a letter to his parents that manifested his honesty and modesty: "Some hearts, it may be, are now swelling with the desire for military distinction, and some heads becoming dizzy with anticipation of earthly glory. But I confess I am either too cowardly or too stupid to belong to either class. They may win the laurels, provided our cause triumphs."

On the battlefield at First Manassas on July 21, Hugh and his fellow soldiers from Lexington were described as "more than brave men" by their commanding general, who earned his famous nickname, "Stonewall," in the battle. But for Hugh, the victory and the attendant commendation were bittersweet. A dozen of his friends had been killed. "The scenes in which I am now engaged are very sad; yet the taste of victory, though bought by precious blood, is sweet," he wrote his parents. "But to preach would be far better. . . . Brother James and I heartily unite with you in praising the Grace which has spared our lives in this bloody battle. He and I joined in the pursuit beyond the Stone Bridge. . . . The next day we buried our dead. . . . Brother James had religious service over the graves. It is a great victory; but may I never pass through such a scene again. Death and hell may rejoice on the battlefield, but let man be silent. May God who has won this victory for us, now give us peace."

On September 13, Hugh was promoted to sergeant. Over the next six months, he remained true to his military duties. Nonetheless, he also reaffirmed his life's calling. In March 1862, he wrote the folks back home, "Let me hear how the seminary prospers. I cannot be there, but still I am anxious to hear how many are there. The war has put a great barrier across my path, but one which cannot be avoided. It must be crossed. If I get through safely, I shall enter upon the work of the ministry with unspeakable delight. I long to spend my life in the work of saving souls."

The Confederate losses at Kernstown, Virginia, on March 23, 1862, created vacancies in the ranks of the Stonewall Brigade. Hugh White, much to his surprise, was elected captain. He wrote his brother Henry, "Promotion in itself brings neither peace nor happiness, and unless it increases one's usefulness it is a curse. An opportunity is now afforded for exerting a wider influence for good, and if enabled to improve this aright I shall then be happier than before. My life is now given to the army, and will be spent in it, even to the end of the war. But if my life is spared to see the end, and we are successful in our struggle, it will be the delight of my heart to spend the remainder of it in the work of the ministry. I am not fond of the army. Indeed many things in it are hateful to me; but nothing is so much as the invader of my native soil."

As a captain, Hugh played a more conspicuous role in brigade activities. Accordingly, his sterling character came to influence more of his fellow soldiers. One of his lieutenants recalled, "As a soldier and officer he was a model. . . . I have never known one as young as he so faultless." Regarding the captain's bravery on the battlefield, the same junior officer wrote, "In action he was perfectly fearless, yet his courage was controlled by a sound discretion. On such occasions he was possessed with a peculiar enthusiasm—an unconquerable zeal and determination to meet the foe—and consequently he was always seen among those gallant spirits who go fartherest in the direction of the foe. His command never was 'go on,' but always 'come on.'"

While encamped on the banks of the Rappahannock River on Sunday, August 24, 1862, Hugh wrote his last letter to his father. In it, he complained that the constant thunder of artillery and the rigors of camp robbed him of the opportunity to properly observe the Sabbath. He enclosed three hundred dollars with instructions that part of it be used to buy supplies for the cavalry and that the remainder be donated to the Confederate States Bible Society. "I ought now more than ever to seek my strength, my happiness, my all in God," he wrote. "How could I live without Him? With Him no storm can disturb my peace, no danger can come nigh, no harm can befall which will not do me good."

Soon after that, the Stonewall Brigade was rushed to the very place where Hugh White had first witnessed bloodshed in a war that seemed to have no end in sight. On Friday, August 29, the vicious fighting of Second Manassas got under way. When hostilities ended for the night, Colonel W. S. H. Baylor, the acting commander of the Stonewall Brigade, summoned Hugh White to his headquarters. There, Baylor—whose promotion to brigadier general was waiting for him in Richmond—confided, "I know the men are very much wearied out by the battle today, and that they need all of the rest they can get to fit them for the impending struggle of tomorrow. But I cannot consent that we shall sleep tonight until we have a brief season of prayer to thank God for the victory and preservation of the day, and to beseech His protection and blessing during the continuance of this terrible conflict." Hugh White hastily organized a prayer meeting. In short order, most of the men of the Stonewall Brigade and many soldiers from other commands assembled at Baylor's headquarters for what one soldier termed "a tender precious season of worship . . . in full hearing of the enemy."

On the morrow, White and his compatriots found themselves in the thick of the fight. In the midst of an afternoon counterattack by the Confederates, Colonel Baylor grabbed the flag of the Thirty-third Virginia as it fell from the hands of a wounded colorbearer. Anxious for his veteran warriors to press ahead, he shouted encouragement as he stormed toward the enemy. At his side was Captain Hugh White. In but a few moments, a ball crashed into Baylor's body. As the colonel collapsed, Hugh took hold of the flag. Waving the colors in one hand and his sword in the other, he raced to the head of the assault, where he exhorted his comrades to follow him to victory. As he disappeared into a cloud of smoke, his voice rang out a final command for the onrushing Virginians: "Come on! Come on!"

The lifeless body of Captain White was subsequently found face down on the battlefield. His head was resting in his hands, and his pistol and unsheathed sword were at his side. A bullet had pierced his breast. Crumpled near his corpse were the bodies of a number of the soldiers who had attended his prayer meeting the night before.

While reviewing the important victory earned by his army on August 30, 1862, Stonewall Jackson reflected on its terrible cost: "In the second battle of Manassas I lost more than one personal friend. Among them was Captain Hugh A. White. We were members of the same church, and had been co-laborers in the same Sabbath school. . . . In the army he adorned the doctrine of Christ his Saviour. . . . Though his loss must be mourned, yet it is gratifying to know that he has left us a bright example, and that he fell, sword in hand, gallantly cheering on his men, and leading them to victory in repelling the last attack of the enemy upon that bloody field."

Unidentified Confederate Soldier

Praying with a Stranger

Washington, D.C.
September 27, 1862

"I pray the Lord my soul to take; / And this I ask for Jesus' sake."

In human terms, America paid a horrific price during the Civil War. More than four hundred thousand soldiers suffered nonfatal combat wounds during the four years of warfare. Many were treated at makeshift medical facilities in the field and then transported by train or wagon to hospitals in the North and the South. More than two score of these military hospitals were located in and around Washington, D.C.

Save for the subsequent assassination of President Abraham Lincoln, the mood in the "Federal City" was never so somber during the war than in the aftermath of the Battle of Sharpsburg. In the days and weeks following September 17, 1862—the single bloodiest day in American history—thousands upon thousands of wounded soldiers from that Maryland battlefield arrived at hospitals throughout the District of Columbia.

No one in the capital of the United States was more concerned about the suffering wrought by the deadly clash at Sharpsburg than Abraham Lincoln. His visits to Washington-area hospitals to comfort wounded Yankee warriors were already legendary when he set out on a full-day mission in the

President Abraham Lincoln with his son
COURTESY OF *HARPER'S PICTORIAL HISTORY OF THE CIVIL WAR*

early-morning hours of Saturday, September 27, 1862. At each facility, beginning at Georgetown University Hospital, the lanky chief executive sat or knelt at the bedsides of countless men. He held their hands, touched their battle-scarred faces, and offered words of gratitude for their courage, sacrifice, and attention to duty.

Darkness cloaked Washington when President Lincoln made his final visit of the day, at the United States Navy Yard Hospital. Stopping at each bed, he provided solace to soldiers who had shed their blood for the United States. After a time, he came to the bed of a seriously wounded Confederate who had been captured in the battle. According to the president, the soldier was "little more than a child." In a soft, sincere voice, Lincoln extended words of compassion to the boy and then uttered a silent prayer for him before moving on to the next bed.

Upon the completion of the visit, the time was at hand for the president to return to the White House. Noticeably fatigued by the long day, Lincoln made his way to the carriage waiting for him. But before the driver could pull away, a nurse hurried out of the hospital and hailed Lincoln. She informed him that the Confederate lad, who was on the verge of death, had requested to see the president again.

Despite his exhaustion, the president hastened to the bedside of the fast-failing Southern soldier. Looking into his weak eyes, Lincoln asked tenderly, "What can I do for you?"

Each word was a struggle, but the boy managed to mutter, "I am so lonely and friendless, Mr. Lincoln, and I am hoping that you can tell me what my mother would want me to say and do now."

Lincoln fought to maintain his composure. His voice was warm and caring when he said, "Yes, my boy, I know exactly what your mother would want you to say and do. And I am glad that you sent for me to come back to you. Now, as I kneel here, please repeat the words after me."

Clearly, the end was near as the frail patient struggled to repeat the words spoken by the president of the United States: "Now I lay me down to sleep, / I pray the Lord my soul to keep, / If I should die before I wake, / I pray the Lord my soul to take; / And this I ask for Jesus' sake."

The Confederate soldier said no more. With President Lincoln at his side, he closed his eyes and drifted into his final sleep.

Colonel William Peleg Rogers
Honor at All Costs

Corinth, Mississippi
October 4, 1862

"Men, save yourselves or sell your lives as dearly as possible!"

In just four years, the battlefields of the Civil War robbed the South of a generation of outstanding men. Throughout Dixie, doctors, lawyers, teachers, preachers, businessmen, and statesmen left their professions, families, friends, and homes in order to go to war against overwhelming odds. Many of these leading citizens ultimately gave their lives in combat. Their reasons for fighting and dying for the Confederacy were varied. Some saw the battlefield as a place to earn glory for themselves as well as for the South. For others, the decision to march into the face of death was based upon honor. When Colonel William Peleg Rogers led the Second Texas into a deadly storm of shot and shell at Corinth, Mississippi, on October 4, 1862, it was all about honor.

Born on December 27, 1819, while his parents were on a visit to Georgia, Rogers grew up surrounded by privilege and affluence on the family plantation near Aberdeen, Mississippi. Acceding to his father's wishes, he completed medical school in Kentucky. After practicing medicine in Pontotoc County, Mississippi, he embarked upon the study of law, which culminated in his admission to the Mississippi bar in 1842. All the while, he edited a

The monument to Colonel William Peleg Rogers at Corinth, Mississippi
COURTESY OF *CONFEDERATE VETERAN*

newspaper in his childhood town of Aberdeen.

When the United States went to war with Mexico in the 1840s, many Southern men volunteered to fight for their country. Ultimately, the combat experience proved invaluable when they went to war against their Northern brethren. One such soldier was William Rogers. In the summer of 1846, he was appointed captain of Company K of the First Mississippi Volunteers. His commander was the regiment's colonel, Jefferson Davis, who subsequently served as president of the Confederacy.

In Mexico, Rogers excelled as a junior field officer. On September 21, 1846, he won plaudits as the first American soldier to scale the walls of the fort at Monterey. Less than six months later, the twenty-six-year-old captain rendered conspicuous service in the pivotal American victory at Buena Vista. But despite his sterling battlefield record, all was not well. He and Jefferson Davis frequently argued about the deployment of Rogers's troops. Rogers grew embittered when he perceived that the official reports of Davis and General Zachary Taylor failed to accord the honor due him and the men of

Company K. As the war in Mexico drew to a close, Rogers penned this in his diary: "I am more than tired of a soldier's life, I am disgusted with it."

In 1849, no one was more surprised than William P. Rogers when Zachary Taylor, who had been elected president of the United States, appointed him United States consul at Vera Cruz, Mexico. But two years later, false allegations that one of his agents had embezzled funds so outraged Rogers that he resigned his post. He and his family settled in Texas, where he quickly established a reputation as a brilliant defense attorney. In 1857, when Baylor University established its law school, Rogers served as one of the first professors, donating much of his time. Two years later, the Rogers family moved to Houston, the city named for William's close friend and client, Governor Sam Houston. When the Texas Secession Convention was gaveled to order in January 1861, Rogers was on hand as a delegate. When the ordinance of secession was presented on February 1, he affixed his signature to it.

No sooner had Texas left the Union than Rogers offered his military experience to his adopted state. The Confederate War Department offered him command of the First Texas, which was to be sent to Virginia. Rogers's wife, Martha, interceded and convinced her husband to accept a commission as lieutenant colonel of the Second Texas, which was commanded by a West Pointer, Colonel John Creed Moore.

On the eve of the Battle at Shiloh in early April 1862, the Second Texas was rushed to the scene of action. No Southern soldier made a greater sacrifice to arrive in time than Lieutenant Colonel Rogers. News of the looming showdown in Tennessee reached the bedridden officer at his home, where he had been confined for a month on sick leave. Anxious for battle, he rose from his sickbed and hurried to his men, who were described by General D. H. Maury, the divisional commander, as "one of the finest regiments I have ever seen." W. P. Doran, a Texas soldier who witnessed the return of the ailing Rogers, recalled the electricity of the moment: "On the morning of the first day's fight at Shiloh, the regiment was forming a line of battle when Lieut.-Col. Rogers dashed up on his fine horse. . . . He rose from a sick bed to go into battle and went through the two days' fight unwell. The whole regiment gave a Texas yell, which the officers tried to check, because it would reveal the location of our army to Grant's troops."

Colonel Moore and Lieutenant Colonel Rogers saw more than a third of their men fall at Shiloh. In the battle's aftermath, Rogers disclosed his pride in the regiment in a letter to Martha: "The gallantry of our regiment is spoken of by all." For their bravery and leadership at Shiloh, both Moore and Rogers were awarded promotions. Moore became a brigadier general, and the command of the Second Texas devolved to Rogers, its new colonel.

The reputation of the Second Texas was tarnished somewhat when General William Hardee accused the Texans of cowardice at Shiloh. Outraged by the charge—which was never substantiated—Colonel Rogers swore that he would uphold the honor of his men. Over the six months that followed, he remained true to that promise. Throughout that time, his leadership drew the notice of soldiers beyond the ranks of the Second Texas. In a letter dispatched to the Confederate War Department in August 1862, the commanding officers of almost two dozen regiments requested that Colonel William P. Rogers be promoted to major general and be given command of a full division. Rogers was pleased with the overture, calling it "a very high compliment." But he was also firm in the belief that the letter would either be ignored or rejected when it reached the desk of his old nemesis, President Jefferson Davis.

As September melted into October, the time was at hand for Colonel Rogers and the men of the Second Texas to defend their honor with their blood. Anxious to retake western Tennessee and northern Mississippi from the Federals, the Confederate high command dispatched a twenty-two-thousand-man expeditionary force under the command of General Earl Van Dorn to Corinth, Mississippi, an important railroad hub. There, Van Dorn's army, which included the Second Texas, was to destroy or disperse a well-fortified Union force of similar numbers under the command of General William S. Rosecrans.

When the battle opened on October 3, the Confederates enjoyed some early success. But at twilight, the Yankees gallantly withstood a furious assault. Frustrated by the inability of his forces to gain the upper hand, and impatient to achieve a victory on the coming day, Van Dorn ordered his three division commanders to launch a number of frontal assaults against the well-entrenched enemy.

On the morning of October 4, Colonel Rogers was selected to command the vanguard of the attack on Fort Robinett, the sturdy compound that stood in the very center of the Federal lines. John Crane, adjutant of the opposing Seventeenth Wisconsin, described the obstacle Rogers faced as he rode out to take his place at the front of his command: "We had cut down several acres of timber in our front, forming an abatis as we felled the trees, so that all the tops pointed toward the foe. It made a very formidable obstruction."

Throughout the early morning, Rogers and his infantrymen watched and waited as the opposing artillery batteries traded fire. When the big guns fell silent, an eerie lull pervaded the landscape. At ten o'clock, the order was given for the Second Texas and the other regiments of Moore's brigade to advance. Colonel Rogers's men sprang to attention as their commander unsheathed his sword and yelled, "Forward, Texans!" Captain Oscar Jackson of the Sixty-third Ohio described the spectacle that unfolded: "I thought they would never stop coming out of the timber. As soon as they were ready they started at us with a firm, slow steady step. In my campaigning I had never seen anything so hard to stand as that slow, steady tramp. Not a sound was heard, but they looked as if they intended to walk right over us." Other Union soldiers echoed the sentiment. Adjutant Crane recalled, "The sun glistened on their bayonets as they came forward at right shoulder shift in perfect order, a grand but terrible sight." Brigadier General David S. Stanley noted, "Should God spare me to see many battles, I never expect to see a more grand charge."

In the heat and humidity of the ninety-degree day, no officer displayed greater valor and composure than the colonel of the Second Texas. Adjutant Crane recalled Rogers's bearing as he led his soldiers toward the fort: "At their head, in front of the center, rode the commander, a man of fine physique, in the prime of life, quiet and cool, as though he were taking his brigade on a drill."

Suddenly, the Federal lines erupted with a murderous artillery barrage against the oncoming Confederates. Lieutenant Charles Labuzan of the Forty-second Alabama—the regiment marching alongside the Second Texas—remembered, "We were met by a perfect storm of grape, canister, cannon balls, and Minié balls. Oh God! I have never seen the like! The men fell like grass." As Rogers and his Confederates struggled to make their way through the treacherous abatis, they were greeted by an onslaught of infantry fire. Lieutenant Labuzan described the grim scene: "I saw men, running at full speed, stop suddenly and fall upon their faces, with their brains scattered all around. Others, with legs and arms cut off, shrieking with agony. The ground was literally strewn with mangled corpses. Ahead was one continuous blaze."

At the abatis, realizing he could no longer use his horse, Colonel Rogers dismounted. With Captain George Foster of the Forty-second Alabama at his side, he made his way toward the breastworks of Fort Robinett, his pistol in one hand and the colors of the Second Texas in the other. Inspired by the valor of their leader, the surviving Texans followed Rogers as he scrambled up the work and planted the regimental flag on the parapet. As the Union defenders began to flee, one of their officers observed Rogers's determination: "He looked neither right or left, neither at his own men nor at mine, but with eyes partly closed, like one in a hail storm, was marching slowly and steadily upon us."

For a fleeting moment, the Confederates held control of Fort Robinett. But suddenly, Union reinforcements poured in on both sides of Rogers's command, which had by then lost half of its men in the battle. Above the din, the colonel screamed, "Men, save yourselves or sell your lives as dearly as possible!" As for Rogers, he chose the latter course. Seconds later, a hail of bullets riddled the colonel's body, killing him instantly.

Following the battle, the victorious Union defenders surveyed the carnage. When they came upon the lifeless body of Colonel Rogers, the Yankee soldiers were yet in awe of his courageous performance. His corpse was reverently laid in the shade and his face covered with an overcoat. When General Rosecrans arrived, he directed the soldiers to uncover the colonel's face. Looking upon the fallen officer, Rosecrans remarked, "He was one of the bravest men that ever led a charge. Bury him with military honors and mark his grave, so his friends can claim him. The time will come when there will be a monument here to commemorate his bravery."

Rosecrans was right. Today, a tall obelisk erected in 1912 marks the spot where Rogers fell at Corinth.

Confederate president Jefferson Davis, the man with whom Rogers had quarreled many times in Mexico, paid tribute to the colonel: "The gallantry which attracted the enemy at Corinth was in keeping with the character he acquired in the former service."

But Rogers would have taken the greatest pride in the eulogy offered by General Earl Van Dorn in his official report on the Battle of Corinth: "I cannot refrain, however, from mentioning here the gallantry of a noble Texan, whose deeds at Corinth are the constant theme of both friends and foes. As long as courage, manliness, fortitude, patriotism, and honor exist the name of Rogers will be revered and honored among men."

Colonel William Peleg Rogers died as he had lived, clothed in honor.

Hiram T. Smith, Civilian

The Substitute

Palmyra, Missouri
October 18, 1862

"I can die as easily as drink that water."

Because of its geographic location and the divided loyalties of its citizenry, Missouri was an important border state and a hotbed of both partisan activity and organized combat throughout the Civil War. Only Virginia and Tennessee recorded more battles and skirmishes during the four-year struggle. One of the darkest days of the war occurred in Missouri in 1862 as a result of a desperate attempt by Federal authorities to maintain military control in the northeastern part of the state. Known as the Palmyra Massacre, the tragic affair had as one of its unfortunate victims twenty-two-year-old Hiram T. Smith.

During the first full year of the war, Smith, who could neither read nor write, was a nonparticipant in the military and political affairs dividing Missouri, though his family sympathies were with the South. Smith spent his days as a tenant farmer until the fall of 1862, when a series of events led him to lay down his life for a neighbor condemned to death because of his Southern loyalties.

Two monuments stand today as mute reminders of Smith's sacrifice. On the picturesque courthouse grounds in Palmyra, a life-sized statue of a Confederate soldier surmounts a solid granite pedestal. Erected in 1907,

The monument to Hiram T. Smith and others executed in the "massacre" at Palmyra, Missouri
COURTESY OF *CONFEDERATE VETERAN*

the monument bears the names of Smith and the nine other Confederate sympathizers executed by a Federal firing squad at the Marion County Fairgrounds on October 18, 1862. A grave in the Mount Pleasant Church Cemetery is marked by a stone bearing a simple inscription: "This monument is dedicated to the memory of HIRAM SMITH, the hero who sleeps beneath the sod here, who was shot at Palmyra . . . as a substitute for William T. Humphrey, my father."

The sordid affair that culminated in the Palmyra Massacre began with the disappearance of an elderly local man, Andrew Allsman. Widely known as a Union informant, Allsman sparked the ire of area Confederate sympathizers by turning their names in to the Federal military headquarters at Palmyra. Once pro-Southern men were arrested, their homes were looted by Union soldiers. On September 17, 1862, Colonel Joe Porter led a group of Confederate raiders into Palmyra in an unsuccessful attempt to rid the town of Union occupation. In the process, some of his men captured Allsman. As the Southern soldiers skedaddled out of town with their prize, some of the local ladies made their feelings known: "Don't let old Allsman come back."

Three days later, Colonel Porter grew frustrated because the old man was slowing the movement of his soldiers in their retreat to southern Missouri. He agreed to release Allsman, but the old man refused to make his way back home alone, fearing retribution by the folks living along the way. Allsman prevailed upon the colonel to allow him to choose six soldiers to escort him to the home of the nearest Union loyalist. En route, the escort encountered less sympathetic Confederate troops, who took Allsman into a wooded area, shot him to death, and covered his body with brush and leaves.

On October 8, almost four weeks since Allsman's disappearance, Colonel John McNeil, the commander of Union forces in Palmyra, ordered his provost marshal, William R. Strachan, to publish an ultimatum to Colonel Porter in the *Palmyra Courier*. It read, "Sir: Andrew Allsman, an aged citizen of Palmyra and a non-combatant having been carried from his home by a band of persons unlawfully arrayed against the peace and good order of the State of Missouri and which band was under your control, this is to notify you that unless said Andrew Allsman is returned to his family within ten days from date, ten men, who have belonged to your band and unlawfully sworn by you to carry arms against the Government of the United States and who are now in custody, will be shot, as a meet reward for their crimes, among which is the illegal restraining of said Allsman his liberty, and if not returned, presumptively aiding in his murder."

Four months earlier, Colonel McNeil had been authorized to wage a campaign of death in the area. In a dispatch to him from St. Louis on June 12, General John M. Schofield had ordered, "I want you to take the field in person . . . and exterminate rebel bands in your division. . . . Don't rest until you have exterminated the rascals." Nonetheless, few Palmyra residents believed McNeil would actually make good on the ultimatum, a copy of which was delivered to Colonel Porter's wife.

Well into the ninth day, there was still no response to the harsh directive published in the *Palmyra Courier*. Allsman was nowhere to be found. Meanwhile, Confederate loyalists in Palmyra to report on their paroles were rounded up and thrown into the Marion County Jail. McNeil directed Strachan to proceed to the facility and choose the "worst rebels" for execution. In the selection process, Strachan was ordered to pass over all illiterate prisoners and take only men "of the highest social position and influence."

When it became evident that Colonel McNeil was serious about carrying out the executions, local citizens, including staunch Unionists, pleaded with him to reconsider. McNeil's response was curt and direct: "My will shall be done."

Among the condemned men in the jail were William T. Humphrey and Thomas A. Sidenor, both former Confederate soldiers, and Willie Baker, the sixty-year-old father-in-law of Hiram Smith. Baker had never served in the army, but two of his sons had, and he had harbored them and their companions. After being informed of his fate, the aged man was the most outspoken of the prisoners. He ranted that he had done nothing that could justify his execution and swore that he would see "old McNeil and Strachan miles in hell." Young Thomas Sidenor had served as a captain in the Confederate army until his company was annihilated in battle, after which he returned to civilian life. He was engaged to be married when chosen by Strachan. Like Sidenor, William T. Humphry was no longer an active soldier. He was the father of seven small children.

When news of the impending executions spread into the countryside, friends and family members of the prisoners hurried to town to do what they could to save their loved ones. Mary Humphrey, William's wife, came to Palmyra with all their children, including a two-week-old baby, and called on Strachan at the provost marshal's office. He sent her to see Colonel McNeil. There, she begged for her husband's life, informing McNeil that William had honored his parole by refusing to rejoin Colonel Porter's regiment. Moved by the tearful woman's sincerity, McNeil issued a directive to Strachan: "If the fact can be established that Humphrey was here on parole when Porter was here and refused to leave, reprieve him and do not put anyone in his place."

Upon receiving the directive, Strachan agreed to spare Humphrey but decided to find someone to take his place before the firing squad. He picked up a blank death warrant as he prepared to leave the jail. "For God's sake, take some man that has no family," the chief jailer beseeched him.

In the yard, the provost marshal happened upon a young fellow who had been visiting his imprisoned father-in-law. Strachan asked him, "What is your name?"

"Hiram Smith," the man responded.

Strachan scribbled on the warrant, then looked up and said, "I have a warrant for you."

Smith offered no verbal response. Rather, he cast his eyes toward the open jail window where William T. Humphrey was being comforted by his wife and children. Smith raised his eyebrows as if to inquire of Humphrey, "Are you the man to be saved?" Humphrey nodded his head. Turning to Strachan, Smith finally spoke: "It had better be me than that man with such a family."

During their walk to the jail, when the two men paused at a well for some water, the substitute remarked, "The way it is, I can die as easily as drink that water."

On the following afternoon, the tenth day after McNeil's ultimatum, ten condemned men—five from Palmyra and five brought in from nearby Hannibal—were escorted from the jail and seated in wagons upon their newly made coffins. Then the death caravan set out on its half-mile route to the fairgrounds. Once the short journey was completed, they were ordered to remove their own coffins. An eyewitness described the macabre scene: "The ten coffins were removed from the wagons and placed in a row 6 or 8 feet apart, forming a line north and south, about 15 paces east of the central pagoda or music stand. . . . The arrangements completed, the doomed men knelt upon the grass between their coffins." Only a few feet separated Hiram Smith and the other condemned men from their executioners, thirty men from the Second Missouri State Militia (Union). A reserve force of an equal number formed a second line.

As the end neared, the Reverend R. M. Rhodes prayed for the men about to die. Then, according to an observer, "each prisoner took his seat upon the foot of his coffin, facing the muskets which in a few moments were to launch them into eternity."

Without blindfolds, Hiram Smith and his compatriots stared into the eyes of the men assigned to kill them. Then the order was given. Thirty rifles fired. Only three of the men were killed. One of the condemned, Morgan Bixler, was not hit at all. Moments later, the reserve line stepped forward and finished the deadly work with their pistols at close range.

Newspapers across America and in Europe condemned the executions. Colonel McNeil subsequently defended the killings thus: "Cherishing, as I do, the firm conviction that my action was the means of saving lives and property of hundreds of loyal men and women, I feel that my act was the performance of a public duty." President Abraham Lincoln termed the incident "the darkest crime of the Civil War."

Hiram T. Smith was buried in a neighborhood cemetery. Over the years, the elements took a toll on the simple white board atop his grave. But the Humphrey family would not allow time or nature to erase the memory of Smith's selfless sacrifice. George Humphrey, the son of the man whose life Smith saved, was born two years after the executions. He spent the earnings from his first winter of teaching school to pay for the permanent monument that marks the grave of the substitute, who made his first and only appearance in a Confederate line before a firing squad.

Lieutenant Nathaniel D. Renfroe
The Fighting Parson

Fredericksburg, Virginia
December 13, 1862

"Boys, this is a pretty hot place, and you must get out the best you can."

When the Civil War began, many ordained ministers in the South volunteered to serve as chaplains in the Confederate military service. During the four years of the war, they faced countless dangers and hardships to provide comfort, friendship, and spiritual guidance and to minister to the wounded and dying. Still other clergymen, far fewer in number, chose to take up arms for the Confederacy and to actively participate as combat soldiers. One such individual was the Reverend Nathaniel D. Renfroe, who served as a lieutenant in Company A of the Fifth Alabama Battalion.

Born in Macon County, Alabama, in 1833, Renfroe was reared in a poor but respected family. Both of his parents were dead by the time he was sixteen, so he was taken in by his older brother, an ordained minister. Following four years of theological education at Union University in Tennessee, Nathaniel returned to Alabama in 1859 to accept a pastorate at a Baptist church in Jacksonville. For almost two years, he worked diligently at his calling. But then came the need in 1861 for all able-bodied Southern men to protect their homeland.

A drawing by Alfred R. Waud (1828–91), picturing four dead Confederates at Fredericksburg, where Lieutenant Nathaniel D. Renfroe died in action
COURTESY OF LIBRARY OF CONGRESS

Throughout the spring and much of the summer of 1861, Renfroe wrestled with the difficult decision of whether he should remain at home to minister to his congregation or whether he should follow his burning desire to defend the South. He agonized, prayed, and consulted with his parishioners and fellow ministers. In August, he arrived at a decision. He bade adieu to his weeping church members and volunteered as a private in the Fifth Alabama Battalion. His older brother, commenting on Nathaniel's early military service, noted that he "met the duty of a private for four months with a fortitude and cheerful devotion common to soldiers fighting for liberty, not only complying with every demand upon himself, but frequently taking the place of the infirm and illy clad, when they were ordered on duty."

Near the end of 1861, when the first vacancy for an officer occurred in the Fifth Alabama, Renfroe was unanimously elected as the lieutenant of Company A. Over the next year, he served as a gallant combat leader on the battlefields of Virginia. In camp, he assumed the role of a chaplain, conducting religious services as often as his other duties allowed. A fellow officer observed, "His example was worth more to us than the public preaching of a dozen chaplains." A soldier who served under the command of Lieutenant Renfroe described him as "a living, walking example of Christianity amongst us." Regarding Renfroe's abilities and character, the soldier said, "He knows how to perform his duties as an officer without conflicting his religion. He is ready at all times to get on his knees to pray for the sick soldier, and has a word of comfort and encouragement for all. His example is a standing admonition and a constant finger board pointing out the road to heaven."

In the late spring of 1862, as Major General John McClellan began to marshal his massive Army of the Potomac to threaten Richmond, Lieutenant Renfroe fell victim to typhoid and was transported to the Confederate capital for treatment. When news reached the city that the first battle of what would become the Seven Days' Campaign was about to begin, Renfroe rose from his hospital bed. Against the advice of his physicians, he hurried to the scene of the fighting. Unable to locate his unit, he took to the field with another Alabama regiment. One of its companies lacked a commissioned officer and readily welcomed the lieutenant, who promptly led it into the heat of battle.

When the fighting ended for the day, Renfroe located his own men. For the duration of the fierce battles over the following week, he commanded his soldiers in combat, even though his doctors warned that he should be in bed.

After the Union threat to Richmond subsided, the lieutenant triumphantly marched his soldiers into the city, where he returned to the hospital, seriously ill with a relapse of typhoid. His condition deteriorated. For several weeks, Renfroe teetered at the point of death. Once the crisis passed, his recovery was painfully slow. He was sent home to recuperate, thereby depriving him of the opportunity to fight with his men at Cedar Run, Second Manassas, and Sharpsburg.

By mid-autumn 1862, Lieutenant Renfroe's health was fully restored. As he bade farewell to his brother at the train depot in Talladega, he offered a premonition of his own demise: "Well, brother, now we part, and unless you visit the army soon, we will not meet again on earth; but shed no tears for me—we will meet in heaven."

Back in Virginia, the fighting parson resumed his command. His resolve to defeat the enemy was as great as ever, but he could not rid his mind of the notion that he was about to die. In a letter home, he forewarned his loved ones: "I have some reason to fear that you have not prepared yourself to meet the news of such a fate as may befall me. . . . But I have entered the army to fight for you, and if need be, to die for you and yours. . . . I am willing to go when God calls, and I am willing if He shall call me in any way He pleases."

When General Robert E. Lee learned that the Army of the Potomac, now commanded by Major General Ambrose Burnside, was rapidly approaching Fredericksburg in November 1862, he dispatched the corps commanded by Lieutenant General Stonewall Jackson and Lieutenant General James Longstreet to meet it. Lieutenant Renfroe had this to say about the forced march to Fredericksburg: "We have just completed another march of one hundred and seventy miles, crossing two awful mountains in the time. We were twelve days on the march. I had no wagon, or horse, or any other means of transportation, except my feet for myself and baggage; we rested, only at night—rising at 4½ in the morning and marching until sunset. I suffered much—frequently thinking that I would fall out and rest, but when I would look through the company and see several men barefooted and still keeping up, it would stimulate me, . . . and I would press on. The tramp finished my boots, and both my feet are on the ground, but little prospect of getting any shoes soon. But it is my duty to bear a little hardness as a good soldier of Jesus Christ, and submit to it cheerfully, and without murmur in view of my country's freedom and the honor of my religion."

By the second week of December, the armies were poised for battle on the banks of the Rappahannock. In his last letter to his brother, the lieutenant offered more words of precognition: "We are certainly on the eve of a great battle here—it will be a grand affair—I may not survive the conflict, but, brother, if I die, I shall fall at my post, and I am ready to go."

At dawn on December 13, Nathaniel Renfroe knelt in prayer for his men and the cause they represented. From the onset of the battle that quickly enveloped the city, the Fifth Alabama was in the thick of the fight. Early in the day, the captain of Company A was badly wounded, and his command devolved to Lieutenant Renfroe. As morning wore into afternoon, there seemed to be no end in sight to the bitter fighting. About three o'clock, a gap in the Confederate lines allowed the enemy to effect a rapid flanking movement. In a desperate attempt to buy time until reinforcements could be brought forward, Brigadier General J. J. Archer ordered the First Tennessee and the Fifth Alabama into the breech. When the blue-jacketed attackers threatened to overpower the soldiers from Tennessee and Alabama, the Southern troops manning the gap were directed to retreat. But according to his men, Lieutenant Renfroe did not hear the order to fall back. As the men of the First Tennessee and the other Alabama companies moved away, the gallant Renfroe and his warriors in Company A stood their ground in the face of an overwhelming enemy.

Only a short distance separated the warring factions when the Union troops demanded that Renfroe surrender. Turning to the few Confederates yet at his side, the lieutenant gave his final command: "Boys, this is a pretty hot place, and you must get out the best you can."

His soldiers promptly obeyed and took flight. But not Lieutenant Renfroe. Repeater in hand, he turned toward the enemy and began firing with cool deliberation in a one-man stand until his body was riddled with bullets.

Reflecting on Renfroe's sacrifice, a fellow lieutenant said, "He died at his post as a brave and Christian soldier, for a braver and better man has not fallen in the Confederate army."

Captain Peter Bramlett

Gratitude for a Good Samaritan

Nashville, Tennessee
January 1863

"Tell him I died under the blankets he placed over me."

Just six days after Christmas 1862, Confederate troops under the command of General Braxton Bragg clashed with the Union forces of Major General William S. Rosecrans at Murfreesboro, Tennessee, in one of the deadliest affairs in the Western theater of the Civil War. When the three days of savage fighting ended at the Battle of Stone's River on January 2, 1863, nearly nineteen thousand soldiers had been killed or wounded. During the battle and its aftermath, surgeons and medical corpsmen from both armies labored night and day to save the lives of fallen warriors, often without regard to the side for which the wounded had fought. And so it was with Dr. F. G. Hindman, a Union surgeon, and Captain Peter Bramlett, a Confederate officer from the Second Kentucky.

As the Battle of Stone's River raged, Dr. Hindman and another surgeon toiled in their field operating tent. Their bloody work continued until midnight, when Hindman's exhausted colleague announced, "We will not do any more work tonight." Meanwhile, litter bearers laid an injured Confederate officer outside the surgery tent. Dr. Hindman could

Nashville, Tennessee, as seen from the State Capitol during the Civil War. Captain Peter Bramlett died in a private home in Nashville after the Battle of Stone's River.
COURTESY OF LIBRARY OF CONGRESS

hear the pitiful cries of the soldier, who had sustained gunshot wounds to the chest and leg.

Concerned that the man might not survive the night without medical attention, Dr. Hindman directed orderlies to bring him into the tent. In the course of the examination, Captain Bramlett asked the doctor if his wounds were fatal. Sadly, Dr. Hindman responded that the chances for survival were not great.

After Bramlett's wounds were cleaned and dressed, he was carried to a nearby shed and laid on unbaled cotton. Before he retired for the evening, Dr. Hindman walked out into the bitterly cold night to monitor the condition of the captured Southerner. He provided Captain Bramlett some brandy and water. The dying man was shivering, so the surgeon ordered that a pair of blankets be placed over him. Satisfied that he had made Bramlett as comfortable as possible, Dr. Hindman informed his patient that he would see him the following morning.

But that was not to be. Before Dr. Hindman reached the shed the next day, Peter Bramlett was transported to Nashville. There, he was placed in the private home of a Mrs. Payne for care and comfort. Not long thereafter, Dr. Hindman was taken prisoner when his three ambulances were captured by Southern forces. His captors took the surgeon to Nashville, where he was put to work in a Confederate hospital.

Ten days after his arrival in Nashville, Dr. Hindman was saddened when the death of Captain Peter Bramlett was announced in the local newspapers. About the same time, Mrs. Payne paid one of her frequent visits to the hospital where the captured Yankee surgeon worked. In the course of a conversation with Dr. Hindman, Mrs. Payne informed him that she had ministered to several Confederate soldiers in recent weeks, one of them Captain Bramlett. Noting the surgeon's interest, she related the details of the final minutes of Bramlett's life. As his death approached, Mrs. Payne had vowed to do everything in her power to make the captain's passing as peaceful as possible. When she attempted to remove his coarse blankets and replace them with clean, soft ones, Bramlett had clutched her hand and spoken his last utterance: "No, do not remove those blankets, for they saved my life at Stone's River. They were placed over me that cold night by the hand of an enemy, but a brother. You may come across him sometime; and if you should, tell him I died under the blankets he placed over me that night."

Those special blankets were sent to Captain Peter Bramlett's grief-stricken parents in Paris, Kentucky.

Major John Pelham
The Gallant Pelham

Kelly's Ford, Virginia
March 17, 1863

"Forward boys! Forward to victory and glory!"

Many of the most famous officers in both the Confederate and Union armies were educated at the United States Military Academy. One of the youngest West Pointers to serve in the Civil War was also one of the best. John Pelham graduated in the spring of 1861, at the very time the American nation was splitting. Over the two years that followed, the youthful artillery officer earned the respect and admiration of friend and foe alike through his skill as a soldier, his daring nature, and his excellence of character. He died at the age of twenty-four, cloaked in glory and fame.

It was in 1856 that seventeen-year-old John Pelham left his native Alabama to enroll at West Point. Henry DuPont, a Northern classmate from the famous industrial family, yielded this glimpse of Pelham: "He was of medium height, very straight, and with a remarkably well-proportioned figure. His complexion was not very fair, although his eyes were blue and his hair decidedly blonde. Altogether he was a very handsome youth, with attractive manners, which lent an additional charm to his open and engaging countenance. Although his natural abilities were good, he could not be called clever and did not stand very high in his class, my recollection being that he did not apply himself particularly to his studies. He was, however, a young man of high tone and decided character." Henry DuPont maintained a high class rank, which resulted in his harassment by two classmates from New England. DuPont recalled the showdown that resulted: "I turned at once to John Pelham, who was my second in a pugilistic encounter of twenty-one minutes, from which I emerged victorious, for cadets in those days settled all the difficulties by stand-up fist fights."

Adelbert Ames, a Northern classmate and future major general who came face to face with Pelham's artillery at Manassas and other deadly fields, also had words of praise for the lad from Alabama: "He was a general favorite in the corps of cadets, and, I think I am safe in saying, the most popular man in our class. He was a gentleman in the highest sense of the term. A discourteous act was wholly foreign to his nature. His kindly heart, sweet voice, and genial smile carried sunshine with him always. What he instinctively claimed for himself, he graciously conceded to others."

Pelham's fearless nature was legend before he left West Point. A reporter for the *London Times* wrote, "Then as now, at the academy, a cat,

Major John Pelham
COURTESY OF LIBRARY OF CONGRESS

with its reputed plurality of lives, would be dead a dozen times in taking the chances the laughing cadets would eagerly seek in the cavalry drill, but Pelham excelled them all." That legend was to grow during the young soldier's two years on the battlegrounds of the Civil War.

The dashing Pelham was extremely popular with members of the opposite sex. Several of his female acquaintances called him "as grand a flirt as ever lived." In fact, that nature enabled Pelham to make it home to Alabama just as the Civil War was beginning. After successfully completing his final examinations in 1861, Pelham resigned his cadetship without receiving his commission in the United States Army. Federal authorities refused to allow him to travel south. Undaunted, he disguised himself as one of General Winfield Scott's couriers and journeyed to Jeffersonville, Indiana, on the Ohio River, where he met a lovely young lady who fell madly in love with him. Her confidence secured, Pelham divulged his intention to travel to Alabama. Under the guise of taking a pleasure trip down the river, the couple rowed across the Ohio to the Kentucky shore. There, they embraced in a tender farewell, and Pelham made haste to Montgomery.

His homecoming was short lived. After accepting a Confederate commission as a first lieutenant of field artillery, Pelham was dispatched to Virginia. At First Manassas, Jeb Stuart was so impressed with Pelham's performance that a six-gun battery was organized for the newly promoted captain of Stuart's "Horse Artillery."

Pelham's reputation grew with every fight. With but one gun available to him at the Battle of Gaines Mill on June 27, 1862, he steadfastly held his own against three heavy enemy batteries. As the fighting raged, Stuart reported to Stonewall Jackson, "General, all your artillery on the left is idle; nobody is firing except Pelham." Once the battle was over, Stonewall rode over to the young artillery captain and gently placed his hand on him in appreciation.

Two months later, Pelham again won Stonewall's praise. After the Confederate victory at Second Manassas, Jackson quipped to Stuart, "General, if you have another Pelham, give him to me." Pelham was promoted to major following the battle.

Six weeks later, Pelham, who had just celebrated his twenty-fourth birthday, was assigned to command the artillery on the Confederate left at Sharpsburg, Maryland. His guns successfully protected Jackson's left flank, the most important portion of the Confederate line. After escaping what would have been a disastrous defeat at Sharpsburg, Stonewall remarked, "With a Pelham on each flank, I believe I could whip the world!"

In the Confederate retreat from Sharpsburg, Pelham was assigned to the rear guard. Three days after the battle, Union forces attacked the Confederate rear at Shepherdstown, Virginia. For hours, Pelham's guns roared. Upon receiving orders from Stuart to fall back, he pleaded to remain at his post. Pelham's men fled to safety, but their commander fought on. The enemy was closing in when he offered a staggering blast from a big gun, then mounted the lead horse and began to escape with his gun carriage. Union marksmen killed the horse, forcing Pelham to cut it away. Two more horses in the team were killed during the major's successful flight.

In all of military history, few soldiers have displayed greater gallantry and determination than Pelham at Fredericksburg on December 13, 1862. Before the battle, Generals Lee, Jackson, and Stuart rode up and down the Confederate lines. Stuart called Pelham aside, after which the young artillerist galloped over to his guns. Moments later, a horseman followed by a two-gun battery lumbered down the heights. It was Major Pelham! Once the two guns—a Napoleon and a Blakely rifle—were in place, Pelham shouted an order, and they thundered fire to herald the opening of the battle. At least a half-dozen Union batteries trained their salvos on the two Confederate guns. By design, Pelham caused the enemy to concentrate its fire on him. Union commanders reasoned that their infantry could not advance until those guns were silenced.

After the Blakely was put out of action, Jeb Stuart grew concerned for the major's safety. He dispatched Major Heros von Borke, the Prussian giant, to suggest that Pelham withdraw. The response was as Stuart expected. "Tell the General I can hold my ground," Pelham relayed.

While they waited to go into action, Confederate infantrymen watched in awe as Pelham cheered his small contingent of gunners in keeping the lone Napoleon busy against countless enemy field pieces. Realizing that Pelham was defying the odds, Stuart sent another message: "Get back from destruction, you infernal, gallant fool, John Pelham!"

Not until his caissons were nearly empty did the major end his effort. After holding off the entire Army of the Potomac with just two guns, Pelham ordered his men to retire. Inspired by the fearless artillery commander, the

Army of Northern Virginia proceeded to repulse the enemy in a terrible slaughter. After personally witnessing Pelham's heroics, Robert E. Lee remarked, "It is glorious to see such courage in one so young." In his subsequent report on the Battle of Fredericksburg, Lee made note of "the gallant Pelham." No other officer below the rank of major general was mentioned in his official report.

During a lull in combat in the winter of 1862-63, Pelham aided Jeb Stuart in his harassment of the enemy. As the winter drew to a close and the spring offensive neared, a nomination for Pelham's promotion to lieutenant colonel was forwarded to Richmond.

On St. Patrick's Day, Pelham was enjoying the company of some beautiful ladies in Culpeper County, Virginia, during a brief respite from his military duties when he detected the distant rumble of artillery. Ever anxious to do his duty, he galloped to the scene, a minor cavalry skirmish at Kelly's Ford. His command was not on the field upon his arrival, so he hastily joined the Third Virginia Cavalry in its thunderous charge. Rising in his stirrups, Pelham waved his hat and offered encouragement to the Virginians: "Forward, boys! Forward to victory and glory!" Seconds later, a fragment from an exploding shell struck him in the back of the neck and penetrated his brain. Comrades transported the mortally wounded major to the home of his fiancée, Bessie Shackleford, in Culpeper County. He died within hours.

Although hardened by the cruelty of war, Jeb Stuart was shocked by Pelham's death. He lamented, "His loss is irreparable." In announcing Pelham's passing to his division, Stuart wrote, "His eyes glanced over every battlefield of this army. . . . His record has been bright and spotless. . . . He fell—the noblest of sacrifices—on the altar of his country, to whose glorious service he had dedicated his young life from the beginning of the war."

The coffin bearing the lifeless body of "the gallant Pelham" was transported to Richmond, where it lay in state. In the days to come, Pelham's promotion was approved posthumously.

His grieving fiancée later married another, but she never forgot the magnificent blue-eyed officer from Alabama. "A boy, yet a man, that was Pelham," Bessie said. "You could not help being drawn to him. He was really fascinating. . . . Sometimes I used to sit and just look at him and wonder if it could be true that he was the man they were all talking about, the man who could aim those guns so they would kill and kill. . . . There wasn't a single line of hardness in his face. It was all tenderness and softness, as fresh and delicate as a boy's who liked people and who found the world good. I used to say to myself, 'A man like that—this boy?' That is really what he was, you know, a boy, a splendid boy."

Lieutenant General Thomas Jonathan Jackson

Stonewall

Guiney's Station, Virginia
May 10, 1863

"Let us cross over the river and rest under the shade of the trees."

Other than Robert Edward Lee, no name in Confederate military history is more recognized, honored, and revered than that of Stonewall Jackson. Countless historians have speculated that, had Jackson not died of complications from wounds sustained in friendly fire on May 2, 1863, the South might have won the Civil War. Acclaimed as one of the greatest battlefield tacticians in world history, Stonewall carried into every battle his unwavering faith in God. It was that steadfast faith that sustained the general in his last hours.

No distinguished general in American history rose from more humble beginnings than Thomas Jonathan Jackson. He was born on January 21, 1824, at Clarksburg, deep in the mountains of that portion of Virginia that would become West Virginia. When Jackson was two years old, his father, a struggling attorney with mounting debts, and his infant sister died of typhoid fever. In the four years that followed, the widow Jackson and her three surviving children were virtual wards of the town.

When Jackson's mother remarried, Tom, as Jackson was called, was sent

Lieutenant General Thomas Jonathan "Stonewall" Jackson
COURTESY OF LIBRARY OF CONGRESS

to live with an uncle who operated lumber and grist mills. Two years later, his mother died. Without either parent, the boy became shy and withdrawn.

Fortune shined on Jackson in 1842 when the initial appointee from his congressional district decided to forgo a military education at West Point. Jackson availed himself of the opportunity and enrolled at the United States Military Academy as an eighteen-year-old mountain boy who was quite awkward and lacking social graces. Few in his class came to the institution with less preparation and academic skills.

During his four-year tenure at the academy, Cadet Jackson made few friends. Rather, he devoted his time and energy to his studies. By the time he graduated in 1846, he had risen from the bottom in academic standing to rank seventeenth in a class of fifty-nine.

When Jackson was commissioned as a lieutenant in the Third Artillery, the United States was at war with Mexico. His performance in that conflict earned him citations for gallantry. By war's end, Tom Jackson held the rank of brevet major. None of his classmates—including the likes of A. P. Hill,

George McClellan, George E. Pickett, George Stoneman, and Cadmus Wilcox—did so well in the war.

Before the beginning of the 1851-52 academic year at Virginia Military Institute, Jackson resigned his army commission in order to accept a position as professor of artillery tactics and optics at the Lexington, Virginia, school. Over the next ten years, an immortal bond was forged between V.M.I. and Jackson. Many of Jackson's students considered him eccentric, and they detested his strict discipline. But all who knew him in Lexington came to admire his integrity, attention to duty, determination, and loyalty.

Upon his arrival in town, Jackson joined Lexington Presbyterian Church and quickly became a strong adherent of the Calvinist doctrine. His daily life was guided by his inflexible faith. He found great comfort in his frequent prayers.

In 1857, three years after his first wife died in childbirth, Jackson married Mary Anna Morrison, the daughter of a distinguished Presbyterian minister in North Carolina. Two of Mrs. Jackson's sisters likewise married Confederate generals—Daniel Harvey Hill and Rufus Barringer.

When tensions mounted between North and South in the months before the Civil War, Jackson expressed his strong desire that the Union be preserved. But when he perceived that his native Virginia was being subjected to coercion by the government in Washington, his attitude changed. Among the first volunteers who stepped forward to defend Virginia when it seceded was Tom Jackson. On April 20, 1861, he left Lexington with a group of V.M.I. cadets bound for war.

When Jackson reported for duty in Richmond, he looked anything but the great officer he was to become. He was thirty-seven years old, stood five foot ten, and weighed 170 pounds. His forehead was extended, his nose sharp, his thick beard black, his hands and feet unusually large, and his voice high pitched. Mounted on a horse, Jackson presented an awkward appearance. He rode with his body bent forward, as if he were leaning into a brisk breeze.

But when it came to Jackson the soldier, appearances were deceiving. Once he donned the Confederate uniform, he exuded professionalism and confidence. To Jackson's way of thinking, the struggle with the North was a holy war to regain God's favor. Accordingly, he waged war in the Old Testament tradition of Gideon, Joshua, and the other great warriors of his faith.

Jackson was already a brigadier general when he received one of most famous nicknames in American history on July 21, 1861, at Manassas, Virginia. In the early afternoon, Federal forces broke through the first line of Confederate defenders and swept up Henry House Hill in anticipation of victory. Jackson rushed his brigade to the crest of the hill, where it held so strong during the hours of horrific fighting that General Bernard E. Bee was moved to shout to his faltering South Carolinians, "Look men! There stands Jackson like a stone wall! Rally behind the Virginians!" At Manassas, the South earned a critical victory in the early stages of the war and gained its first genuine hero—Stonewall Jackson.

In October, the Confederate high command elevated Jackson to major general. Greater battlefield glory was forthcoming. During his Shenandoah Valley Campaign in the spring of 1862, he displayed military genius in the deployment of his troops. One Federal officer lamented that Jackson's strategy resulted "in the complete derangement of the Union plans in Virginia."

On the battlefield, the general was cold as steel. His apparent lack of emotion while surveying his dead in the wake of combat was sometimes perceived as callousness. To the contrary, Jackson saw death in battle as the price that all Confederate soldiers must be willing to pay to promote the cause of the South and God. On many occasions, he pronounced his willingness to die in battle. In a letter in 1862, he wrote, "God has fixed the time for my death. I do not concern myself about that, but to be always ready, no matter when it may overtake me. . . . That is the way all men should live, and then all would be equally brave."

During the summer and autumn of 1862, Stonewall's reputation as a master of battlefield tactics continued to grow. Over time, his name became legend throughout the world. Lord Roberts, the commander in chief of the British armies in the early twentieth century and a student of military history, once remarked, "In my opinion Stonewall Jackson was one of the greatest natural military geniuses the world ever saw. I will go even further than that—as a campaigner in the field he never had a superior. In some respects I doubt whether he had an equal."

When the Army of Northern Virginia was reorganized in October 1862, Robert E. Lee promoted Jackson to lieutenant general and placed him in command of half of that army. If ever two generals worked well together, they were Lee and Jackson. "So great is my confidence in General Lee that I am willing to follow him blindfolded," Jackson remarked.

On May 1, 1863, Lee faced his most formidable task to date. His 60,000 troops were posed against the 130,000 men of the Army of the Potomac near the crossroads settlement of Chancellorsville, Virginia. A day later, after conferring with Lee, Jackson executed his famous flanking movement. After completing the circuitous twelve-mile march, his 28,000-man corps stormed General Joseph Hooker's unprotected right. By the time darkness enveloped the battleground, the routed Federals had fled two miles. Not satisfied that the Confederate victory was complete, Jackson, for the first time in the war, rode forward to make a personal reconnaissance of the enemy's position. As he returned through the thick woods known as "the Wilderness," North Carolina troops mistook him for Union cavalry. They opened fire.

Jackson was hit three times. One of the balls splintered the bone in his left arm below the shoulder. Surgeons were forced to amputate the limb, but they did not consider the wound life threatening.

When Lee learned of Jackson's injury, he promptly sent a telegraph to his invaluable corps commander: "General: I have just received your note, informing me that you were wounded. I cannot express my regret at the occurrence. Could I have directed the events, I should have chosen for the good of the country to be disabled in your stead. I congratulate you upon the victory, which is due to your skill and energy."

When an aide read him Lee's dispatch the following morning, Sunday, May 3, Jackson turned his face away and said, "General Lee is very kind, but he should give praise to God." Jackson, who seemed to be feeling much better, directed his staff members to resume their regular duties. An aide was dispatched to Richmond to bring Mary Anna Jackson to her husband.

In a subsequent telegraph to Jackson on May 4, Lee wrote one of the most enduring sentences of the entire war: "You are better off than I am, for while you have lost your left, I have lost my right arm."

The following day, Jackson was transported to the railroad at Guiney's Station in anticipation of a transfer to a Richmond hospital. However, he rapidly developed pneumonia, making further movement impossible. A pulmonary specialist from the Confederate capital hastened to his side.

After treating their patient for several days, Jackson's doctors had little choice on May 8 but to warn him that the pneumonia might prove fatal. "I am not afraid to die; I am willing to abide by the will of my Heavenly

Father," Jackson told his physicians. "But I do not believe that I shall die at this time; I am persuaded the Almighty has yet a work for me to perform."

A day later, Jackson tossed and turned, his body racked with fever.

Sunday, May 10, 1863, broke sunny, clear, and bright at Guiney's Station. But inside the house where Jackson was being treated, there hung a heavy pall of gloom. On innumerable fields of combat, Jackson had displayed a unique brand of bravery, but never was he more gallant than on the day he lost the battle for his life.

His medical team concurred early in the day that nothing more could be done to save him. They called Mrs. Jackson from her husband's side to inform her that he had but hours to live. Mary Anna had somehow expected the doleful news, but she could not hold back her tears. Many times, Stonewall had told her that although he was ready to die at any time, he would prefer to have notice of his impending demise. As hard as it was, Mrs. Jackson knew that she must be the one to tell him.

Upon regaining her composure, she walked into the sickroom. Although his illness had weakened his senses, Jackson immediately acknowledged his wife. She had to speak her message several times before he seemed to understand: "Do you know the Doctors say you must very soon be in Heaven?"

His face displayed no anxiety as he replied, "I prefer it. I prefer it."

"Well, before this day closes, you will be with your blessed Saviour in His glory," she said.

Stonewall answered, "I will be an infinite gainer to be translated," a biblical reference to the Book of Hebrews.

When the general's young daughter, Julia, was brought in and placed on the bed beside her father, he brightened and exclaimed, "Little darling! Sweet one!" Father and daughter traded smiles until Stonewall lapsed into unconsciousness.

When Jackson revived, Alexander "Sandie" Pendleton, his beloved adjutant general, was at his side. To the man who would dress his body for burial, Stonewall said in a weak voice, "Sandie, it is the Lord's Day; my wish is fulfilled. I have always desired to die on Sunday."

As the end neared, Jackson's chaplain, the Reverend Beverly Lacy, was not at his side. Instead, he was preaching to Stonewall's corps, in accord with the general's directions. When Lacy prepared to return to Jackson, Lee remarked, "When a suitable occasion offers, give him my love, and tell him that I wrestled in prayer for him last night, as I never prayed, I believe, for myself." But the Reverend Lacy was unable to deliver the message.

As Jackson drifted in and out of consciousness, one of his attendants offered to give him some brandy. He refused, saying, "It will only delay my departure and do no good. I want to preserve my mind, if possible, to the last."

A short time later, about three in the afternoon, Jackson's thoughts seemed to be on the battlefield when he called for his West Point classmate A. P. Hill to come. Suddenly, he stopped, and his face beamed the smile that had endeared him to the entire Confederate nation. Then he spoke his last: "Let us cross over the river and rest under the shade of the trees."

Robert E. Lee subsequently weighed the loss: "If I had had Stonewall Jackson at Gettysburg, I would have won that fight; and a complete victory there would have given us Washington and Baltimore, if not Philadelphia, and would have established the independence of the Confederacy."

But even more than Lee's words, an incident on the road to Gettysburg would have brought Jackson great happiness. As Confederate troops poured through the streets of Chambersburg, Pennsylvania, Robert Stiles of the Richmond Howitzers asked a local lady if he could get a drink of water from her well. From her seat on the front porch, she gave him permission and asked him to sit down for a rest. In the course of their conversation, the elderly woman inquired if Stiles had ever seen Stonewall Jackson. When he responded in the affirmative, the matron spoke with the utmost conviction: "I expect to see him soon, for if anyone ever has left this earth and gone straight to heaven, it was he."

Captain William Francis Corbin

A Worthy Example

Johnson's Island, Ohio
May 15, 1863

"I was fighting for a principle, which in the sight of God and man, and in the view of death, which awaits me, I believe I am right."

Numerous Confederate soldiers were executed during the Civil War. According to some Union officers, these men were put to death not simply to punish them for their conduct, but also to make an example of them. In a number of cases when Southern men died on the gallows or before the firing squad, the harsh punishments did not fit the alleged offenses. Consequently, these executions served as examples in ways neither intended nor desired by the officials who prescribed them. The executed men were often looked upon by Southern soldiers and civilians as martyrs. Their deaths away from the battlefield drew the ire of the people in Dixie and served to stiffen their resolve to fight to the bitter end.

When the Civil War began in 1861, William Francis Corbin's native Kentucky assumed a stance of armed neutrality, whereby the state militia was to be the only military force allowed within its borders. But over the

Captain William Francis Corbin
COURTESY OF *CONFEDERATE VETERAN*

first twelve months of the war, both the Confederate and Union armies regularly violated that neutrality and crossed into the state to lay claim to various towns and other strategic positions. To further complicate matters, the state militia splintered into pro-Southern and pro-Northern factions.

Corbin was a first lieutenant in one of the Kentucky state militia companies that sympathized with the Confederacy. After all, from the time his company was organized in the summer of 1860, it had worn regulation gray. When Major General Edmund Kirby-Smith invaded Kentucky with an army of six thousand Confederate troops in late August 1862, the Federals countered with an army of like size. Suddenly, the time was at hand for Kentuckians to take sides.

With twenty-five of his fellow militiamen, Corbin slipped through the Federal lines to Paris, Kentucky. There, he was sworn into the Confederate army, commissioned a captain, and assigned to duty in the Fourth Kentucky Cavalry. During the winter of 1862-63, he served with the regiment in the Virginia mountains. His comrades came to admire Captain Corbin for his integrity, bravery, and generosity. George R. Rule, one of his messmates, remembered Corbin thus: "Will Corbin's camp life was not different from his home life. He was always a Christian gentleman. Everybody was his friend."

As spring 1863 approached, his commander dispatched Corbin to Kentucky, where he was to raise a company. Operating out of his home county, the captain enjoyed a large measure of success. Once his assignment was complete, he began the return journey to Virginia. En route, Corbin and his recruits stopped in Pendleton County, Kentucky, at the home of Garrett Daniel, where the captain had arranged to rendezvous with his comrade and friend Jefferson McGraw. Corbin and his men waited and waited, but McGraw did not show. Concerned that misfortune had befallen his friend, the captain directed his men to proceed to Paris while he maintained the lonely vigil for McGraw.

For a brief moment, Corbin's anxiety was transformed into relief when McGraw bounded into the Daniel residence. But hot on his heels were Yankee troopers. In seconds, the place was surrounded by more than a dozen soldiers from the 118th Ohio. With no means of escape, the two Confederates were forced to surrender.

His captors assured Corbin that he and his friend would be treated as prisoners of war. At worst, Corbin reasoned, they would be confined in a Federal military prison until they were exchanged.

But forces were at work that would make Corbin's term of imprisonment extremely brief. On April 13, 1863, five days after Corbin's arrest, General Ambrose Burnside issued General Order No. 38, which provided that "hereafter all persons found within our lines who commit acts against the benefit of our country will be tried as spies and traitors and if convicted will suffer death." Although Corbin and McGraw had been arrested prior to the order, Burnside decided that it should be applied to them.

Within days, the two Confederate soldiers were tried in Cincinnati before a military court comprised of nine Union officers. Corbin tendered a plea of not guilty to the charges of recruiting men within the lines of Federal forces and carrying secret mail. Captain J. M. Cutts, the judge advocate, had little with which to work in presenting his case. Lieutenant S. A. Nickerson, the commander of the Union squadron that had captured Corbin, testified, "The only papers I found in his possession was a commission for one Humphrey and also a blank book with a blank form of oath on it, and a list—supposed to be a list of recruits. . . . I recognized the papers [as] what I understand to be a recruiting commission, authorizing election of officers when a number of men [were] recruited." Then Cutts examined Private F. M. Stockdale, who related to the court, "There were other men in the neighborhood where Corbin was captured, because the men who were captured said that there were more, that if they had all been together, they would have give us a pretty tight rub." Finally, a sergeant offered perjured testimony to the effect that Corbin had admitted taking part in the burning of bridges on the Kentucky Central Railroad.

Unaware that he was being tried under the dictates of General Order No. 38, Captain Corbin offered no defense.

Following their deliberations, the members of the court-martial returned with a verdict of guilty and sentenced Corbin to be "shot to death . . . at such time and place as the Commanding General shall direct, subject to the approval of the President of the United States."

Following Corbin's trial, McGraw was likewise tried and sentenced on the same evidence presented in the first trial.

When news of the death sentences reached Melissa Corbin, the sister of the Confederate officer, she and Captain J. C. DeMoss traveled to Cincinnati to intercede. Their petitions to General Burnside were summarily rejected. He informed them that he intended to make an example of the two men and would not recommend mercy to the president.

Undeterred by Burnside's rebuff, Melissa Corbin and DeMoss boarded a train to Washington, D.C., where they again made impassioned pleas for the lives of the two men. After enlisting the aid of the minister of the church where Abraham Lincoln worshiped, they called at the White House. The president refused to give any consideration to their entreaties. In the presence of DeMoss, Lincoln declared that the condemned men "were bridge burners and bad men and should be punished." He would not overturn Burnside's order. The fates of Corbin and McGraw were sealed when Lincoln wrote, "The foregoing sentence approved: A. Lincoln, May 4, 1863."

Meanwhile, the two condemned Confederates were transported to the military prison on Johnson's Island near Sandusky, Ohio. Officials there delayed the executions until all hope was lost. With only hours to live, Corbin led a worship service in the small chapel used by the prisoners. Captain DeMoss described the scene: "To see this man, standing in the presence of an audience composed of officers, privates, and prisoners of all grades, chained to and bearing his ball, and bearing it alone, presenting the religion of Christ to others while exemplifying it himself, was a scene which would melt the strongest heart, and when he took his seat every heart and every eye [was] bathed in tears."

Before he sat down to await his fate, Corbin proclaimed, "Life is just as sweet to me as any man; I am ready to die, and I do not fear death; I have done nothing I am ashamed of, but I acted on my own convictions, and I am not sorry for what I have done; I was fighting for a principle, which in the sight of God and man, and in the view of death, which awaits me, I believe I am right."

At 1:20 P.M. on May 15, 1863, Corbin and McGraw, bound securely and under heavy guard, were led from the prison compound, placed on a wagon, and ordered to ride atop their coffins. As a Federal band played the death march, the execution detail made the short trip to the lakeshore. There, a chaplain offered final prayers for the two Confederate soldiers. Blindfolds were placed on their heads, and the death squad of thirty-two men stepped forward. Then the order was given, and more than a dozen balls ripped into the breast of each man. Both died without struggle.

Captain Will Corbin was laid to rest in his native Kentucky in a family cemetery overlooking the Ohio River. Subsequent investigations yielded incontrovertible evidence that he had not been involved in the burning of any bridges during the war. Southern partisans, still smarting over Corbin's execution, retaliated by capturing and killing Major Abraham F. Wileman of the Eighteenth Kentucky (Union) when he arrived in Pendleton County, Kentucky, for a furlough in October 1863.

Colonel William Orton Williams

The Curious Case of Colonel Williams and Lieutenant Peters

Franklin, Tennessee
June 9, 1863

"Let us die like brave men!"

Espionage was important to the governments in Washington and Richmond throughout the Civil War. Spies, secret agents, scouts, and the like operated behind the lines to gather intelligence and sabotage enemy plans. Among the strangest affairs involving secret operations in the war was the capture, arrest, and execution of Colonel William O. Williams—a cousin of General Robert E. Lee—and Lieutenant Walter G. Peters by Federal officers in Franklin, Tennessee, on June 9, 1863.

No one could question the allegiance of Colonel Williams's family to the United States. He was a descendant of George Washington. His father, a West Point graduate, died in action at Monterey, Mexico.

Orton, as Williams was known to family and friends, graduated from the University of Virginia and then served as a second lieutenant in the Second United States Cavalry. Immediately prior to the Civil War, he was the aide-de-camp and secretary to General Winfield Scott, the ranking American general. When Williams informed General Scott that his loyalties were with the South, he was initially sent to Governor's Island, New York, be-

A drawing depicting the hanging of Colonel William O. Williams and Lieutenant Walter G. Peters
COURTESY OF *HARPER'S PICTORIAL HISTORY OF THE CIVIL WAR*

cause he had been privy to sensitive information. Three months later, Federal officials allowed him to go home, where he made himself available for military duty.

Well aware of Williams's service in the army and his family background, the Confederate high command commissioned him as a colonel of artillery and assigned him to General Leonidas Polk, "the Fighting Bishop." But a subsequent incident between Colonel Williams—a strict disciplinarian—and one of his men resulted in the soldier's death. Though Williams performed admirably at Shiloh, his immediate commander had lost faith in him. A transfer was in order. Accordingly, General Braxton Bragg accepted Williams as his assistant chief of artillery.

Following Bragg's disappointing performance at the Battle of Stone's River in early January 1863, Williams began to devise a daring enterprise against the Union army. Family members knew that Orton was fond of drink and considered him a bit reckless. They were little surprised, then, when he embarked upon a career in espionage. To mask his identity and plans, Colonel Williams was assigned to the cavalry under the name of Colonel Lawrence W. Orton. Friends and family speculated that he was about to embark upon covert operations in Europe and Canada. However, the colonel chose to begin in Tennessee.

Because of his association with General Scott in the old army, Williams was well versed in the issuance of paperwork in the Federal military. Thus, he took elaborate measures to ensure the success of his initial mission. A cousin of his, Lieutenant Walter G. Peters, was also to take part. Dressed in Yankee blue, the two Confederate agents, mounted on fine horses, rode up to the entrance of Fort Granger near Franklin, Tennessee, on the afternoon of June 8, 1863. After announcing themselves as Colonel Auton and Major Dunlap, they presented to the Union sentry purported orders from the United States secretary of war wherein the two were directed to "inspect immediately the departments of the Ohio and Cumberland." Their passes, bearing the forged signature of General James A. Garfield, the chief of staff of the Army of the Cumberland, looked authentic. However, the guard was bewildered because the two officers had arrived without baggage. Williams allayed his concern by explaining that they had been forced to abandon their belongings in their flight from a Confederate patrol.

Once they gained entry into the fortified compound, Williams and Peters were introduced to the post commander, Colonel John P. Baird. Following a thorough inspection of the fort, the two Southerners carried their ruse a step closer to the absurd. Lamenting their loss of money during the supposed encounter with Confederate raiders, they induced Baird to lend them fifty dollars. The inspectors then merrily mounted their horses, satisfied that their visit was a complete success. But as they exited the fort, Colonel Louis D. Watkins happened to ride past them. After taking a close look at Williams's face, he hurried to Colonel Baird and inquired about the identity of the strangers. Baird declared rather matter-of-factly, "They are inspecting officers of the United States army, and they have just been making us a visit." Watkins responded, "There must be some mistake. I think I recognized one of these men as an old army officer in the Confederate service."

After a brief discussion, Watkins and his orderly took up pursuit and ultimately caught Williams and Peters. With guns pointed at them, the disguised Confederates accompanied the Yankee colonel to be searched. Inscribed on the blades of their swords were their actual names, followed by the initials *C.S.A.*

Following their arrest, Williams and Peters were returned to Fort Granger. An investigation was immediately initiated. General William Rosecrans and General Garfield notified Colonel Baird that no such men could be found in the Union army. By midnight that same day, Baird received a dispatch instructing him to immediately convene a court-martial.

At three o'clock in the morning on June 9, the hastily convened military tribunal completed its business and found the two men "guilty of the charge of being spies found within the lines of the United States Army." An hour later, Colonel Baird received another telegraph from General Garfield, this one with ominous overtones: "The general commanding directs that the two spies, if found guilty, be hung at once."

Meanwhile, the post commander had become unnerved when he discovered that one of the condemned men was related to General Robert E. Lee. Baird's distress was evident in a telegraph to General Garfield: "Colonel Watkins says Colonel Williams is a first cousin of General Robert E. Lee. . . . We are consulting. Must I hang him? If you can direct me to send him to hang somewhere else, I would like it."

Garfield was adamant. Even the telegraphic entreaty of Colonel Williams fell on deaf ears: "Will you not have any clemency for the son of Captain Williams who fell at Monterey, Mexico? As my dying breath, I protest our innocence as spies. Save also my friend."

By daylight, Union soldiers were hard at work constructing a scaffold. Convinced he was about to die, Williams scrawled a letter to his sister, Martha. It read, in part, "Do not believe that I am a spy. With my dying breath I deny the charge. Do not grieve too much for me. . . . Altho I die a horrible death, I will meet my death with the fortitude becoming the son of a man whose last words to his children were, 'Tell them I died at the head of my column.' "

Colonel Baird was perplexed about the intent of Williams and Peters. He noted, "They were not spies in the ordinary sense. Said they were going to Canada and something about Europe. . . . They would not disclose their true object. Their conduct was very singular, indeed; I can make nothing of it."

By nine o'clock in the morning on June 9, the officer in charge of the execution reported to Colonel Baird that all was ready. Williams and Peters were escorted to the scaffold, which was enclosed by the garrison of Fort Granger. In open sight were two plain coffins.

When Lieutenant Peters's eyes fell upon the apparatus of death, terror engulfed him, and he began to weep. Williams snapped, "Dry those tears and die like a man!" Soon, the ropes were placed around the necks of the condemned men. Williams struggled to embrace his comrade and said, "Goodbye, Peters. Let us die like brave men!"

Then the order was given and the execution completed, thus bringing to an end a bizarre chapter in the annals of military espionage.

Private Stringfellow Houston

The Indefatigable Spirit of Youth

Vicksburg, Mississippi
Early summer 1863

"No, Captain, they have not killed me; they have just shot out my eye."

Of the many sad chapters of Civil War history, none is more tragic than that of the teenage soldiers who bled and died in large numbers in both armies. Long before they were able to vote, these young warriors participated in combat on virtually every field of battle during the four-year conflict. Despite their tender age, they displayed the same valor, tenacity, and ferocity as their older comrades. And the boy soldiers manifested a special spirit that is reserved to the young. No lad of the Confederacy exhibited more determination and sacrifice than Private Stringfellow Houston, a poor farm boy from Charlton County, Missouri.

In May 1862, when Claiborne F. Jackson, the newly elected governor of Missouri, issued a call for fifty thousand state troops to repel the invading Federal army, Stringfellow Houston was living with his widowed mother on a small farm in the north-central part of the state. As the youthful "man" of the house, "String," as Houston was known, had been forced to forgo any formal education in order to assist his mother in keeping the farm going. But he and his mother agreed that String must answer the call of the

A drawing showing combat during the siege of Vicksburg, where Private Stringfellow Houston died
COURTESY OF *HARPER'S PICTORIAL HISTORY OF THE CIVIL WAR*

governor to come to the defense of Missouri. Accordingly, he volunteered for one year of duty in the Missouri state forces, commanded by General Sterling Price.

Though only a private, String Houston quickly won the admiration of officers and men alike. His captain, Albert B. Danner, offered this: "String never missed a fight unless he was in the hospital recovering from a wound, for he was one of the wounded in nearly every engagement, but usually back with his company ready for the next battle. Always cheerful and keen to be in the fight, he did many daring deeds. If in a charge, he was just a little ahead of the line, for he was active and strong and impulsive. If on skirmishing or picket duty, the officer in charge would always have something to say about the efficiency shown by String. This boy was hopeful, bright, full of fun, and really seemed to enjoy the risk and excitement of a battle."

With the passage of time, severe attrition occasioned by battlefield casualties and desertion was a source of discouragement for the Missouri troops fighting for the South. But String, owing to his conviction that he was fighting for a just and honorable cause, maintained a boundless optimism that the Confederacy would prevail.

Only when he received sorrowful letters from home did String's youthful exuberance flag. On one such occasion, he called at the tent of Captain Danner. There, he asked the officer to read his mother's letter, which had somehow made it through enemy lines. In the missive, Mrs. Houston related the dire straits she faced. Her resources were depleted, and her situation was hopeless unless her son could return home to help her. String deeply loved his mother and could not bear to lose her, yet he was duty bound to the Southern war effort. Captain Danner sympathized with the boy. After a lengthy discussion, he pointed out a stark reality: If String attempted to return to his home, the military forces then in control of that part of Missouri would likely kill him. Consequently, he would be unable to help his mother. Danner's rational words led String to stay with his company.

Not long after that fateful decision, String and his comrades were among the Confederates surrounded by the enemy at Vicksburg, Mississippi. From the river, the Union fleet bombarded the Southerners, who were forced to live in trenches around the city, which was encircled on land by General U. S. Grant's enormous army. For more than forty days, String was among those who exposed themselves to great danger as they worked tirelessly about the ditches to fortify their position.

During some of the heaviest fighting of the siege, Captain Danner was scrambling to get an order to the front line when he encountered a group of soldiers carrying a battle casualty on a stretcher. One of the litter bearers called out, "Captain, this is String Houston." Danner cried, "Poor String, they have got him at last." Then the captain heard the voice of the young private he had come to love as a son. More than a half-century later, Danner recalled the moment: "I did not forget and have never forgotten the tone nor the words of String Houston as he was being carried, as I supposed, to his deathbed. There was no whining or shadow of complaint; without hope of special attention or reward of any kind, he offered his life and took what came to him."

String, his face so smudged with blood and powder that his features were unrecognizable, spoke from the stretcher in a voice filled with remarkable cheerfulness: "No, Captain, they have not killed me; they have just shot out my eye, and when I get back from the hospital I can shoot that much faster, as I won't have to shut it."

Much to Danner's surprise, String returned from the hospital to fight with one eye. But his return was short lived, for he fell with a mortal wound in a trench at Vicksburg, surrounded by members of his company.

Several years after the war, Captain Danner traveled to Brunswick, Missouri, in a quest to locate String's mother. He was anxious to comfort her with a living testimony to the valor and sterling example of her son. But try as he might, Danner could never ascertain what had become of the woman. In his despair, he paid tribute to her and the other mothers of young Confederate warriors: "Doubtless if she survived the war she waited anxiously, hoping for the return of her boy day after day. I imagine that during the night a candle was left burning in the window to light him on his way; and with every noise—a footstep in the road, the bark of a dog, the blowing of the wind in the trees—she would start up to greet her boy."

Colonel Henry "Harry" King Burgwyn, Jr.
The Boy Colonel

Gettysburg, Pennsylvania
July 1, 1863

"Tell the General my men never failed me at a single point."

In the annals of Confederate military history, no name ranks higher on the roll of honor than that of Colonel Harry Burgwyn, Jr. A lieutenant colonel at the age of nineteen and a full colonel before his twenty-first birthday, he was widely known as "the Boy Colonel of the Confederacy." Despite being one of the youngest regimental commanders in either army, Burgwyn led the Twenty-sixth North Carolina into battle with the skill, boldness, wisdom, alacrity, and gallantry of a graying veteran. Nowhere was his valor more conspicuous than at Gettysburg on the first day of the pivotal battle. There, he fought to the death.

Reared on a plantation in northeastern North Carolina, Burgwyn enjoyed a life of privilege. His early education came from plantation tutors, but when as a teenager he aspired to attend West Point, he traveled to New York for preparatory study. His subsequent request for an appointment to the United States Military Academy was denied by President James Buchanan. Consequently, Burgwyn returned home and enrolled at the University of North Carolina. Ironically, when he graduated in 1859, the commencement speaker was President Buchanan.

His abiding desire for a military education led Burgwyn to enroll at Virginia Military Institute soon after obtaining his degree in Chapel Hill. Thanks to his prior education, he was a member of the class of 1861 at V.M.I., where he drew the praise of his instructors, particularly Thomas Jonathan Jackson. In the spring of 1861, the bright young graduate set out for North Carolina, where he would offer his sword in defense of the South. With him, he carried Jackson's recommendation that he would "make an ornament not only to the artillery, but any branch of the military service."

In the wake of North Carolina's secession on May 20, Burgwyn was commissioned a major. After participating in a brief recruiting expedition to the western part of the state, he went to Raleigh, where he was named lieutenant colonel of the Twenty-sixth North Carolina on August 27. An entry in his journal noted as "Strictly Private" expressed Burgwyn's feelings about his promotion: "I am now 19 years, 9 months & 27 days old & probably the youngest Lt. Col. in the Confederate or U.S. service. . . . May Almighty God lend his aid in discharging my duty to him and to my country."

Commanded by Colonel Zebulon B. Vance, the Twenty-sixth North Carolina spent six months in the defense of the North Carolina coast. During that time, Vance gave the regiment its unique esprit de corps, while Burgwyn instilled discipline in the men and aided them in perfecting their military skills.

In March 1862, the officers and men of the Twenty-sixth fought with distinction in the Confederate loss at New Bern. As the last man to make his escape across Brice's Creek in the Southern retreat, Harry Burgwyn earned the admiration of his men and the praise of his colonel. Vance lauded him for "great coolness and efficiency."

Following the Southern debacle on the North Carolina coast, the regiment was dispatched to Virginia, where Vance and Burgwyn capably led their soldiers in the Seven Days' Campaign around Richmond. A month or so later, Vance left the Twenty-sixth to become governor of North Carolina. With complete disregard to the grousing by Brigadier General Robert Ransom that he did not want any "boy colonels" in his brigade, the men of the Twenty-sixth twice voted for Burgwyn as their new commander. And thus, he was elevated to the rank of colonel several months before his twenty-first birthday. When he stepped to the front of the regiment as its new

Colonel Henry "Harry" King Burgwyn, Jr.
Courtesy of The North Carolina State Archives

colonel for the first time, he enjoyed the confidence of the rank and file. One of his charges wrote, "Harry was very much beloved by all his men & officers & much respected for his courage & competency by all who knew him."

Because of Ransom's reservations about the new colonel, the Twenty-sixth was transferred to the brigade of General James Johnston Pettigrew. For Burgwyn, the change was fortuitous because Pettigrew, a fellow North Carolinian, shared many of his character traits, among them intelligence, dedication to duty, and modesty. One member of Burgwyn's regiment declared, "It seemed as if Pettigrew and Burgwyn were made for each other. Alike in bravery, alike in action, alike in military bearing, alike in readiness for battle and in skillful horsemanship, they were beloved alike by the soldiers of the Twenty-sixth. Each served as a pattern for the other, and in imitating each other they reached the highest excellence possible in attainment in every trait which distinguishes the ideal soldier."

In less than a year, Colonel Burgwyn molded the Twenty-sixth into the fighting unit that some historians have deemed the most distinguished regiment North Carolina provided to the Confederacy. In the words of one of Burgwyn's officers, "[A] finer body of men never gathered for battle. [These] men were patriots; they loved their country, they loved liberty. . . . They were quick to see, quick to understand, quick to act."

Morale was at a peak when Harry put his eight-hundred-man force on the march on June 15, 1863, as Lee's invasion of the North began. One private in the ranks offered a description of the scene: "What a fine appearance the regiment made as it marched out from its bivuoac near Fredericksburg that beautiful June morning. The men beaming in their splendid uniforms, the colors flying, and the drums beating, everything seemed propitious of success." Little did Colonel Burgwyn or his men know that they were soon to achieve their greatest glory at an unimaginable price.

On the steamy afternoon of Wednesday, July 1, the men prepared for combat at a small town in southern Pennsylvania. Major John T. Jones described the position of the regiment at Gettysburg as Burgwyn impatiently waited for orders to attack: "In our front was a wheat field about a fourth of a mile wide, then came a branch (Willoughby Run) with thick underbrush and briers skirting the banks. Beyond this was an open field with the exception of a wooded hill (McPherson's Woods) directly in front of the Twenty-sixth Regiment, and about covering its front."

As Burgwyn's men watched and waited, they saw that the regiment was about to go into combat against overwhelming numbers, just as it had many times before. Infesting McPherson's Woods were three lines of Federal artillery and infantry, including the vaunted Twenty-fourth Michigan, better known as "the Iron Brigade."

At two o'clock, the long-awaited call of "Attention!" spread down the long line of three thousand Confederates in the division of Major General Henry Heth. Manning the center was the Twenty-sixth North Carolina. Colonel Burgwyn moved to the front of his troops. His lieutenant colonel, John R. Lane, stood on the left, and Major John T. Jones on the right. Color Sergeant J. B. Mansfield stepped four paces to the front with the regimental flag, and the eight color guards promptly assumed their places. Burgwyn shouted, "Forward, march!" George C. Underwood, assistant surgeon of the regiment, recalled what happened next: "All to a man stepped off, apparently as willingly and proudly as if they were on review."

Yankee guns suddenly blazed from the wooded heights. Some North Carolinians fell, but most of the Union marksmen aimed too high. On stormed Burgwyn and his warriors over the three hundred yards that separated them from the enemy. Dr. Underwood remembered, "All kept the step and made as pretty and perfect a line as a regiment ever made, every man endeavoring to keep dressed on the colors."

When the Tar Heels reached the branch, a heavy enfilading fire from artillery caused some temporary disorganization in the ranks, but as soon as the crossing was effected, Burgwyn's men closed up in good order. He then directed his charges up the Yankee-held hill in the face of withering fire. According to Dr. Underwood, "It seemed that the bullets were as thick as hail stones in a storm." As they slowly, steadily made their way up the slope, the North Carolinians unleashed the Rebel yell. "Their advance was not checked," noted Colonel Henry Morrow of the Iron Brigade, "and on they came with rapid strides, yelling like demons."

Unaware that the Twenty-sixth had smashed through the first Federal line, Lieutenant Colonel Lane hurried over from his post to confer with Burgwyn, who screamed with excitement, "It is all right in the center and on the left; we have broken the first line of the enemy!" Lane replied confidently, "We are in line on the right, Colonel."

As Burgwyn's men poured into the second enemy line, the fighting became more intense. Suddenly, he came face to face with Captain W. W. McCreery, the assistant inspector general of General Pettigrew's brigade. McCreery bore a special message for Burgwyn from Pettigrew: "Tell him, his regiment has covered itself in glory."

Inspired by the compliment, Burgwyn spread it through the ranks to rally his men, for already the regimental colors had fallen ten times. All of his colorbearers were down when Captain McCreery, a West Pointer, seized the flag and waved it proudly as he stormed to the front, where a ball plowed through his heart. Immediately, twenty-eight-year-old lieutenant George Wilcox raced forward, picked up the blood-drenched banner, and attempted to lead the charge atop the ridge. Though he managed but a few steps before he was wounded in the right side, Wilcox stumbled forward, flag in hand. Another wound, this one to the left foot, sent him crashing to the bloody landscape. When the flag remained on the ground, the onrushing Confederates began to hesitate.

Sensing a crisis was at hand, Burgwyn pulled the flag from Wilcox's grasp. Flag in his left hand and saber in his right, the colonel moved to the front. There, he called out, "Dress on the colors!" From the ever-thinning ranks came Private Frank L. Honeycutt, who pleaded with the colonel to allow him the honor of advancing the banner. Honeycutt took the staff from Burgwyn's hands and managed just two steps before he was killed by a bullet to the head. At the same time, Burgwyn was hit by a ball that entered his body on the left side, pierced both lungs, and sent him spiraling to the ground.

Lieutenant Colonel Lane rushed to the side of his fallen commander. Kneeling, he asked, "My dear Colonel, are you severely hurt?" Burgwyn's head was slumped, and he could not speak, yet he managed to press the lieutenant colonel's left hand. "He looked as pleasant as if victory were on his brow," Lane remarked. The lieutenant colonel was reluctant to leave, but he knew he must assume command.

After reorganizing the attacking force, Lane caught sight of the regimental banner beside the lifeless body of Private Honeycutt. At the same moment, Lieutenant Milton B. Blair took hold of the flag. As he began to hoist it, Lane said, "Blair, give me them colors!" Blair was quick to respond, "No man can take these colors and live!" But Lane asserted, "It is my time to take them now." Acceding to his commander's wishes, Blair warned, "You will get tired of them."

Hoisting the colors high, Lane rallied his Tar Heels in a last grand charge to send the Federals into retreat. From his command position on nearby Herr Ridge, General Pettigrew watched with excitement as the survivors of the Twenty-sixth followed their flag to victory. Describing the performance of Colonel Burgwyn's regiment on July 1, Pettigrew observed, "It is the bravest act I ever saw."

As the Union soldiers fled the battle, one of their sharpshooters was attracted to the splendid bearing of Lieutenant Colonel Lane. His musket resting on a tree, the Yankee fired at thirty paces. His well-placed shot struck the Confederate officer in the back of the neck just below the brain and smashed through his jaw and mouth. When Lane fell, so did the colors of the Twenty-sixth North Carolina, for the fourteenth and final time on July 1.

In the aftermath of the hard-earned Confederate triumph, the regiment counted its casualties. Of the 800 effectives who had taken the field, only

216 were fit for duty when the sun went down. In less than six hours, the ranks had been diminished by nearly 75 percent.

Without question, the most costly loss was Colonel Burgwyn. Just moments after Lieutenant Colonel Lane left Burgwyn's side, Lieutenant Wilcox, wounded himself, crawled forward to render aid to his fallen commander. Wilcox later wrote, "He motioned to his side and tried to speak but seemingly in agony of the death, and amidst the terrible din and confusion of arms, I could not understand what he said." Anxious to get the colonel out of harm's way, Wilcox directed several privates to put Burgwyn on a blanket and carry him down the hill away from the fight.

Burgwyn was placed on the ground at Willoughby Run. His frock coat was removed and his wounds bathed. Captain Louis Young arrived on the scene, cradled the colonel in his arms, and said, "I regret to see you as wounded as you are." Burgwyn responded with resignation, "The Lord's will be done. We have gained the greatest victory in the war. I have no regret at my approaching death. I fell in the defense of my country."

Federal shells were exploding nearby, so Burgwyn's attendants summoned an ambulance. While they maintained their death vigil, he lapsed into unconsciousness. To revive him, they pulled a flask of French brandy—a gift from Burgwyn's father—from his frock coat. Captain Young managed to get him to swallow a small quantity of the spirits, which revived him. He asked that his friends send his love to his family.

Private William Cheek was holding the colonel's hand when the ambulance finally arrived. But it was of no use. The end was very near. Burgwyn inquired about his men and was assured that they had carried the day. He was pleased. "I know my gallant regiment will do their duty," he said. "Tell the General my men never failed me at a single point." Then he asked for his sword. Once it was placed at his side, he indicated that he was "entirely satisfied with everything." Seconds later, he said very quietly, "The Lord's will be done." He spoke no more.

Burgwyn's comrades and friends buried him under the shade of a walnut tree about two miles from Gettysburg near the Chambersburg Pike. Private Cheek, who was at his commander's side when he died, offered a perfect description of the Boy Colonel of the Confederacy: "I never saw a braver man than he."

Colonel Isaac Erwin Avery
Cemetery Hill

Gettysburg, Pennsylvania
July 2, 1863

"Tell my father I died with my face to the enemy."

When a brigadier general was incapacitated by a battle wound or injury, the temporary command of his brigade usually devolved to its senior colonel. For that colonel, the elevated position was fraught with danger as well as opportunity. Courageous, skillful leadership of the brigade could make the colonel a new general, or it could get him killed. Isaac Erwin Avery, the thirty-four-year-old colonel of the Sixth North Carolina, was well aware of the promise and the peril when he assumed command of Brigadier General Robert F. Hoke's brigade of Tar Heel soldiers in the spring of 1863.

General Hoke went down with a gunshot wound to his left shoulder at Salem Church, Virginia, on May 4. Three weeks later, as Robert E. Lee developed his plan "to transfer the war into the enemy's country" and to make Union forces leave Virginia, it became apparent that Hoke would not be able to lead his soldiers on the ambitious expedition to Pennsylvania. Colonel Isaac Avery was the logical choice as his replacement.

Avery was the consummate field officer. Descended from a politically prominent family that produced five Confederate officers, four of whom died as a result of the war, the bachelor left his plantation in Burke County, North

Colonel Isaac Erwin Avery
Courtesy of The North Carolina State Archives

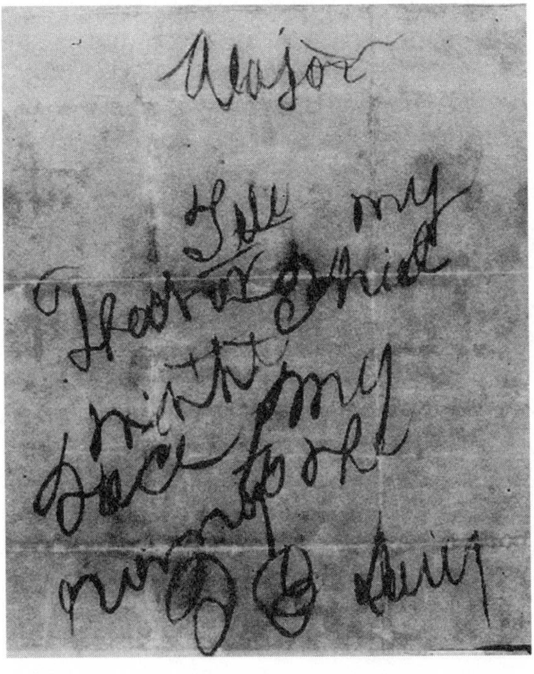

A photograph of the handwritten message found near Colonel Isaac Erwin Avery's hand on the battlefield at Gettysburg on July 2, 1863. Avery was mortally wounded while leading General Robert F. Hoke's brigade up Cemetery Hill. The note reads: "Major Tell my father I died with my face to the enemy. I.E. Avery."
Courtesy of The North Carolina State Archives

Carolina, at the outbreak of the war to assist his business associate, Colonel Charles Fisher, in organizing the Sixth North Carolina. Receiving his baptism by fire at Manassas in July 1861, Avery, then a captain, witnessed Fisher lose his life while leading the regiment into the fray. Almost two years later, Avery would be called on to make the same sacrifice.

About eleven o'clock in the morning on Thursday, June 4, 1863, Hoke's brigade, with Avery in command, struck camp at Hamilton's Crossing, Virginia, and joined the other brigades in the division of Major General Jubal Early on the long march north. Over the month that followed, Avery demonstrated that he was ready to step up to the next level of command. A number of prominent generals including Early, John Bell Hood, William Dorsey Pender, and Evander Law recommended him for promotion to general, but the cruel fate of war would intervene all too soon.

In the wake of the fighting at Winchester, Virginia, on June 15, Avery's command was depleted when one of his four regiments and a battalion of sharpshooters were detached for other duties. On the morning of July 1, Avery's three remaining regiments were pushing through Heidlersburg, Pennsylvania, when Early received a dispatch from Lieutenant General Richard Ewell directing him to move his division swiftly to Gettysburg. Marching seven miles in that direction at a rapid pace, Avery and his men saw the town's spires to the south as noon approached.

As the colonel and his senior officers and staff discussed the booming artillery, Early's adjutant galloped up with an order directing the brigade to make haste to the battle, which was raging on the west and northwest sides of the town. Dropping their blankets and other nonessential encumbrances, the North Carolinians quick-stepped toward the action. They could see a cloud of smoke hovering over the town and could hear the raging battle.

Early's division was deployed on the Confederate left. Colonel Avery positioned his forces on the extreme left of the division. About three o'clock that afternoon, as a refreshing mist began to fall, the order was given for Early's division to advance. Avery's three regiments moved out slowly in the face of an enemy protected by stone fences on a hill on the northeast side of town. Separating the warring factions was Rock Creek, a slow-moving stream with rugged banks. When Avery's troops reached the creek, just two hundred yards from the Federal position, Union artillery opened up on them. Instantly, Avery gave the order to charge. His soldiers scrambled through the water and surged up the hill to the stone wall protecting the enemy.

On that day, the Tar Heels were unstoppable. Captain John A. McPherson of Company E of "the Bloody Sixth"—the nickname of Avery's regiment (see pages 12-15)—praised his fellow North Carolinians in a letter to Avery's father on August 3, 1863: "I never saw men fight better or act more gallant than the men of our Brigade. Col. Avery rode up and down the lines and some of the time he was in front of the Brigade gallantly leading and cheering on his Brigade. He rode to within 30 or 40 yards of the enemy before we broke their lines but at last they broke and we drove them to town."

Jubal Early was overwhelmed by the Confederate success, deeming it "a brilliant victory." Hamilton Jones, one of Avery's fellow colonels, proclaimed, "It looked indeed as if the end of the war had come." However, Lieutenant General Ewell failed to follow up on the victory, and the Union forces who escaped capture took refuge on Cemetery Hill and the surrounding heights. Avery's brigade and Brigadier General Harry Hays's demi-brigade of Louisianians settled down for the night in a wheat field in a ravine near the base of East Cemetery Hill.

As the new day dawned, the Southerners at the base of the hill discovered that their adversaries had done a miraculous job of strengthening their position at the summit. Union artillery batteries, well placed behind newly constructed breastworks, lined the hill. German immigrants in Leopold von Gilsa's New York brigade formed a strong skirmish line, protected by the artillery and the stone fences and trenches at the crest of the hill. These skirmishers offered heavy fire throughout the morning and afternoon, forcing the soldiers of Avery and Hays to remain prone in the wheat field under a sweltering sun.

Around four o'clock that afternoon, Confederate artillery on both flanks of Early's division opened fire on the Union strongholds on Cemetery and Culp's Hills, thus signaling that the long wait for the infantry was nearing an end. When the enemy artillery offered a response, Major James F. Beall of the Twenty-first North Carolina noted that "it fell like music upon our ears." Avery's men were anxious for another chance to smash the Union lines.

The sun was low in the western sky by the time Avery was instructed to ready his brigade for combat. After a bit of deliberation, the colonel decided that he would lead the attack up the hill on horseback. His mount at Gettysburg was General Hoke's big black war-horse.

When the time for the infantry assault was at hand, the Confederate batteries facing Cemetery Hill fell silent, their loud blasts replaced by the blare of Confederate bugles. Quickly, the two diminutive brigades—Hays had but twelve hundred men and Avery nine hundred—sprang to attention. To the surprise of the Union forces defending the heights, the twenty-one hundred Confederates rose, moved forward at double-quick speed from the low ridge protecting them, and marched into open view. It took more than an hour for the North Carolinians to work their way across the seven hundred yards of rocky Pennsylvania landscape. Onward they came in the face of a murderous shower of grape and canister from the sixteen big guns atop Cemetery Hill and another half-dozen on Culp's. Lines of well-entrenched sharpshooters, firing from behind stone walls on the incline, took a deadly toll.

As the twilight on July 2 gave way to darkness, the galling fire from the Union guns opened wide holes in the Confederate lines, but the surviving Southern soldiers continued forward. They drove back the troops manning the enemy's main line of works, then scrambled up the hill. Fewer than seventy-five men from Avery's regiment and a smaller number from the Ninth Louisiana reached the summit. They silenced and spiked the guns there and planted the colors of the Sixth North Carolina atop Cemetery Hill. General Hays remarked on the sudden quiet: "At that time, every piece of artillery that had been firing at us had been silenced."

For a fleeting moment, the troops of Colonel Isaac Avery occupied the hill on the outskirts of Gettysburg that will forever represent the apogee of the Confederate war effort. Captain Neill Ray of the Sixth North Carolina noted, "We had full possession of East Cemetery Hill, the key to Meade's position, and we held it for several minutes." Historian Glenn Tucker subsequently pointed out the significance of the Tar Heels' accomplishment: "Here was a high point, possibly the high point, of Lee's invasion of the Free States." Walter Clark, the youngest commissioned officer in the Confederate army, who later served as chief justice of the North Carolina Supreme Court, termed it "undisputable fact that on the evening of the second day Hoke's brigade . . . together with Louisianians from Hays brigade, climbed Cemetery Heights, being farther than any other troops ventured during the three days [at Gettysburg]."

But Colonel Avery was not on hand to enjoy the fleeting Confederate success at the top of the hill. He had fallen early in the assault. As the only mounted officer in the charge, he had proven a perfect target for the enemy skirmishers at the base of the hill. A bullet pierced his neck on the right side and, according to field reports, "plowed its way through the great blood vessels and nerves that supplied the upper extremities." Critically wounded, he slumped off his horse and fell to the ground. Few, if any, of Avery's onrushing men saw their commander fall, owing to the darkness and the dense smoke from the guns that blazed on the hillside.

As he lay bleeding to death far from his home in western North Carolina, the colonel was unable to speak. He managed to pull from his frock coat a pencil and a scrap of Confederate notepaper. His right arm paralyzed by the wound, Avery used his left to scrawl a few words to his hometown friend and junior officer, Major Samuel M. Tate. His usually beautiful penmanship was now reduced to indistinct characters, but Avery's last words, jumbled on a small bit of paper, presented a clear message that would be uttered time and time again far beyond the bloody battlefield at Gettysburg: "Major: Tell my father I died with my face to the enemy. I. E. Avery."

When litter bearers reached the unconscious colonel, they found the bloodstained note beside his hand. Colonel Isaac Erwin Avery died within hours at a field hospital.

Decades later, Lord James Bryce, the British ambassador to the United States, happened to notice a dingy piece of Confederate notepaper on display at the North Carolina Department of Archives and History in Raleigh. Deeply moved by Avery's last official act as commander of Hoke's brigade, Bryce remarked, "The message of that soldier is the message of our race to the world."

Brigadier General William Barksdale

Living and Dying the Dream

Gettysburg, Pennsylvania
July 3, 1863

"Tell my wife I am shot, but we fought like hell."

From the Confederate perspective, no battle of the Civil War was more symbolic of what might have been than Gettysburg. On a number of occasions, particularly during the first and second days of that pivotal battle in early July 1863, the Southern dream of crushing Federal lines on Northern soil and thereby forcing Washington to sue for peace was close to reality. A case in point was the gallant charge of Brigadier General William Barksdale's Mississippians through the famed Peach Orchard toward Little Round Top on the evening of July 2. At the head of the deadly assault, the forty-one-year-old Barksdale lived and died the dream of Southern independence.

Born in Tennessee on August 21, 1821, Barksdale lived most of his adult life in Columbus, Mississippi, where he practiced law and edited a pro-slavery newspaper. Following Barksdale's military service as an officer in the Mexican War, Mississippi voters elected him to four consecutive terms in the United States House of Representatives. Known in Washington as a staunch advocate of states' rights, the barrel-chested Barksdale resigned from Congress when Mississippi seceded in March 1861. Casting his lot with the military fortunes of the South, he served as quartermaster general of his state for a brief period

Brigadier General William Barksdale
COURTESY OF *HARPER'S PICTORIAL HISTORY OF THE CIVIL WAR*

until he was appointed colonel of the Thirteenth Mississippi in May 1861. Over the year that followed, his regiment was involved in almost every major battle in the East.

His skillful regimental leadership led to Barksdale's rapid promotion to brigadier general on August 12, 1862. His new command consisted of his former regiment and three others from Mississippi. He quickly molded the brigade into a crack fighting unit. A Confederate major from Virginia termed Barksdale's brigade "the finest body I ever saw . . . almost giants in size and power . . . and almost without exception fine shots."

Less than a month after his promotion, General Barksdale and his command drove Federal troops from the crest of Maryland Heights, thus sealing Stonewall Jackson's victory at Harpers Ferry. Even brighter days followed just four days later, on September 17, when Barksdale played a conspicuous role in the Confederate attack that led to the rout of General John Sedgwick's Union division at Sharpsburg. As he witnessed the bold charge that drove the Yankees from the West Woods, Barksdale's immediate commander, Major General Lafayette McLaws, noted that the Mississippi general fought with "radiant wild joy."

Three months later, a sizable Union force threatened to cross the Rappahannock River to capture Fredericksburg, Virginia. Barksdale was ordered to occupy the city and repel the anticipated enemy crossing until Robert E. Lee could marshal his army into a defensive position. Despite a heavy artillery bombardment from big Union guns, the Mississippians managed to hold the Federal pontoon-bridge builders at bay for sixteen hours. At one point during the horrific fight, Barksdale dispatched a courier to his superiors with a bold message: "Tell General Lee if he wants a bridge of dead Yankees I can furnish him with one!"

In early May 1863, Barksdale's warriors again defended Fredericksburg while Lee and Stonewall Jackson did battle with the Army of the Potomac at nearby Chancellorsville. Barksdale, known for his willingness to fight against overwhelming odds, successfully protected the rear of the Confederate army from his position at Marye's Heights with forces that were heavily outnumbered.

On the afternoon of July 2, 1863, Barksdale's battle-tested veterans were ready for action near the Peach Orchard along the Emmitsburg Road in Gettysburg. Their general was itching to take part in the echelon attack designed to break through General George Meade's famous "fishhook." From the Confederate lines, it appeared that Meade and his subordinate, General Dan Sickles, had ignored the Southern threat at the Peach Orchard. Here was a great opportunity.

On that day as on all the others, Barksdale was the epitome of confidence. He proclaimed to his soldiers, "We have never been whipped, and we can never be!" According to one of his men, the general exhibited a face "radiant with joy" and exuded "a thirst for battle glory." With the enemy just six hundred yards away, the Mississippi commander begged Major General McLaws to allow him to clear the orchard of Federal soldiers: "General, let me charge. General, let me go!" But McLaws was duty bound to wait from orders from Lieutenant General James Longstreet.

As the moment of decision neared, Barksdale drew his regimental commanders together and provided them one final directive: "The line before you must be broken—to do so let every officer and man animate his comrades by his personal presence in the front line."

In a few minutes, General Longstreet rode up. Barksdale rushed to his side and, pointing to the Yankees in the distance, pleaded, "I wish you would let me go in, General; I will take that battery in five minutes." Longstreet reassured Barksdale that the fight was forthcoming: "Wait a little. We are all going in presently."

Not long thereafter, around six-thirty, Barksdale received the order he sought. The drums of the brigade began to sound, and the general galloped to the front of the Thirteenth Mississippi, his old regiment. There, he took his place about the regimental flags. In a loud, confident voice, he shouted, "Forward, men, forward!"

With Barksdale leading the charge, the Mississippians, approximately fifteen hundred in number, burst from the woods, their voices united in the Rebel yell. As they moved toward the enemy, not one of them fired a shot. Rather, they scrambled over rail fences and reached the Peach Orchard in less time than even Barksdale had calculated. A Federal officer who witnessed the electrifying spectacle termed it "the grandest charge that was ever made by mortal man."

Upon encountering the Union soldiers of the Third Corps, Barksdale's men delivered a savage assault. Within minutes, General Charles K. Graham's blue-jacketed brigade lost half its men. Graham himself went down with a serious wound, and General Sickles was toppled from his horse by a gunshot wound that would cost him his leg.

In short order, the Federal forces in the Peach Orchard were reeling. From the Union position atop Cemetery Hill, Lieutenant Frank A. Haskell reported, "The Third Corps, after a heroic but unfortunate fight, is being literally swept from the field."

All the while, Barksdale was at the head of his brigade. One of his junior officers, Major John J. Hood, recalled, "Barksdale stood on the turnpike watching the movements of his heroes as they drove the enemy before them. His bright eyes flashed as though lit by a spark from the fires eternal. His face beamed with the glow of glorious victory. His thin lip curled with that haughty smile which meant defiance. He stood the perfect picture of a true hero."

After breaking the enemy line, the Mississippians ran into stiff resistance as they moved in the direction of Plum Run. One observer indicated that Barksdale was "almost frantic with rage" at the changing fortunes of battle. Unwilling to watch his victory snatched from him, he raised his saber and screamed to his warriors, "They are whipped! We will drive them beyond the Susquehanna!"

A volley of shots rang from the Federal lines. Barksdale fell from his saddle, critically wounded in the lung and leg. Battlefield tradition holds that an enemy officer directed that a full company train its guns on Barksdale as he inspired his soldiers to keep charging.

Shortly after losing their commander, the soldiers of the Mississippi brigade retreated, and the Union line was restored. Barksdale was taken prisoner. He lingered through the night in intense pain. In the early-morning hours of July 3, he feebly looked up at a Federal surgeon and gasped his parting words: "Tell my wife I am shot, but we fought like hell."

Colonel James Keith Marshall

Sinking at the High-Water Mark

Gettysburg, Pennsylvania
July 3, 1863

"We do not know which of us will be next to fall!"

When it was released in 1993, the epic historical drama *Gettysburg* reacquainted many Americans with the gallant but futile attempt by Confederate forces to break the Union lines on Cemetery Ridge during the final day of the great battle in Pennsylvania. Although the movie paid homage to the gallantry and sacrifice of the four Virginia brigades in the division of Major General George E. Pickett, the so-called Pickett's Charge on Friday, July 3, 1863, actually involved many soldiers from four additional states. Forty regiments—eighteen from Virginia, fifteen from North Carolina, three from Tennessee, three from Mississippi, and one from Alabama—were arrayed in three divisions commanded, respectively, by Pickett (a Virginian), Brigadier General James Johnston Pettigrew (a North Carolinian), and Brigadier General Isaac Trimble (a Marylander). And it was an adopted North Carolinian from Virginia who led a brigade of Tar Heel soldiers to the stone wall on Cemetery Ridge on that fateful afternoon. Colonel James Keith Marshall gave his life at the place thereafter known as "the high-water mark of the Confederacy."

A drawing of the Battle of Gettysburg,
where Colonel James K. Marshall was killed on July 3, 1863
COURTESY OF *HARPER'S PICTORIAL HISTORY OF THE CIVIL WAR*

Just three years earlier, on July 4, 1860, Marshall, known to his friends as Jimmy, had graduated from Virginia Military Institute at the age of twenty-one. An outstanding student and leader, he served as first lieutenant of one of the cadet companies and was selected by the Society of Cadets as final orator at graduation ceremonies. Born on April 17, 1839, into a distinguished family in Fauquier County, Virginia, he moved to northeastern North Carolina two months after graduation. There, he settled in the colonial capital of Edenton to take charge of a private school and to study law in his spare time.

As his adopted state reluctantly moved toward secession in the spring of 1861, patriotic zeal led Jimmy to join the many volunteers who stepped forward to defend North Carolina. Cognizant of Marshall's leadership skills and military education, his comrades in the Chowan Dixie Boys elected Jimmy as their commander. Two days later, the unit was mustered into service as Company M of the First North Carolina Volunteers. For the duration of 1861, Captain Marshall proved to be a capable junior officer as he deployed his troops in the Tidewater area of his native state.

When North Carolina reorganized its troops in 1862, Jimmy was promoted to colonel and awarded command of the Fifty-second North Carolina. Assigned to the brigade of General Pettigrew, the regiment operated in and around Petersburg, Virginia, during much of the last half of the year. In the course of his duties there, Jimmy enjoyed one of his greatest military successes. On October 4, while on picket duty at Joyner's Ford on the Blackwater River, he received intelligence that three United States Navy gunboats were making their way up the blackwater from Albemarle Sound to join a Federal cavalry force in an attack on a Confederate pontoon bridge at Franklin. With great dispatch, Jimmy posted his best marksmen along the overgrown banks of the river with instructions to shoot every man who appeared on the decks of the approaching warships. In short order, the Tar Heel sharpshooters dropped a large number of Union soldiers, thereby forcing the Northern vessels to reverse course and abandon their mission. Meanwhile, Colonel Marshall and the remainder of his regiment chased away the enemy land forces assigned to destroy the bridge. A subsequent report in the *Richmond Enquirer* lauded Jimmy's efforts: "His repulse of the enemy's land and naval forces on the Blackwater is the first recorded victory of riflemen over gunboats."

As 1862 drew to a close, Marshall and his men were dispatched to eastern North Carolina, where they participated in Major General Daniel Harvey Hill's unsuccessful attempt to capture the coastal towns of New Bern and Washington. When the Fifty-second was ordered back to Virginia during the first week of May 1863, it arrived too late to take part in the pivotal Confederate victory at Chancellorsville. But the regiment's day of glory was soon to come, for by early June, General Robert E. Lee had matured his plan to take the war into the enemy's country. On June 14, Marshall ordered his men to strike camp at Fredericksburg. The invasion of the North was under way.

Over the course of his year or so as colonel of the Fifty-second, Jimmy had won the admiration of his men. Regimental adjutant John H. Robinson said, "Of his rank the Confederate Army had few equals and no superiors. [Marshall's] regiment was greatly attached to him; his uniform courtesy, coupled with great firmness and rigid discipline in camp, as well as on the march, had won the entire confidence of his men."

Pettigrew's brigade reached Cashtown, Pennsylvania, on Monday,

June 29. The following morning, Marshall's regiment and several others in the brigade were dispatched to Gettysburg, located six miles southeast, in search of shoes and other supplies. Thus was Marshall swept into the vortex of events that culminated in the titanic battle during the first three days of July 1863.

En route to his assigned destination, General Pettigrew came across a Confederate scout who informed him that Gettysburg was occupied by three thousand Yankee cavalrymen under General John Buford. In haste, the Southerners returned to Cashtown, where Pettigrew informed his superior, Major General Henry Heth, of the enemy presence. When General A. P. Hill arrived in Cashtown with his corps later that day, the decision was made to send the divisions of Heth and William Dorsey Pender after the Yankees on the morrow.

Early on the morning of July 1, Colonel Marshall put his Tar Heels on the march as part of the Confederate vanguard. That afternoon, Heth's division was ordered to strike the heavily fortified enemy on McPherson's Ridge. In the first major clash of the three-day battle, Pettigrew's North Carolinians were pitted against the famed Iron Brigade, considered the finest fighting unit in the Army of the Potomac. Captain Louis G. Young, a Confederate staff officer, described the scene as Colonel Marshall and the other regimental commanders led their troops into action: "When the order came to advance, Pettigrew's Brigade, about 3,000 strong, marched out in perfect alignment, and under a hot fire as was ever faced, moved steadily through the wheat, reserved its fire for close range."

Marshall's North Carolinians, positioned on the right flank of the brigade, yelled like demons as they stormed the enemy. Major John T. Jones, who participated in the ferocious assault against the Iron Brigade, recalled the success enjoyed by Marshall and his charges: "The enemy did not perceive the Fifty-second, which flanked their left, until they [the Fifty-second] discovered themselves by a raking and destructive fire into their [the Federals'] ranks, by which they were broken. On this second line the fighting was terrible—our men advancing, the enemy stubbornly resisting, until the two lines were pouring volleys into each other at a distance not greater that 20 paces. . . . At last the enemy was compelled to give way."

Jimmy Marshall played an important role in the Confederate victory that first day at Gettysburg. But success did not come without significant casualties, including Major General Heth, disabled by a severe head wound.

Colonel Marshall's men and the others in Pettigrew's brigade were allowed to rest and recuperate on July 2. Jimmy and his commanding general were given new assignments. Because of Heth's injury, temporary command of his division was awarded to Pettigrew. Jimmy Marshall was charged with the leadership of Pettigrew's brigade.

Most of the morning of July 3 was spent in preparation for the great assault by the three Confederate divisions against the Federal lines, which were entrenched behind rock walls near a copse on Cemetery Ridge. To inspire his warriors, Jimmy directed a regimental band to play "Lorena," "Dixie," and other popular airs.

At one o'clock, two guns were discharged by the Washington Artillery, the prearranged signal for the massive Confederate cannonade to commence. For more than two hours, Jimmy's soldiers waited in the shade of forested Seminary Ridge as the 140 big Southern guns traded salvos with Union field pieces.

Suddenly, the deafening roar was supplanted by an eerie silence. The time of decision was at hand. Captain Young described the scene: "The day was beautifully clear; the smoke from the guns of the artillery, which was to have concealed our start, had been blown away. Before us lay bright fields, and a fair landscape, embracing hill and dale and mountain; and beyond, fully three-fourths of a mile loomed up Cemetery Ridge, for two miles, its heights capped with cannon, and behind them the whole Army of the Potomac waiting for our little band."

When the order was given, more than thirteen thousand Confederate soldiers stepped out of the woods. The divisions of Pettigrew and Pickett formed the front line, which stretched a mile in length. As the Southern soldiers stood at attention awaiting the order to attack, General Pettigrew rode over to Jimmy Marshall, the officer now in command of his brigade, and said, "Now, Colonel, for the honor of the good old North State, forward!"

Captain Samuel A. Ashe, a North Carolinian in Trimble's division, recollected what happened next: "They moved in quick time and with admirable precision, as if on some gala day parade. It was a glorious spectacle, evoking admiration from foe and friend alike, and being the theme of unstinted praise from everyone who witnessed it."

Marshall led on horseback as his soldiers pressed toward the waiting enemy. Heavy enfilading artillery fire from Little Round Top and Cemetery Hill ripped large gaps in the North Carolina line. The men quickly closed ranks and surged onward. In the face of deadly infantry fire, they hurdled fences and charged the stone wall protecting the Union marksmen. Lieutenant B. F. Little of the Fifty-second recalled the desperate struggle: "I was shot down when in about fifty yards of the enemy's works, and the ground between where I lay and the works was thickly strewn with killed and wounded, some of them having fallen immediately at the works."

As they neared the wall, Pettigrew and Marshall continued to rally their thinning ranks. After being jolted from his horse by an explosion, Jimmy remounted and galloped forward. Amid the hail of iron and lead, he yelled to Captain Stockton Heth, "We do not know which of us will be next to fall!"

Upon reaching "the high-water mark" of the Southern war effort, the decimated brigade of North Carolinians limped back across the field in retreat. Of the seventeen hundred effectives in the brigade who took the field at the opening of the battle, only six hundred were left standing when the fighting ended on the afternoon of July 3. Among the dead was Colonel James Keith Marshall, the twenty-four-year-old Virginian who laid down his life for the South just one day short of the eighty-seventh birthday of the United States of America.

Ironically, much of the constitutional and legal framework of that nation had been established by Chief Justice John Marshall, Jimmy's grandfather.

Brigadier General Lewis Addison Armistead

That Sublime Four-Letter Word

Gettysburg, Pennsylvania
July 5, 1863

"Men who can subsist on raw corn can never be whipped."

Robert E. Lee once said, "Duty is the sublimest word in our language. Do your duty in all things. You cannot do more. You should never wish to do less."

If ever a soldier in the Army of Northern Virginia embodied Lee's words, it was Lewis Addison Armistead. Born into a family of military distinction, Armistead was a dutiful soldier all of his adult life. And when death came calling on the battlefield at Gettysburg, duty remained foremost on his mind.

Armistead was born on February 18, 1817, in New Bern, North Carolina, while his mother was visiting her parents. Duty to country was ingrained in the lad at an early age. His maternal grandfather, John Wright Stanly, played a pivotal role in the struggle for American independence and subsequently served in Congress. It was the military service of his family, however, that attracted the interest of "Lew," as young Armistead was known. His Virginia-born father, Brevet General Walter Keith Armistead, was the youngest of five brothers who served in the United States Army. One of Lew's uncles, Lieutenant Colonel George A. Armistead, achieved enduring fame as "the hero of Fort McHenry." He was the commander of the fort in

Brigadier General Lewis Addison Armistead
COURTESY OF *CONFEDERATE VETERAN*

Baltimore Harbor in September 1814 during the bombardment that inspired Francis Scott Key to write "The Star-Spangled Banner."

No one in the Armistead family was surprised when young Lew aspired to a career in the military. Following in the footsteps of his father, a member of the second class to graduate from the United States Military Academy, Lew was admitted to West Point on September 1, 1834. Although the seventeen-year-old cadet was bright, he did not graduate. On January 16, 1836, Armistead was insulted by a fellow cadet on the parade grounds at the academy. In retaliation, he broke a plate over the head of his antagonist, Jubal Early, a future Confederate general. Rather than face expulsion, Armistead tendered his resignation on January 29.

Undaunted in his quest to become a soldier, Lew completed his military education in North Carolina. On July 10, 1839, the United States Army commissioned him as a second lieutenant and assigned him to the Sixth Infantry. His first action came during the Seminole War, when he operated under the command of his father and General Zachary Taylor. Lew's subsequent service in the war against Mexico saw him breveted three times for gallantry. He was promoted to major after he led the attacking force at Chapultepec.

Following the Mexican War, Armistead spent the final fourteen years of his United States Army career on the Western frontier. There, he developed close friendships with many of the officers against whom he would fight in the Civil War. Among his most treasured military friends in the West was Winfield Scott Hancock, a future Union general.

As the crisis between the North and the South worsened in 1860, soldiers on the American frontier pondered their future. To cheer one of his pessimistic comrades, Lew declared, "I know but one country and one flag. Let me sing you a song and drive away your gloom." He proceeded to sing a song created in part thanks to the heroism of his family—"The Star-Spangled Banner." But over the next year, Armistead's beliefs and allegiance would change.

On May 26, 1861, he resigned his commission in the United States Army. He promptly traveled from San Diego to Los Angeles to bid farewell to Hancock and his wife, Almira. To his former comrade in arms, Armistead said, "Hancock, goodbye; you can never know what this cost me, and I hope God will strike me dead if I am ever induced to leave my native soil, should worse come to worse." Turning to Almira, Lew placed a satchel in her hands with instructions that it not be opened unless he died. Among its contents was Lew's personal prayer book. On the flyleaf of the book, Armistead had inscribed, "Trust in God and fear nothing."

Armistead's grueling cross-country journey came to an end on September 15, 1861, when he reported in Richmond, Virginia, and requested assignment in the Confederate army. For two weeks, he served as a major. By the end of September, he was colonel of the Fifty-seventh Virginia.

Lew Armistead entered the war much older than most of his compatriots. He had buried two young wives and a little daughter—all victims of epidemic diseases—on the frontier while serving in the United States Army. Yet the career officer had no doubts about his decision to fight for the South. In the early days of the war, he wrote to a friend, "I have been a Soldier all my life—I was an officer in the Army of the U.S., which service I left to fight for my country, and for, and with, my own People—and because they were right, and oppressed."

During his six-month tenure as a regimental commander, Armistead instilled in his men a strong sense of duty. One of his junior officers, Rawley M. Martin, observed, "He was a strict disciplinarian, but never a martinet. Obedience to duty he regarded as the first qualification of a soldier. For straggling on the march or neglect of duty on the part of his men he held the officer in immediate command strictly responsible. The private must answer to the officer, but the officer to him."

On April 1, 1862, Armistead was promoted to brigadier general. His baptism under fire in the Civil War came two months later at the Battle of Seven Pines. There, his brigade of Virginians performed miserably. As the fighting grew in intensity, most of the soldiers broke and ran. But Armistead, after his horse was killed, fought alongside the twenty stalwart men who stood their ground against heavy enemy fire.

A month after Seven Pines, the brigade performed gallantly in a charge against deadly enemy fire at Malvern Hill. Armistead lost nearly four hundred men in the battle.

Over the next thirteen months, Lew and his charges saw very limited battle action. For a time during the summer of 1862, he served as provost marshal of the Army of Northern Virginia. Once he resumed his command, the brigade was deployed at Sharpsburg on September 17. During the ensuing battle, Armistead's men were held in reserve. As Lew stood at the head of his brigade, fuming over its inactivity, a cannonball flew over a hill and hit him on the foot, temporarily incapacitating him.

When he returned to duty later in the fall, his brigade had been assigned to the division of Major General George E. Pickett. Lew reasoned that now he would finally be in the thick of the action. To his chagrin, however, the division was dispatched to procure supplies in coastal Virginia in early May 1863, while Lee and Jackson were achieving a magnificent victory at Chancellorsville. But Lew's day of glory, final duty, and death was soon to come.

On July 1, as Confederate forces routed the enemy at Gettysburg, Armistead was again miles from the big fight, his men deployed in the destruction of the railroads at Chambersburg. But a day later, Pickett was ordered to march his division twenty-six miles east to Gettysburg to participate in what would become the most famous charge of the entire war. In the middle of that grand assault would be Lew Armistead.

As the sun rose on July 3, 1863, Armistead's men from the Ninth,

Fourteenth, Thirty-eighth, Fifty-third, and Fifty-seventh Virginia assumed their positions in the Confederate lines on Seminary Ridge. Throughout the morning, the final plans were laid for the mighty charge against the center of the Union lines. Armistead thought about the adversary awaiting across the field he and his men must cross. It was General Winfield Scott Hancock, his dear friend and the commander of the Federal Second Corps.

Notwithstanding Hancock's presence, Lew was bound to his duty. When he learned that, by luck of the draw, his brigade would march last in the forthcoming action, Armistead requested that one of Pickett's staff officers intercede with General James Longstreet, Lee's immediate subordinate at Gettysburg. In response, Longstreet offered words of assurance: "You can tell General Armistead to remain where he is at present, and he can make up the distance when the advance is made."

Lew's brigade, the largest in Pickett's division, was ready to face the enemy. According to Colonel Rawley W. Martin, one of Armistead's regimental commanders, "The *esprit du corps* could not have been better; the men were in good physical condition, self-reliant and determined. They felt the gravity of the situation, for they knew well the metal foe in their front; they were serious, resolute, but not dishearten[ed]. None of the usual jokes, common on the eve of battle, were indulged in, for every man felt his individual responsibility."

Indeed, Armistead had instilled a strict sense of duty in his men. But his example was never greater than on the day that proved his last as their commander. At one o'clock that afternoon, the long line of Confederate artillery positioned in front of Seminary Ridge opened a barrage, and the big Federal guns boomed their reply. Though balls exploded all about, Armistead remained on his feet during the entire cannonade, calming his men and urging them to remain low. One of his soldiers, Robert Tyler Jones, the grandson of President John Tyler, recalled Armistead's splendid bearing: "For hours we watched the hero as he moved with easy step in front of our lines, surveying the field and marking the effect of the cannonade." When some of the men exhibited their unease about the barrage, Armistead said, "Lie still, boys, there is no safe place here." At one point during the artillery exchange, Robert Tyler Jones sprang to his feet in an attempt to join his commander as he paced. Jones remembered, "Once I rose upon my feet when he ordered me to lie down; and when I justified myself by his own example, he replied, 'Yes, but never mind me; we want men with guns in their hands.' "

Once the artillery fell silent, Armistead readied his men for the deadly work ahead. His voice boomed up and down the lines. John H. Lewis, a lieutenant in the Ninth Virginia, noted, "If I should live a hundred years I shall never forget that moment the command was given by Lewis A. Armistead on that day. He was an old army officer and was possessed of a very loud voice." Armistead proclaimed, "Rise, men!" In an instant, his troops stood to prepare themselves to march into combat. Robert Tyler Jones, a member of the color guard, described the scene: "Now, as his stentorian voice rang out like a bugle blast in the air, every man rose to his feet like clockwork, our line representing the precision and regularity of a dress parade."

Armistead drew his sword and hurried to the front of the brigade. Standing to the right of Leander C. Blackburn, his color sergeant, he inquired, "Sergeant, are you going to put those colors on the enemy's works today?" The response from his lead colorbearer brought pleasure to the general: "I will try, sir, and if a mortal man can do it, it shall be done." In gratitude, Armistead pulled a flask from his frock coat and offered a drink to the gallant soldier who would die within the hour.

"Men, remember what you are fighting for!" Armistead exclaimed. "Your homes, your firesides, and your sweethearts! Follow me!" He loosened his collar, tossed his cravat aside, and affixed his black slouch hat on the tip of his sword. Drums pounded as the brigade stepped forward some minutes after three o'clock. As the Confederates marched, the Union artillery opened up again, this time with greater intensity. Huge gaps were blown in his lines, but Lew continued to inspire his soldiers, cautioning, "Steady, men, steady!"

When the time to charge came, the Virginians unleashed the Rebel yell and stormed ahead amid shot and shell. Through it all, the forty-six-year-old general managed to stay at the forefront. Upon seeing the colors fall, Armistead called to Robert Tyler Jones to pick up the flag: "Run ahead, Bob, and cheer them up!"

Over the next few minutes, Lew managed to make it to the rock wall at the copse of trees on Cemetery Ridge, the very target of the Confederate offensive. Staring into the face of two guns of the Fourth United States

Artillery, he jumped onto the wall, placed his hand on one of the cannons, and shouted, "Give them cold steel! Who will follow me?"

As his 150 survivors followed him over the wall, rifle fire from Pennsylvania soldiers brought Armistead to the ground thirty yards from their lines. The fallen general flashed the Masonic sign of distress, which prompted several nearby Yankee soldiers to seek permission to render aid. They hurried him to the rear on a stretcher, where Henry H. Bingham introduced himself as a member of Hancock's staff. Lew said, "Tell General Hancock for me that I have done him and you all an injury which I shall regret the longest day I live." Little did Armistead know that Hancock had also been seriously wounded in the battle.

Before he was transferred to a hospital, Lew was placed on a cot at a makeshift medical facility on the field. To the physicians and nurses, he cried out, "Don't step so close to me." To a courier for General Abner Doubleday, Armistead hinted that he was not going to make it: "Tell General Doubleday in a few minutes I shall be where there is no rank."

Union surgeons, however, determined that Armistead's injuries were not life threatening. After examining and treating his wounds, Dr. Daniel G. Brinton noted, "They were two in number, neither of them of a serious character, apparently. The one in the fleshy part of the arm, the other a little below the knee . . . His prospects of recovery seemed good."

But Lew suffered from extreme exhaustion. That, coupled with shock and blood loss, led to his death on July 5. In Armistead's last hours, W. H. Moore of the Ninety-seventh Volunteers admired the Southern officer's "intense, all-consuming desire for the Confederates to win the battle" and his fervent wish "to die like a soldier."

Federal surgeons examined Armistead's wounds as he struggled for his last breaths. With his final bit of energy, he reached in the pocket of his trousers and produced a few kernels of raw corn. With the corn in plain view, he looked into the eyes of one of the physicians and whispered, "Men who can subsist on raw corn can never be whipped." His head then slumped in death.

Captain James E. Poindexter of the Thirty-eighth Virginia proclaimed the greatness of his fallen commander: "Not Wolfe at Quebec, not Ney at Waterloo ever exhibited a grander example of heroism and devotion than that displayed by our lamented chief."

In reflecting upon the loss, Robert E. Lee declared that Armistead died as he had lived, "discharging the highest duty." In his official report on the Battle of Gettysburg, the commander of the Army of Northern Virginia praised Armistead for a "devotion that never faltered and courage that shrank from no danger" and memorialized him for dying in the "highest duty of patriots." No one could have said it better about Lew Armistead, the veteran soldier whose long military career was guided by Lee's sublime four-letter word.

George Cummings, Body Servant

Undying Loyalty

Maryland
July 1863

"We'll meet again, ober de ribber."

Volumes have been written about the tragic institution of slavery in early American history. Countless stories of cruelty and sadness have been chronicled about that dark chapter that reached a crisis in the middle of the nineteenth century. Amid the myriad accounts of misery, torment, and injustice suffered by black Americans, there survive a few heartwarming stories of the special bond that developed between some masters and slaves during the Civil War. One such relationship was that of C. C. and George Cummings.

C. C. Cummings and his lifelong friend George grew up together on a plantation in Mississippi during the antebellum period. C. C. was the son of the plantation owner, and George was born to slaves owned by the Cummings family. When the North and the South went to war in 1861, C. C. volunteered for service in the Seventeenth Mississippi. Like many affluent sons of the South, the young planter took with him a body servant to attend to his personal needs on the march, in camp, and on the field. Upon being informed of his assignment, George indicated that he would be delighted to accompany his master "when he left de ole plantation in Massippi for war."

A postwar photo of C. C. Cummings during his judicial career. George Cummings was C. C. Cummings's body servant during the Civil War.
COURTESY OF *CONFEDERATE VETERAN*

As sergeant major of his regiment, C. C. Cummings took part in most of the significant battles in the Eastern theater during the first two years of the war. All along the way, George was there, displaying loyalty and affection for his master. Many years after the war, C. C. described George as "a faithful man in black who followed me through First Manassas, Leesburg, where he assisted in capturing the guns we took from Baker to the Peninsular, the Seven Days from Richmond, Fredericksburg, the bombardment of the city December 11, and the battle, two days after, at Marye's Heights, and the terrible struggle at Sharpsburg (Antietam now), and last, Gettysburg."

On the second day of the Battle of Gettysburg, Sergeant Major Cummings went down with a severe wound in the fierce fighting in the Peach Orchard. Throughout the night and the next day, when the battle was decided, George stayed by the side of his injured master, providing care and comfort.

When General Robert E. Lee ordered the Confederate retreat on July 4, the misery of the defeated Southern forces was intensified by a cold, steady rain. To ensure safe passage for his master, George secured an ambulance. But the movement out of Gettysburg was at a snail-like pace, the roads jammed with hundreds of wagons mired in the mud. C. C. noted, "All day long we moved slower than any funeral train over the pike, only getting eight miles."

On the night of July 4, Sergeant Major Cummings's condition deteriorated. Unable to travel any farther, he was carefully removed from the medical wagon and placed in a barn at the side of the road. George clung to his master. Over the next twenty-four hours, he provided as much care as possible, given the trying conditions.

At sunset the following day, word came that the Yankees were fast approaching. With alarm in his voice, George reported to C. C. that enemy troops were separating the "black folks from dar masters." He informed the wounded officer that the Union medical corps would soon arrive to render treatment. In the meantime, George reasoned that he would disappear into the night, make his way over the mountains, and catch up with the Seventeenth Mississippi, which was preparing to cross the Potomac at Williamsport. In that way, they could, according to George, meet again "ober de ribber."

C. C. recalled passing a settlement of free blacks in the vicinity of Gettysburg as his ambulance had snaked its way out of town. He strongly urged George to take his freedom by joining that settlement. But this time, George was unwilling to follow the instructions of the man who was not only his master but also his friend from childhood. Maintaining that he wanted to stay with C. C., he insisted on following his own plan.

As the time neared for what was intended to be a temporary separation, George broke his master's sword at the hilt and hid the weapon in a crack of the barn, as directed by the injured officer. Years later, C. C. remembered the moment: "I can see that faithful black face and the glint of the blade as the dying rays of that day's sun flashed upon them." Sergeant Major Cummings and his colonel, W. D. Holder, were sprawled amid thirty other wounded Confederates when George rendered his final act of service to his master. "A canteen of water and some hard tack was the last token of his kindly care for me," C. C. later recalled.

Upon his capture, the sergeant major was ministered to by Union medical corpsmen, and his right hand was amputated. Following his recovery, he was incarcerated at Chester, a few miles from Philadelphia.

Concerned about George's welfare, C. C. made numerous inquiries as the war drew to a close in the spring of 1865. Finally, a member of the Seventeenth Mississippi related the bittersweet tragedy that had befallen the dedicated servant. George had made it safely to the rear of the regiment on its retreat from Gettysburg. Along the route, he came upon a lady who was the mother of a soldier in the Seventeenth. George was able to report to her that her son had survived the battle but had been taken prisoner. In the course of that conversation, a patrol of Yankee troopers appeared without notice. George, attired in gray, bolted. Convinced that he was a Confederate soldier, the Federals offered a deadly fire. As he breathed his last, the ever-faithful man offered a parting message and a promise to his friend: "We'll meet again ober de ribber."

After the war, C. C. Cummings enjoyed a distinguished career as a judge in Texas. But he never stopped missing George, whom he described as "the truest and best friend I ever had."

Brigadier General James Johnston Pettigrew

From High Tide to Falling Waters

Bunker Hill, Virginia
July 17, 1863

"It is time to be going."

If any solider of the Civil War can accurately be described as a Renaissance man, then surely it was General James Johnston Pettigrew. Highly intelligent and multitalented, Pettigrew was deemed by noted nineteenth-century scientist Matthew Maury as "the most promising young man of the South." Some historians have subsequently proclaimed Pettigrew the most brilliant man ever produced by North Carolina. In matters military, the Tar Heel citizen-soldier was largely self-taught. Nonetheless, his innate abilities enabled Johnston, as he was known to friends and family, to lead a division to "the high-water mark of the Confederacy" on July 3, 1863. That moment of glory proved fleeting. The Confederacy's fortunes of war promptly began to recede. And just eleven days after the Battle of Gettysburg, the thirty-five-year-old general sustained a mortal wound in Maryland at a place ironically named Falling Waters.

Born on July 4, 1828, on Bonarva Plantation in eastern North Carolina, Johnston Pettigrew descended from a family that had already made its mark in the social, religious, and political affairs of the state. Johnston was something of a child prodigy. Ebenezer Pettigrew, a one-time congressman who was never known to boast of himself or his family, said of his son, "He is unequivocally the most talented person of his age that I have ever seen." Family tradition holds that the boy, in his preteen years, read the three thousand volumes in the massive plantation library. In mathematics, he was a genius. And despite suffering much sickness as a child, Johnston developed great proficiency in sports, particularly fencing and boxing.

To enable his son to achieve his unique potential, Ebenezer enrolled him in the finest preparatory school in the state. In 1843, one month before his fifteenth birthday, Johnston passed the entrance examination at the University of North Carolina. Soon thereafter, he embarked upon a brilliant scholastic career on the Chapel Hill campus. From his first day until his graduation four years later, he was the university's undisputed academic leader. His grades were the highest ever attained there. Professor Elisha Mitchell, the Chapel Hill professor for whom the highest peak east of the Mississippi River is named, referred to Pettigrew as "the pride of the college." Kemp Battle, the president of the university, said, "I have never seen a man with a more penetrating mind than Pettigrew. He seemed to me the ablest man I ever met."

When Johnston delivered the valedictory address at the graduation ceremonies of 1847, the audience included several distinguished graduates, including United States president James Knox Polk and Secretary of the Navy John Mason Young. Prior to the commencement, President Polk and Secretary Young had observed the senior examinations in mathematics and astronomy. So impressed were they with Pettigrew that he was awarded an appointment as assistant professor at the Naval Observatory in Washington, D.C.

Although Johnston made a profound impression on famed oceanographer Matthew F. Maury, the head of the observatory, he grew bored with his job and left within six months to pursue the study of law. For a year or so, he practiced law with a relative in a distinguished firm in Charleston. Then, anxious to broaden his horizons, he went to Europe for foreign study in 1849. From Germany, where he enrolled at the University of Berlin, he traveled throughout the continent on foot and horseback for two years. During his stay, he learned six languages, including Arabic and Hebrew, acquired a wealth of knowledge in French and Prussian military science, and mastered the piano. Johnston developed a special fondness for the people and customs of Spain. Accordingly, he adopted the dress of a Spanish nobleman and cut his mustache in the style of the Spaniards.

Upon his return to America in 1852, he resumed his law practice in

Brigadier General James Johnston Pettigrew
Courtesy of The North Carolina State Archives

Charleston. Four years later, voters elected him to the South Carolina legislature. In 1859, news reached South Carolina that war had broken out in Europe between Austria and Italy. Johnston made haste to Italy, where he volunteered to aid in the fight for Italian independence, only to learn that the conflict had ended. Despite the sudden turn of events, he decided to sojourn in Europe, where he acquired a deeper understanding of military logistics and tactics.

Tensions between the North and the South were growing when Pettigrew returned to Charleston in the fall of 1859. His knowledge of European military techniques made him a popular instructor for local militia units in coastal South Carolina. Meanwhile, Johnston cast a wary eye at radical Northern politicians he believed would draw the South into war.

While national events played out over the next year just as Pettigrew predicted, he was busy writing and publishing a book based on his travels in Spain. *Notes on Spain and the Spaniards in the Summer of 1859, With a Glance at Sardinia* was released in early 1861, at the very time the war came to South

Carolina. As the chief military aide to Governor Francis W. Pickens, Pettigrew was swept into the vortex of events in Charleston Harbor universally recognized as the beginning of the Civil War.

Following the capture of Fort Sumter on April 12, several offers of command were tendered to Pettigrew, but he disdained them because he wanted to be close to the action in Virginia. As a result, he entered Confederate military service as a private. But while he was passing through his native state en route to Virginia, a telegram was delivered to him whereby he was notified of his unsolicited election as colonel of the Twenty-second North Carolina.

Walter Clark, a teenage Tar Heel soldier who would ultimately become chief justice of the North Carolina Supreme Court, offered a contemporary description of the new colonel: "He was slender of build, swarthy of complexion, dark hair and mustache, and with dark eyes the most brilliant and piercing. He was quick in his movements and quick in perception and in his decision. . . . As gentle and modest as a woman, there was an undoubted capacity to command, which obtained for Pettigrew instant obedience, but a kindness and bearing which won affection, and chivalry and courtesy which marked him as every inch a gentleman."

From September 1861 through March 1862, Colonel Pettigrew skillfully led his regiment at its post on the lower Potomac. His service brought several offers of promotion to brigadier general, but he rejected them all, citing his unwillingness to command men he had never led into action. Later in the spring, Jefferson Davis appointed Pettigrew to command the brigade to which the Twenty-second North Carolina belonged. At the time, he was one of a small number of general officers in the Confederate army who was neither a powerful politician nor had served in the United States military.

Pettigrew's initial command of a brigade in the Peninsula Campaign was short lived. On June 1, 1862, he led a gallant charge at the Battle of Seven Pines. In the course of the action, he was ascertaining the position of the enemy when he was seriously wounded and captured. Pettigrew subsequently described the incident: "The ball entered the lower part of the throat, striking the windpipe, glanced to the right, passed under the collar bone, struck the head of the shoulder, and glanced again upward, tearing the bones. It unfortunately cut an artery, and I would have bled to death had it not been for Colonel [Gustavus A.] Bull. I became entirely unconscious. I subsequently received another shot in the left arm and a bayonet in the right leg, spent the night on the battlefield, and little before day was carried to a Yankee camp. My right leg is still partially paralyzed, but I am recovering the use of it."

After the general was stabilized by Union physicians, he was incarcerated as a prisoner of war. Pettigrew detested his imprisonment, especially the six weeks he spent at Fort Delaware. The two-month ordeal in Federal custody made an indelible impression on him.

A prisoner exchange in early August led to Pettigrew's release. Although his arm was paralyzed and his leg was stiff, he insisted upon returning to active duty. James Louis Pettigru, his first cousin and law partner, expressed disdain about Johnston's decision to take to the battlefield again: "There's no hope for genius." But the general saw it differently. His soldiers cheered him upon his return, leading Johnston to remark, "The Yankees say that it is very hard to kill the North Carolinians entirely, and it does seem so, though they wound a great many of us. Those of us, who had the bad luck to fall into their hands are now more anxious than ever to have another trial."

A new brigade consisting of five North Carolina regiments was assigned to Pettigrew. From September 1862 to the spring of 1863, it was deployed in eastern North Carolina, where it participated in a number of small engagements. As he prepared to return to Virginia with his soldiers in May 1863, Johnston succinctly summarized the campaign: "We whipped the Yankees every time we could get at them."

The stay in Virginia was brief because Robert E. Lee quickly matured his plans for the Confederate invasion of the North. On June 14, Johnston received orders to pull four of his regiments from the trenches at Fredericksburg. Excitement grew as the march on the North got under way.

In the early afternoon on July 1, Pettigrew positioned his three-thousand-man command to attack the enemy at McPherson's Woods as the curtain was set to rise at Gettysburg. In the ensuing battle, he led his soldiers in one of the most heroic and bloodiest charges of the Civil War. The Yankees were routed, but at a heavy price to both armies. Among the casualties was Johnston's divisional commander, Major General Henry Heth, who sustained a painful head wound. Command of Heth's division devolved to Pettigrew.

On July 3, Robert E. Lee made his final, desperate attempt to break the Union lines at Gettysburg by sending three divisions into battle. Commanding them were Pettigrew, George E. Pickett of Virginia, and

Isaac R. Trimble of Maryland. When the time for the grand assault neared, Pettigrew, attired in his gray uniform and soft gray hat, held the reins of his gray horse in his left hand as he galloped up and down the lines to ready his men.

In the course of Pickett's Charge—so named by the Richmond press—Johnston Pettigrew led his division to a point at least six hundred yards beyond the famed stone wall of the enemy. On that hot July afternoon, he and his men reached what has been termed "the high-water mark of the Confederacy." During the fighting, Johnston's horse was hit by enemy fire and the general sustained gunshot wounds to the arm and hand. Yet he fought on with grim determination, hoping for reinforcements that never came.

When the order came for the Confederates to fall back, Pettigrew and his surviving warriors could not believe their ears. Major John T. Jones, one of the general's field officers, lamented, "At the very moment I thought victory was ours, I saw it snatched from our hands. . . . The day was lost." Johnston, reluctant to concede defeat, was one of the last Confederate soldiers to leave the field that fateful day.

Back at Seminary Ridge, the place where the Confederates had begun their charge, General Lee offered words of comfort and praise as he moved among Pettigrew's battered troops. Suddenly, Pettigrew appeared from within the ranks to present himself to Lee for further orders. General Lee leaned from his saddle, took hold of Pettigrew's left hand, and said, "General Pettigrew, it is all my fault. The fault is mine, but it will be all right in the end." Then, noticing Johnston's bloody arm, he added, "General, I am sorry to see you wounded."

After Lee departed, Pettigrew was reduced to tears, not because of his injuries but as a result of the bitter outcome of the battle. Not willing to ascribe blame to Lee, he said to Major Jones, "My noble brigade had gained the enemy's works, and would have held them had not [another] brigade given way. Oh! Had they have known the consequences that hung upon their action at that moment, they would have pressed on."

When dawn spread over the gruesome Gettysburg landscape on Saturday, July 4, the new day was the anniversary of the birth of both General Pettigrew and the United States. Instead of celebrating his thirty-fifth birthday, Johnston busied himself in the massive Confederate retreat south. The early-morning drizzle intensified to thunderstorms in the afternoon, causing the roads to become quagmires. Wagons filled with wounded and dying Southern soldiers were stuck in the sloppy mess. The weather and the attendant misery seemed an omen of things to come for Johnston and the cause for which he fought.

His wounded arm was in a sling as he assumed command of the rear guard of the massive retreat. Although his post of duty was a high honor, it was also fraught with peril. Concern grew when his command reached the Potomac, since there was no artillery left to protect the rear.

On July 14, Johnston's worst fears were realized. At Falling Waters, Maryland, a troop of fifty Union cavalrymen attacked the general and his staff as they were having breakfast. During the skirmish, the general used his "free" arm—still weak from the wounds at Seven Pines—to steady his rearing horse, which ultimately threw him. As he struggled to pick himself up, Johnston came face to face with a burly Union corporal who had already killed several men. The general drew a small pistol from his coat. To his dismay, it misfired. In a split second, the corporal fired his Colt at Pettigrew's abdomen, and the general fell. Johnston's men quickly overtook the corporal and crushed him to death with a large stone. The other soldiers of the enemy squadron were killed or captured.

The badly wounded Pettigrew was hastily transported across the river. Several Confederate surgeons were dispatched to the rear to render aid. They determined that Pettigrew's life could be saved only if he were completely immobilized. In an attempt to convince him to remain behind, they argued that the pursuing Union army would render the care necessary to assure his survival. But Johnston would not agree. He would prefer death over being taken prisoner again. Acceding to his wishes, Pettigrew's concerned staff gently laid him on a stretcher and assembled a group of litter bearers. Over the course of that day and night, the general was carried twenty-two miles by details of four men.

Even though the position in the rear was extremely dangerous, General Lee rode alongside the stretcher, trying to comfort Pettigrew as he was jostled in the hasty retreat. Despite his pain, Johnston attempted to boost the spirits of the men bearing the stretcher by saying, "Don't be disheartened. Maybe I will fool the doctors yet."

On the night of July 15, the ailing general was placed in the home of the Boyd family in Bunker Hill, Virginia. An Episcopal minister stopped by the following afternoon to ask if he wanted to take the sacraments. Responding in the negative, he whispered, "It is not from a want of faith or a want of disposition, but from a feeling of unworthiness. I fear to incur the guilt of presumption." As darkness began to cloak the Appalachian Mountains of western Virginia, Johnston's condition worsened. Morphine was administered to relieve his pain.

At 6:25 on the morning of July 17, the general looked up at Louis Young, his trusted aide-de-camp, and said, "It is time to be going." With that, General James Johnston Pettigrew drew his last labored breath.

Reflecting on the death of his commander, Major Jones wrote, "In him our state lost one of her brightest stars, and the Confederacy one of her ablest defenders."

Many years later, Douglas Southall Freeman, the eminent Civil War historian, offered an eloquent tribute to Johnston Pettigrew: "For none who fought so briefly in the Army of Northern Virginia was there more praise while living or more laments when dead."

Brigadier General Benjamin Hardin Helm

Brother-in-Law vs. Brother-in-Law

Chickamauga, Georgia
September 20, 1863

"Victory! Victory! Victory!"

When the North and the South went to war in 1861, the conflict created deep divisions in America's most cherished institutions. Churches and fraternal organizations were torn asunder on the basis of geographic and political loyalties. Even the American family was not immune to the rancor that characterized the period. In a number of instances, father was pitted against son, and brother took up sword against brother. One of the most noteworthy cases of family discord involved two brothers-in-law—Benjamin Hardin Helm, a brigadier general in the Confederate army, and Abraham Lincoln, president of the United States.

Benjamin Helm was born in Bardstown, Kentucky, on June 2, 1831, the son of John Larue and Lucinda Hardin Helm. His maternal grandfather was one of the foremost attorneys and politicians in antebellum Kentucky. His father, also a distinguished attorney, served as governor and lieutenant governor of the state.

Close to his twentieth birthday, Benjamin graduated ninth in a class of forty-two at West Point. But ill health forced him to resign his commission as a second lieutenant in the United States Army after little more than a year's

Brigadier General Benjamin Hardin Helm
COURTESY OF LIBRARY OF CONGRESS

service. After studying law at the University of Louisville and Harvard University, Helm settled in Elizabethtown, Kentucky, to practice law with his father. Voters elected him to the state house of representatives in 1855. Following one term there, he served as the commonwealth's attorney. He married Emily Todd, the sister of Abraham Lincoln's wife, in 1856.

As war clouds gathered in 1860, Kentucky officials appointed Helm—who was not yet an ardent supporter of Southern independence—to serve as an assistant inspector of the state guard. Meanwhile, his illustrious brother-in-law was canvassing to become president of the United States. Helm greatly admired Lincoln's quick wit, kindly nature, and gift of oratory. Lincoln, himself a native Kentuckian, was deeply attached to Helm, whom he regarded as polished, scholarly, and handsome.

Less than sixty days after he was sworn in as the sixteenth president of the United States, Lincoln invited Helm to visit him in Washington. At the White House on April 27, 1861—the same day that Robert E. Lee resigned from the United States Army—the president handed his brother-in-law a sealed envelope and said, "Ben, here is something for you. Think it over by yourself, and let me know what you will do." Inside the envelope was Helm's official nomination as paymaster of the United States Army with the rank of major. Here was an opportunity very few men could afford to turn down. Helm responded, "I will try to do what is right. . . . You shall have my answer in a few days."

For Helm, the decision was not about personal advancement or emoluments. Rather, it had to do with honor and his duty to Kentucky. Moreover, during the early days of President Lincoln's administration, Helm had grown increasingly suspicious of his brother-in-law's intentions toward the South. Accordingly, his answer to the president's offer was short, impersonal, and direct: "Helm, Ben Hardin; nominated for paymaster in the United States Army, April 27, 1861. Declined."

Abraham Lincoln and Benjamin Hardin Helm would never again have a face-to-face meeting. Instead, they would indirectly square off against each other on countless battlefields, for Helm chose to throw his allegiance to the Confederacy. Less than four years later, both brothers-in-law would be dead, each sacrificing his life in a war that divided their native state and tore apart the American nation.

Back in Kentucky, Helm immersed himself in the patriotic fervor that was manifesting itself. He recruited and raised many of the companies that formed the First Kentucky Cavalry. Once Southern forces entered Kentucky in the fall of 1861, the regiment was incorporated into the Confederate army. Helm was named its colonel on October 19.

Helm spent much of his first six months of Confederate military service on scouting duty in south-central Kentucky. Shortly after his promotion to brigadier general on March 18, 1862, he used his brigade to protect the Confederate flanks at the Battle of Shiloh. A new assignment came three weeks later when he was transferred to the infantry to command the Third Kentucky Brigade in the division of Major General John C. Breckinridge—the very man who had been defeated by Abraham Lincoln in the presidential election of 1860.

In July 1863, Helm was given yet another command, the First Kentucky Brigade. Better known as the Orphan Brigade, this was the most famous military organization produced by Kentucky during the war. Tracing its origins to the prewar state guard, it acquired its famous nickname in 1862 after the Confederate army evacuated Kentucky, thereby cutting off the men of the First Kentucky from their native state for the remainder of the war. Excellent commanders including Simon Bolivar Buckner and John C. Breckinridge were instrumental in developing the brigade into one of the South's finest combat units. But the most beloved general to lead the Orphan Brigade was Benjamin Helm.

Hardened by the realities of war and accustomed to the dangers associated with the rear guard, the usual post of the First Kentucky in the wake of a battle, the Orphans appreciated General Helm's kind, gentle nature. Never did they perform more admirably than under his command. An aide to Jefferson Davis wrote this about the First Kentucky: "Their performance was rapid, yet precise, their appearance tough and active, and they will compare for efficiency with any brigade in the Confederate army." Generals Joseph E. Johnston and John Bell Hood repeatedly praised the Orphan Brigade as the best in the Western theater.

As the spring of 1863 drew to a close, Helm deployed the brigade at Vicksburg to assist Johnston in his unsuccessful attempt to end the siege there. Sharing in the misery of that harsh duty, Helm termed the campaign the most unpleasant and trying of his career.

In the third week of September, the Orphan Brigade went into action when General Braxton Bragg attacked the Union army at Chickamauga, Georgia. At nine-thirty on the morning of September 20, the divisions of Breckinridge and Patrick Cleburne were ordered to move forward. Helm's brigade and the other two in Breckinridge's division drove into the Federal left. General Cleburne's division, which was to strike near the center of the line, was delayed. As a consequence, Helm, whose men were deployed on the extreme left of the advance, was unable to protect his left flank.

Some of the Orphans managed to work their way to within thirty yards of the Federal lines, where, according to Private John Green of the Ninth Kentucky, they were "giving and taking death blows which could last but a few minutes without utter annihilation." Meanwhile, General Helm, leading the remainder of his brigade on horseback, slammed headlong into the well-fortified Union lines. Just as Breckinridge's division gained control of the road to Chattanooga, a marksman from the Fifteenth Kentucky (Union) sent a bullet that plowed into Helm's chest and toppled him from his horse.

After the general was borne from the field, surgeons determined that his wound was mortal. Helm hung on for several hours until the battle was done. The fast-fading thirty-two-year-old general asked which army had prevailed.

When assured that the Confederates had carried the day, he muttered, "Victory! Victory! Victory!"

In his official report on the Battle of Chickamauga, General Daniel Harvey Hill wrote that Benjamin Helm's "gallantry and loveliness of character endeared him to everyone." In a letter to Emily Helm, General Breckinridge said, "Your husband commanded them [the men of the Orphan Brigade] like a thorough soldier. He loved them, they loved him, and he died at their head, a patriot and a hero."

When Helm's brother-in-law, the president of the United States, was informed of the general's death, he locked himself in a private room and wept uncontrollably.

Lieutenant Richard Rowland Kirkland

Death of an Angel

Chickamauga, Georgia
September 20, 1863

"You can do me no good. Save yourselves and tell Pa good-bye and I died right."

Amid the grim carnage on the killing fields of the Civil War, several Americans won enduring fame as angels of mercy. Acclaimed an angel because of her tireless efforts to provide medical care to sick and injured soldiers, Clara Barton emerged from the war as one of the most famous women in American history. Even in the heat of battle, there were some warriors who earned the soubriquet *angel* by rendering aid to soldiers of the opposing army. No battlefield angel was more beloved than Richard Rowland Kirkland, who was celebrated as "the angel of Marye's Heights" at Fredericksburg in December 1862 and who died at Chickamauga less than a year later.

Born in August 1843 in north-central South Carolina, Kirkland was the son of parents who traced their ancestry to Revolutionary War patriots. He inherited a strong sense of duty. As war clouds gathered over South Carolina in early 1861, seventeen-year-old Richard and three of his brothers volunteered to defend their native state. As a member of the Second South Carolina, Richard was on hand for the capitulation of Fort Sumter in mid-April.

Lieutenant Richard Rowland Kirkland
Courtesy of *Confederate Veteran*

By May, the Second South Carolina was in Virginia, where it participated in the titanic struggle to protect the Confederate capital. At First Manassas and in all the battles in which his brigade was engaged in the Old Dominion in 1861 and 1862, Richard Kirkland rendered effective service. Because of his reliability, he was promoted to sergeant when he reenlisted at the expiration of his original one-year term of duty.

Four months after his nineteenth birthday, Sergeant Kirkland was among the 75,000 soldiers assigned by General Robert E. Lee to defend Fredericksburg, located on the west bank of the Rappahannock River. Desperate for a victory against the outnumbered Army of Northern Virginia, President Abraham Lincoln had put a 130,000-man army under the command of General Ambrose Burnside. On December 13, 1862, a bitterly cold day, Burnside unleashed a furious attack against the well-fortified Confederates in Fredericksburg.

As part of Lieutenant General James Longstreet's corps, Kirkland and his comrades in Joseph Kershaw's brigade were positioned along a ridge known as Marye's Heights. Adding to the strength of their position were a stone wall and a sunken road, known as Telegraph Road, at the base of the hill. In a vain attempt to sweep away the Confederate defenders, Burnside recklessly sent wave after wave of blue-clad troops toward Marye's Heights. The onrushing Yankees came face to face with the rifles of Southern marksmen waiting behind the stone wall. As Kirkland and his compatriots leveled the charging enemy hordes, a fresh line of Confederate sharpshooters scrambled to the wall while the prior line reloaded. Through the long, frigid day, the deadly work continued. Not one Union soldier made it to the stone wall.

By the time the sun began to descend, the temperature was below freezing. From his vantage point on Marye's Heights, Sergeant Kirkland surveyed the bloody outcome of the battle. Ten thousand wounded and dead enemy soldiers were strewn about the frozen landscape. Badly injured men unable to crawl back to their lines used the bodies of their expired comrades for cover. Fearing the lethal weapons behind the rock wall, no Federal soldier dared to attempt a rescue. Kirkland struggled to stay warm that desolate night. Nothing could silence the groaning and crying coming from the suffering men at the base of the hill. The pitiful pleas for water from men bleeding to death made sleep impossible for the sergeant.

Once the fog lifted on the new day, Kirkland was appalled to see that some of the wounded soldiers had frozen stiff in the night. Still, cries for help by those clinging to life permeated the air. Although he had become accustomed to death on numerous battlefields, the ghastly sights and sounds of Fredericksburg tormented Kirkland. At his wit's end, he left his position at the stone wall and hurried up the hill to the Stevens House, which served as the headquarters of General Joseph Kershaw. When it was announced to the general that he had a visitor, Kershaw graciously welcomed the son of one of his old friends from South Carolina. From the sergeant's facial expression, the general discerned that something was wrong.

Without wasting time on pleasantries, Kirkland got to the point: "General, I can't stand this!"

"You can't stand what, Kirkland?" Kershaw asked.

"Those poor fellows out there are our enemies; it is true, but they are wounded and dying, and they are helpless!" the sergeant said. "I have come to ask leave to carry water to them."

Touched by Kirkland's request, Kershaw glanced out the window, which offered a panoramic view of the thousands of wounded and dying Yankees.

He then looked at the young soldier from his own county and said, "Why, Kirkland, don't you see the danger? If you were to place your cap on your ramrod and elevate it above the wall behind which our line is formed, it would be riddled with bullets instantly."

Politely but firmly, the sergeant responded, "Yes, Sir. I know that; but if you will let me, I am willing to try it."

"What you propose is so noble and indicates so magnificently what a glorious soldier you are that I cannot say no," the general said. "Go, my dear boy, perform your mission, and may God shield and preserve you!"

Kirkland saluted the general and said, "Thank you, Sir!" With that, he bounded down the steps. But suddenly, he reversed his course. Convinced that the sergeant had changed his mind, Kershaw was surprised when Kirkland asked, "General, can I show a white handkerchief?"

Kershaw replied in the negative, explaining that such a gesture might be taken as a signal of surrender. Kirkland would be on his own. There would be no cease-fire.

"All right, I'll take my chances," the sergeant said.

From the window of his office, the general monitored Kirkland as he headed back to his unit. There, the young man borrowed more than a dozen canteens, filled them from a well near the Stevens House, and hurried back to the stone wall.

Sharpshooters manning the Federal lines watched in stunned silence as a lone Confederate soldier climbed over the wall onto the battlefield. Under the firm belief that he was going to rob the lifeless bodies of their fallen comrades, the Yankee pickets opened fire. As bullets whizzed about him, the unarmed Southerner went about his mission of mercy. Crouching and running low, he reached a wounded enemy soldier. There, he knelt, gently lifted the man's head, tilted the canteen, and then made the soldier as comfortable as possible. On to another man he went. Before long, the hostile fire ended. The Federals looked on in awe while Kirkland quenched dry lips and throats, adjusted broken and mangled limbs, arranged knapsacks to serve as pillows, buttoned the jackets of freezing soldiers, covered corpses with coats, and offered words of reassurance to the wounded and of comfort to the dying. One mortally wounded soldier thrust a letter addressed to his family into Kirkland's hand. In all directions, the surviving battlefield casualties raised their hands to attract the sergeant's attention.

Once the canteens were dry, Kirkland sprinted back to fill them. Then he resumed his mission. Thoroughly exhausted after ninety minutes, the sergeant jumped back over the wall for the final time on December 14. He was unharmed. To show their appreciation, the soldiers in blue and gray offered up a spontaneous tumult of cheers. From that day forward, Sergeant Richard Rowland Kirkland was known to both armies as "the angel of Marye's Heights."

When the war moved north in the summer of 1863, so did Kirkland. At Gettysburg, he fought with distinction at the Peach Orchard and in the Wheatfield. For his service in Pennsylvania, he was promoted to lieutenant.

As the summer drew to a close, Kershaw's South Carolinians were ordered to do battle on yet another hill. On September 20, Lieutenant Kirkland and his fellow soldiers charged up Snodgrass Hill at Chickamauga, Georgia. For a fleeting moment, the Confederates gained control of the hill, but Federal reinforcements necessitated a retreat. In the process, Kirkland sustained a serious chest wound. Despite galling fire from enemy guns, his friends attempted to carry him from the field. But Kirkland eschewed their aid. Recognizing his wound to be fatal, he muttered, "No, I am done for. You can do me no good. Save yourselves and tell Pa good-bye and I died right. I did my duty. I died at my post."

Death came to "the angel of Marye's Heights" on that Georgia battlefield just one month after his twentieth birthday. In eulogizing Kirkland, General Kershaw noted that he "bequeathed to the American youth—yea, to the world, an example which dignifies our common humanity."

First Lieutenant John E. Wilson

Brothers in Blood

Chickamauga, Georgia
Late September 1863

"We have gained the needed time. I am willing to die."

Among all the units of military organization in the Confederate army, the company was the most closely knit. Not only were the soldiers in a company from the same state, most came from the same geographic area within that state. Fathers and sons, siblings, cousins, and other family members often volunteered with friends, neighbors, and other local citizens to fight together in the same unit. As they shared the camaraderie of camp, endured the hardships of war, and stared death in the face on the battlefield, they bonded as brothers in blood, for each man in the company realized that the next engagement might be his last. Commanding each company was a captain or lieutenant who earned the respect of his soldiers by being in the forefront of the fight. One such lieutenant was John E. Wilson of Company G of the Sixth Florida. In his final charge of the war, he led his men on his hands and one knee up Snodgrass Hill at Chickamauga, Georgia, on September 20, 1863.

The war was not yet a year old when, on March 11, 1862, Wilson, a resident of Quincy, Florida, and a number of local men were mustered into

A monument on Snodgrass Hill, where First Lieutenant John E. Wilson was fatally wounded
COURTESY OF *CONFEDERATE VETERAN*

the Confederate army as Company G at the Arsenal, an old fort near Apalachicola constructed by General Andrew Jackson. Over the next eighteen months, Lieutenant Wilson provided inspirational leadership. His fearless nature, indefatigable spirit, noble character, devotion to duty, and willing sacrifice made him a sterling example to the Floridians in Company G.

On no field of battle did Wilson's star shine brighter than at Chickamauga. In the middle of September 1863, Union major general William S. Rosecrans, the commander of the Army of the Cumberland, forced General Braxton Bragg to move a large portion of the Army of Tennessee from Chattanooga into northern Georgia. Anxious to strike back, Bragg prepared his sixty-six-thousand-soldier command for a savage assault that would culminate in the bloodiest two-day battle of the war. In the middle of that bloodshed were Wilson and his brethren in Company G.

On Saturday, September 19, Wilson was poised to take part in the great battle that would prove the last Confederate victory in the Western theater. Early that day, Bragg's army struck in the rugged, mountainous area of northern Georgia near Chickamauga Creek. The Cherokee name Chickamauga means "river of death." As casualties mounted during that first day, the creek turned crimson as blood poured from the thousands upon thousands of fallen men on both sides.

When Sunday dawned, the air was frigid and a heavy frost carpeted the battlefield, already littered with corpses. The fog lifting from the blood-heated waterway blended with the smoke lingering from the previous day's combat. Desperate to vanquish Rosecrans, Bragg sent his warriors back into action.

By late afternoon, the tide of battle turned in favor of the South. Only the division of Major General George Thomas offered resistance in the wake of a massive Union retreat. Perched atop Snodgrass Hill, a spur of Missionary Ridge, Thomas and his blue-clad warriors made a determined stand so as to enable the bulk of the Federal army to flee to safety. Among the many Southern officers ordered to try to dislodge the Yankees was John Wilson. Because the Sixth Florida had already suffered heavy casualties, Lieutenant Wilson took command of a force comprised of the survivors of his own company and several others. C. F. Duncan, a private in Company G, described the action: "We were ordered to take a battery from an Ohio regiment stationed on top of the hill. Twice we had gone up the hill to be repulsed with terrible loss."

Lieutenant Wilson quickly regrouped his ever-thinning ranks and implored the men to follow him in yet another charge. Up the hill they stormed amid shot and shell as thick as rain. As he ran behind Wilson, Private Duncan witnessed what he described as "the bravest act of all those long, hard four years of war." In the vanguard of the assault, Lieutenant Wilson proved a perfect target for the Ohio gunners. A cannonball smashed into his leg, shattering the bone. Blood gushed from the wound as Wilson fell to the ground. From the landscape of death, he shouted for his men to continue charging. Then, in a determined effort to keep the attack alive, he crawled on his hands and one knee in the direction of the Union artillery.

In short order, the Floridians captured the big guns, thus silencing the last Federal battery. Flush with victory, the ragged survivors of Company G hurried to the side of their leader. "We have gained the needed time. I am willing to die," John Wilson told them. But Private William M. Miller said, "You are too good a man to die, and you shan't die here." He gently gathered his lieutenant in his arms and bore him to a field hospital.

As darkness cloaked the foggy battlefield, Company G assembled for a roll call in the wake of the Southern triumph. Only 54 of the 154 men who had charged up Snodgrass Hill could present themselves for duty. The others were dead or wounded. John Wilson was not there. Private William McDaniel explained his absence: "He was carried to a farmhouse in the valley which had been temporarily converted into a hospital. . . . His leg was cut off by the army surgeon. I was waiting outside and I saw his leg when they threw it out of a window on top of a pile of arms and legs that would have filled a wagon."

Not long after the battle, Lieutenant John E. Wilson joined many of his blood brothers of Company G in death. They were among the 18,454 casualties suffered by the Southern army in its Pyrrhic victory at the place so aptly known as the "river of death."

Private Samuel Davis

But One Life to Give

Pulaski, Tennessee
November 27, 1863

"I would rather die a thousand deaths than betray a friend or be false to my country."

Few, if any, Civil War privates attained the fame of Sam Davis. Long before the war was over, his name was legend throughout the South. Even in the North, it was whispered with reverence in many homes and public places. But it was not on a battlefield that the young Tennessean won the admiration of Yankees and Confederates alike. Rather, it was on a hanging scaffold in his native state where Davis wrote one of the most memorable chapters in American history. The heroism, loyalty, and devotion to duty he exhibited as he stared death in the face earned him a measure of immortality.

The world in which Sam Davis was raised offered little hint of the fame he would achieve in the last moments of his life twenty-one years later. Born on a farm in Smyrna, Tennessee, in 1842, he spent his childhood outside Nashville, where he perfected his horsemanship and other skills that enabled him to render exemplary service as a Confederate scout.

When war became inevitable in early 1861, Davis closed his schoolbooks and bade farewell to his instructors, Edmund Kirby-Smith and Bushrod Johnson, both future Confederate generals. He volunteered to fight for the

South and was assigned to the First Tennessee. His endurance, cleverness, and derring-do attracted the attention of his superiors, including General Braxton Bragg, the commander of the Army of Tennessee. Aware that his army needed sensitive information about the enemy—which invaded Tennessee in 1862—Bragg established a company of scouts, known as Captain Coleman's Scouts, under the secret command of Captain Henry B. Shaw. Among the first of the hand-picked soldiers chosen for the elite group was Private Sam Davis (see pages 196-200).

As Davis and his fellow scouts went about their perilous missions in enemy territory, they wore regulation Confederate gray, knowing well their fate if captured. Month after month, Sam Davis rode swiftly and secretly in his quest to keep the Southern army apprised of the position and strength of the enemy. Hairsbreadth escapes were common.

Sam's greatest test came in November 1863 as the Sixth Corps of the Union army, commanded by General Grenville M. Dodge, began to move north from Corinth, Mississippi, in anticipation of reinforcing Grant at Chattanooga. Captain Shaw, alias Captain Coleman, summoned his scouts and informed them that they must keep the lines of communication open to General Bragg. Joshua Brown, one of Sam Davis's compatriots, recalled the warning the scouts were given: "When we received our orders we were told that the duty was very dangerous, and that they did not expect but a few of us to return; that we would probably be captured or killed, and we were cautioned against exposing ourselves unnecessarily."

To prized scout Sam Davis, Captain Coleman entrusted a large quantity of intelligence meant only for the eyes of General Braxton Bragg. Davis placed the secret documents—which included maps, reports, letters, and other papers—in his saddlebags and boots and rode away. He carried with him a pass signed by E. Coleman that read, "Samuel Davis has permission to pass on scouting duty anywhere in Middle Tennessee or south of the Tennessee River he may think proper. By order of Gen. Bragg."

Meanwhile, General Dodge encamped his army at Pulaski, Tennessee, located just north of the Alabama line and close to the Tennessee River. His cavalry was directed to keep a close lookout for Coleman's Scouts, who were known to be operating in the area.

On Thursday, November 19, a squadron of "Jayhawkers" from the Seventh Kansas Cavalry caught and arrested Sam Davis as he was riding near

A bust of Private Samuel Davis
Courtesy of *Confederate Veteran*

the Tennessee River. After he was escorted to Pulaski, a thorough search of his person and belongings yielded his cargo of confidential information.

General Dodge, anxious to put an end to the activities of Coleman's Scouts, ordered that Davis be brought to his headquarters. Dodge recalled, "I took him into my private office and told him that it was a very serious charge brought against him; that he was a spy, and from what I found about his person, he had accurate information in regard to my army, and that I must know where he obtained it. I told him that he was a young man, and did not seem to realize the danger he was in."

Sam Davis listened intently to the general, then replied in a dignified voice, "General Dodge, I know the danger of my situation, and I am willing to take the consequences."

Neither Dodge nor his men realized that Captain Coleman was Captain Henry B. Shaw, who had also been captured and brought to Pulaski. In his quest to determine Coleman's identity, Dodge "asked [Sam Davis] to give me the name of the person from whom he got the information, that I knew it must be someone near headquarters or who had confidence of the officers of my staff, and I repeated that I *must* know the source from which it came."

Davis insisted that he would provide no information. The general grew somber when he told the prisoner that he had no alternative but to convene a court-martial to try him for his life. Despite the dire threat, Sam looked at Dodge and responded, "I know that I have to die, but I will not tell you where I got the information, and there is no power on earth that can make me tell. You are doing your duty as a soldier, and I am doing mine. If I have to die, I do so feeling that I am doing my duty to God and my country."

Moved by Davis's strength of character, the general tried again: "I pleaded with him and urged him with all the power I possessed to give me some chance to save his life, for I discovered that he was a most admirable young fellow, with the highest character and strictest integrity."

Sam Davis would not relent. "It is useless to talk to me," he said. "I do not intend to do it. You can court martial me, or do anything else you like, but I will not betray the trust imposed in me." He then thanked General Dodge for his kindness and was escorted back to his cell in the Giles County Jail.

A court-martial was convened on November 20. After hearing the case of Samuel Davis, it sentenced the Confederate scout "to be hanged by the neck until he is dead." His execution was scheduled for November 27 between the hours of ten in the morning and two in the afternoon. Captain W. F. Armstrong of the Ninth Illinois, the provost marshal, delivered the news to Sam. Upon learning that he would die by hanging rather than by firing squad, he showed his dismay. But there was no expression of fear, only resignation.

As he awaited his fate, Sam, now twenty-one years old, was visited on a number of occasions by an enemy soldier of the same age. Private C. B. Van Pelt of the Eighty-first Ohio developed a warm friendship with the prisoner. "I paid him daily and almost hourly visits between capture and execution," Van Pelt recalled. "He always met me with a smile, and would say, 'You are very kind to me.' " On more than one visit, Private Van Pelt pleaded with Sam to save his own life by providing the information requested by General Dodge. With perfect serenity, Sam replied, "I am true to my cause. What would you do in my position?" With the day of execution fast approaching, he remarked to Van Pelt, "My friend, I have loved ones at home, so have you; and when you left, their prayers followed, that if you returned alive you might return in honor, no matter in what channel of service military orders might place you."

On the eve of his hanging, Sam took up a pen and wrote a farewell letter to his family. In part, it read, "I wish I could see you all once more, but I never will any more. Mother and father, do not forget me. Think of me when I am dead, but do not grieve for me. It will not do any good."

At ten o'clock on the morning of Friday, November 27, a drum roll began as a regiment of Federal infantry marched to the jail. A wagon with a plain pine coffin on top pulled up to the building. Provost Marshal Armstrong stepped inside the building and emerged with Sam Davis. After guards bound his hands and shackled his legs, the prisoner struggled to get into the wagon. Once aboard, he stood and gazed at his fellow prisoners, who were looking at him through their cell windows. Sam acknowledged his friends, smiled, bowed a final farewell, and then took a seat on his coffin.

Attired in an overcoat with a cape dyed dark brown after Sam had taken it as booty on one of his adventures, he manifested a peaceful countenance on the short, slow ride to the scaffold on the outskirts of Pulaski. Leading the procession were Yankee soldiers with fixed bayonets. A military band played a funeral dirge along the route.

When the wagon reached its destination, Sam saw the gallows surrounded by a solid square of Union troops. He descended from the wagon at the steps leading to the scaffold. A. W. Bill, a young private in the Sixty-sixth Illinois, recounted the scene: "Davis lifted his face and gazed long and steadily at the hills and fields and sky. Then it was that I saw the noble profile, the black eyes, the close-pressed lips, the white, white face of a young man only two years and a little older than myself, and who might have been earlier a playmate had I lived in Tennessee, and then my heart gave way."

While the death squad readied the apparatus, Sam took a seat on a bench under a tree. He asked the provost marshal, "How long have I to live, Captain Armstrong?"

With regret in his voice, Armstrong replied, "About fifteen minutes."

Anxious to hear news about his Southern brethren fighting at Missionary Ridge, Sam asked, "What is the news from the front?" After Armstrong related details of General Bragg's defeat, the prisoner said graciously, "Thank you, Captain; but I'm sorry to hear it." Then Sam's lips quivered as he looked at the provost marshal and remarked, "The boys will have to fight their battles without me."

Upon that comment, Captain Armstrong lost his composure. "Sam, I would rather die myself than to execute the sentence upon you," he confessed.

Attempting to comfort his executioner, Sam said, "Never mind, Captain. You are doing your duty. Thank you for all your kindness."

"I am sorry to be compelled to perform this painful duty," Armstrong said.

Sam smiled and replied, "It does not hurt me, Captain. I am innocent, though. I am prepared to die, and do not think hard of it."

Their conversation was interrupted when an emissary from General Dodge came bounding up on a fleet horse. With Chaplain James Young of Ohio at his side, the general's agent identified himself as Captain Chickasaw, chief of the Union scouts. To Davis, he said, "It is not too late yet!" Three times, Chickasaw made the offer: If the Southern scout would tell the name of the man who had given him the information, General Dodge would spare his life. In the days leading up to the execution, Captain Henry B. Shaw (a.k.a. Captain Coleman) had begged Sam to reveal his identity. But Sam would have none of it.

Seated in the shadow of the gallows, Sam shook his head as the offers of clemency were tendered. When the final offer was issued, Sam stood up for a moment of personal introspection. A Federal officer offered a vivid description of the moment: "The boy looked about him. Life was young and promising. Overhead hung the noose; around him were soldiers in line; at his feet was the box prepared for his body, now pulsing with young and vigorous life; in front were the steps that would lead him to disgraceful death, and that death it was in his power to easily avoid. For an instant he hesitated, and then put aside the tempting offer."

Sam's eyes flashed defiance as he gave his final response to Captain Chickasaw: "No, I cannot! I would rather die a thousand deaths than betray a friend or be false to my country."

After asking that his gratitude be extended to General Dodge, Sam ascended the platform. Chaplain Young offered a prayer for him, after which Sam said confidently, "I am ready, Captain."

Upon Armstrong's order, the trapdoor dropped, and it was over. Private Van Pelt, the young Union soldier who had befriended Sam in his last days, noted, "On that day when his life went out I felt as if I were going to my execution."

J. A. M. Collins, a member of the Second Iowa Volunteers, witnessed the execution. "To my mind Davis was of the highest type of manhood," he wrote.

In 1909, an impressive monument was unveiled as a memorial to Private Samuel Davis on the grounds of the State Capitol in Nashville. Among the numerous Federal soldiers who contributed to the monument fund was General G. M. Dodge, the man who had approved the sentence of death. With his donation, Dodge enclosed a personal note about that dark day in November 1863. "All of my command knew I desired to save him," it read in part. "It is not, therefore, necessary for me to state that I regretted to see the sentence executed, but it was one of the fates of war, which is cruelty itself, and there is no refining it."

David Owen Dodd, Telegrapher

Too Young to Die

Little Rock, Arkansas
January 8, 1864

"If I am to die I want to die like a man."

Because of his youth, David O. Dodd was deprived of the opportunity to don the gray and shoulder a rifle for his native South when it was invaded in 1861. But when the seventeen-year-old faced the gallows fashioned by his Union executioners in Little Rock, Arkansas, in early January 1864, he exhibited a measure of courage and loyalty to the Confederate cause rarely equaled on the battlefield during the Civil War.

David was born in Lavaca County, Texas, on November 10, 1846. During his tender years, he moved with his parents to Arkansas. There, he matured into a handsome, beardless teenager with large, dark eyes and flowing, dark hair. When the Civil War erupted, David was living in Little Rock, where he was a student cadet at St. John's Masonic College, which had recently instituted a course of military study. Despite his youth, he fancied the role of a soldier in the Confederate army. Unfortunately, a serious bout of malaria soon ended his college career and his dreams of serving as a Southern warrior.

After recuperating from "the fever," he went to work for the Little Rock telegraph firm of Snow and Ketcham. There, he mastered Morse code and

David Owen Dodd
Courtesy of *Confederate Veteran*

developed outstanding penmanship. As the summer of 1862 drew to a close, his skills as a telegrapher earned him a position in the Confederate telegraph office in Monroe, Louisiana.

For the fifteen-year-old boy, the job was a dream come true. He could aid the Southern war effort by relaying important military dispatches concerning battlefield events and troop dispositions, both North and South. But after several months of sending and receiving telegraphs about the war that was by then raging throughout much of the South, David developed a burning desire to be close to the action. Consequently, he resigned his position on November 24, 1862, and journeyed to Jackson, Mississippi, where he joined his father, Andrew Dodd, who was serving as sutler for the Third Arkansas Dismounted Rifles.

On a number of occasions over the next ten months, the elder Dodd found it necessary to travel to Alabama and Louisiana on business matters. In his absence, David was left in charge of all trade transactions with the Confederates. In the course of his day-to-day interaction with the Southern military encampments, he acquired an intimate knowledge of the war in the Deep South.

David's life took a marked turn on September 10, 1863, when Major General Frederick Steele and a large army of Union soldiers took control of Little Rock. Residing in the city at the time were David's mother and two sisters. Without delay, he was dispatched by his father to the occupied city to ensure the safety of the female family members. In early December, Andrew Dodd arrived in Little Rock with a wagon and moved the entire family south to Camden, Arkansas, in Confederate-held territory.

Once the family was safely settled, the Dodd patriarch decided to send David back to Little Rock to finalize several important business matters. David was only too happy to oblige his father. After all, he had made the acquaintance of several charming young ladies during his recent three-month sojourn in the state capital. But before Andrew Dodd sent his son through enemy territory, he took steps to gain his safe passage. He penned a document containing evidence of David's age and place of birth and a certification that his son was too young for military service. But there was more to do, too. On Tuesday, December 22, Andrew and David appeared before General James F. Fagan, the Confederate cavalry commander in southern Arkansas. Fagan, an old family friend, agreed to provide David a pass through Confederate lines. As the Dodds prepared to take leave of Fagan, the general looked at David and said, "Of course, I'll expect a full report on your return."

No one knows exactly what Fagan meant by his statement. Perhaps he was merely joking. Or maybe he expected David to bring him a report already prepared by Confederate agents working in and about Little Rock. But David apparently took General Fagan's words as a directive to uncover intelligence about enemy activities.

He completed the journey to Little Rock without incident by Christmas Eve. During his five-day stay in the city, David resided in the home of an aunt and enjoyed holiday festivities in the company of three teenage girls—Mary Dodge, Mary Swindle, and Minerva Cogburn. Mary Dodge was an ardent supporter of the Confederate cause, but her father, a Vermont native, was loyal to the Union and often quartered Yankee soldiers in his home. Much of the information David prepared for General Fagan may have come from Mary Dodge.

Upon completing his father's business in the city, David obtained a pass from the office of General Steele on December 27. Two days later, on a Tuesday morning, he left Little Rock on a mule, which he intended to trade for a horse en route. As he made his way toward an overnight stay at the home of his uncle, Washington Dodd, David encountered a Union sentry, Private Daniel Olderburg. Upon inspecting David's pass, Olderburg inquired the teenager's destination, then noted that the road forked a few miles ahead. When David informed Olderburg that his uncle lived on the Hot Springs Road, the right fork, the guard reasoned that the boy would no longer need his pass, since his destination was beyond the Union lines. Olderburg kept the pass and sent David on his way. Later in the day, he destroyed the pass after he went off duty.

David spent the night at the Washington Dodd house. Early the next morning, he resumed his trek, now armed with a small pistol given to him by his uncle. Not long into the journey, a terrific storm caused him to lose his way and inadvertently ride back across Federal lines. When he came to a duty post manned by Sergeant Frederick Miehr of the First Missouri Cavalry (Union), he informed the officer that another sentry had retained his pass two days earlier. Unwilling to accept the young man at his word, Miehr took him into custody and sent him back to regimental headquarters at Little Rock. There, Captain George W. Hanna and Lieutenant C. F. Stropal began the interrogation process by demanding that David produce some identification. When he related the story about his pass, Hanna directed that he be returned under guard to Private Olderburg's duty station. To David's dismay, the soldier was no longer on duty at the post.

After David was returned to Little Rock later that night, he was thoroughly searched. Among the effects found in his clothing were personal letters, the pistol, currency from several Southern states, and several locks of female hair. Of more importance, his captors found the note of identification written by his father and the Confederate pass authorized by General Fagan. Just as it appeared that David would be released, his boots were searched. Secreted there was a notebook filled with pages written in Morse code.

Early the next morning, December 30, David was brought before Brigadier General John W. Davidson, who immediately asked if he was a telegraph operator. David's nervous, evasive answer prompted the general to direct Captain Robert Clowrey, the assistant superintendent of Union military telegraph operations, to reduce the dashes and dots in David's notebook to words. Captain Clowrey began to read the following: "Third Ohio has four guns—brass. Eleventh Ohio Battery has six guns—brass. . . . [There are] three regiments in a brigade commanded by Davidson." Clowrey had completed but two pages when General Davidson interrupted him to announce that David O. Dodd was under arrest and would be tried as a spy.

A military tribunal of six officers was convened the following day. David tendered a plea of not guilty. His attorneys, William Fishback and T. D. W. Yonley, produced character witnesses and offered several defenses, to no avail. The verdict was guilty. In a desperate attempt to save their client's life, the defense team urged the judges to take David's tender age into consideration. But by a four-to-two vote on January 2, 1864, the young prisoner was sentenced to die by hanging in just six days.

As the news of the verdict and sentence circulated throughout Little Rock, passions were inflamed. Most citizens reasoned that Major General Steele would intervene to spare David's life in order to prevent a riot in the city. Publicly, the general washed his hands of the matter, stating that he had no legal or military authority to abrogate the death sentence. Behind the scenes, however, Steele made several personal appeals to David: If the prisoner would provide a list of his accomplices, his life would be spared. David disdained the offer each time it was presented.

Ice was on the ground in Little Rock on the clear, cold morning of Wednesday, January 8, 1864. There was yet hope. No gallows had been erected at the place designated for the execution—the parade ground of David's old school, St. John's Masonic College. Rumors that General Fagan was sending a rescue party for the prisoner were still alive.

At ten o'clock, David prepared for the worst in his holding cell. In his beautiful script, he inked a final letter to his family. In part, it read, "I was arrested as a Spy and tried and was sentenced to be hung today at 3 o'clock. The time is fast approaching but thank God I am prepared to die. I expect to meet you all in heaven."

Townspeople began to assemble at the parade ground, now the site of the parking lot of the University of Arkansas School of Law. By the time workers commenced construction of the gallows at two-thirty, thousands of civilians surrounded the soldiers guarding the place.

Suddenly, the death procession came into view. Under heavy guard and attired in a dark suit, David sat near the rear of his wagon atop his coffin. Along the route, a tearful Mary Swindle watched from her bedroom window as he passed. But at the R. L. Dodge home, neither Mary Dodge nor her father was home when the death wagon rolled by. Days before, General Steele had dispatched father and daughter to Vermont to avoid further scandal.

Upon arriving at the parade ground, the driver pulled the wagon directly under the gallows. Union soldiers, five ranks deep, pressed close to form a human square surrounding the hanging apparatus. Every person in attendance fixed his attention on the condemned boy, who stared at the noose. Eyewitnesses noted that he looked pale but that he held his head erect and displayed no fear or anxiety.

When the order for execution was read, the atmosphere grew somber. General Steele stepped forward to again offer leniency in exchange for the requested information. Defiantly, David exclaimed, "I have no disclosures to make; hurry up your execution. I can die, but I cannot betray a friend."

Sensing that David's time was short, a minister named Peck dropped to his knees and offered a prayer for the soul of the condemned. In the preceding days, the Reverend R. G. Colburn, the minister of First Methodist Church in Little Rock, had counseled David. But the sight of the teenager standing at the hangman's noose so sickened him that he fled the parade ground.

Colburn was not the only person disgusted by the proceedings. Hundreds of Yankee soldiers not a part of the official death detail turned their backs on the gallows. J. R. Martin, an Iowa soldier assigned as a guard at the execution site, later noted, "It was only our great respect for military discipline that prevented a very demonstration at the time in his favor. . . . We soldiers always spoke of it as murder."

Finally, the time was at hand. As a frigid wind blew David's long hair, the executioner, who was aptly named Dekay, stepped forward to apply the blindfold. Somehow, he had forgotten to bring one! Without losing his composure, David looked the man squarely in the eye and said, "You will find a handkerchief in my coat."

In an instant, David's eyes were covered and his arms bound behind his back. As the noose was placed around his neck, he was heard to whisper, "If I am to die I want to die like a man."

The death order was given, and the tailgate of the wagon was dropped.

Soldiers and spectators alike were horrified at what they observed. Because the hanging rope was too long, David's toes touched the ground. For five long minutes, the bound, blindfolded boy twisted and jerked. Battle-tested warriors vomited on the scene.

In an attempt to put David out of his misery, one soldier climbed atop the crossbar and pulled on the rope while several comrades grabbed the teenager's feet. In the end, they succeeded in completing the bungled execution. Seventeen-year-old David O. Dodd was dead.

J. R. Martin, one of the Union troops ordered to participate in the hanging, paid a fitting tribute to the young Confederate: "His quiet and heroic bearing stamped him as not only one of the bravest of the brave, but not one of us doubted that he met his fate with the same lofty feeling of patriotism that sustained in his last hours, Nathan Hale, the immortal spy of the Revolution."

Major General James Ewell Brown Stuart

Lee's Eyes and Ears

Yellow Tavern, Virginia
May 12, 1864

"I hope I have fulfilled my destiny to my country and my duty to God."

Among the cavalry leaders of the Civil War, none was greater than Major General James Ewell Brown Stuart. Better known throughout the South as "Jeb," the swashbuckling soldier was adept at providing the Confederate high command reliable information about the position and strength of the enemy. As the conflict wore on, he proved almost indispensable to the Southern war effort. Both armies referred to Stuart as "the eyes and ears of Lee's army." His death in the late spring of 1864 left a void that could not be filled.

Born near the North Carolina line in Patrick County, Virginia, on February 6, 1833, Stuart enrolled at West Point in 1850. Four years later, the young lieutenant embarked upon a military career as a cavalry officer. His skill in the saddle quickly came to the fore during his service in the First United States Cavalry. A year after his graduation from the United States Military Academy, Stuart married Flora Cooke, the daughter of Phillip St. George Cooke, who would serve as a cavalry general in the Union army during the Civil War.

In 1859, the United States War Department, cognizant of Stuart's talents, granted him a six-month leave of absence so he could perfect his invention of cavalry accouterments. His patent was subsequently purchased by the government for five thousand dollars. After his return to active duty, Stuart served as a volunteer aide to Colonel Robert E. Lee in the capture and arrest of John Brown at Harpers Ferry. Thus began an association between Lee and Stuart that would grow in significance in the coming years.

Upon learning that his native state had seceded, Stuart resigned his commission in the United States Army and accepted an appointment as lieutenant colonel in the Provisional Army of Virginia in 1861. Soon, he was colonel of the First Virginia Cavalry. In that command, he built a network of outposts in northern Virginia from which his men could monitor activities in Washington, D.C.

General Joseph E. Johnston recommended Stuart's promotion to President Jefferson Davis on August 10, 1861: "He is a rare man, wonderfully endowed by nature with the qualities necessary for an officer of light cavalry. Calm, firm, acute, active, and enterprising, I know of no one more competent than he to estimate its occurrences before him at their true value. If you add to this army a real brigade of cavalry, you can find no better brigadier-general to command it." By September, Stuart was a general. Over the months that followed, he used six regiments of cavalry to monitor the enemy and protect the rear of the Southern army in Virginia.

During the first week of June 1862, Stuart completed a four-day ride around the entire Federal army in the Peninsula Campaign. From the daring venture, General Lee gained invaluable information and Stuart achieved enduring fame. Less than a month later, Stuart's cavalry turned in another stellar performance in the Seven Days' Campaign. As a reward, Lee established a cavalry division in his army and appointed Stuart as its major general.

Over the year that followed, Jeb emerged as a beloved Southern hero. Stories of his scouting forays, his raids of Union camps and towns, and his daring battlefield exploits became legend. His showmanship, his flair for dress, and the pomp surrounding his command added to the myth. Noted nineteenth-century American author John Esten Cooke described Stuart thus: "Young, gay, gallant; wearing a uniform brilliant with gold braid, golden spurs, and a hat lopped up with a golden star and decorated with a black plume; going on marches at the head of his cavalry column, with his banjo

Major General James Ewell Brown "Jeb" Stuart
COURTESY OF *REBELLION RECORD*

player gayly thrumming behind him; leading his troops to battle with a camp song on his lips; here today and away tomorrow; raiding, fighting, laughing, dancing, and as famous for his gallantry toward women as for his reckless courage."

His flamboyance notwithstanding, Stuart was a bold, confident, fearless, and clever soldier. At Fredericksburg, when Lee dispatched a courier for a report on the battle, Stuart responded brashly: "Tell him Jackson has not advanced, but I have, and that I am going on, crowding 'em with artillery." On another occasion, his command was in a tight spot when Stuart was asked what he planned to do next. Without hesitation, he declared, "Go through or die trying."

One of the few blemishes on Stuart's record came during Lee's invasion of the North in the summer of 1863. In his attempt to repeat his famous ride around the massive Union army, he became separated from the main body of Confederates. As a result, he did not reach Gettysburg until the second day of the battle. Though Lee did not lose his confidence in

Stuart, he sternly reprimanded him, remarking that the Confederate army "had been much embarrassed by the absence of cavalry."

After the great debacle at Gettysburg, Stuart spent the remaining ten months of his life in defense of his native soil. In early May 1864, Union cavalry forces commanded by Major General Philip H. Sheridan initiated a series of raids in the direction of Richmond. It was Stuart's job to stop Sheridan. On the morning of May 11, 1864, he decided to make a stand at Yellow Tavern, just six miles from the Confederate capital. To beat back the enemy army of twelve thousand men, he had twenty-four hundred soldiers in Fitzhugh Lee's division, his own cavalry, and fewer than two dozen artillery pieces.

About two o'clock that afternoon, Sheridan unleashed a savage attack against Stuart. For two hours, the beleaguered Southerners held the Federals at bay in ferocious, often hand-to-hand, combat. When George Armstrong Custer's brigade threatened to flank the Confederate left around four o'clock, Stuart sprang into action. He quickly rode to the front, where he was greeted by the men of Company K of his First Virginia Cavalry. His saber extended, the general expressed his delight by saying, "Bully for old K! Give it to them, boys!" Realizing that the battle teetered in the balance, he cried out, "Boys, don't stop to count fours [horses' hooves]. Shoot them! Shoot them!"

Just then, a well-directed shot from a Michigan soldier found its mark. General Stuart pressed his hand to his side and struggled to remain in his saddle. J. R. Oliver of Company K rushed to the aid of his commander and asked, "General, are you hit?"

"Yes," responded Jeb.

"Are you wounded badly?" inquired Oliver.

Stuart replied, "I am afraid I am. But don't worry, boys, Fitz will do as well for you as I have done." To a nearby lieutenant, the general said, "Yes, I am done for, but don't let my men know it. Get me another horse!" Captain Gus Dorsey rode up and attempted to render aid, but Stuart was more interested in the battle. He shouted, "I am shot; Dorsey, save your men!"

Another horse was brought up, but Stuart was unable to mount it. His attendants carefully placed him in the saddle and rode alongside holding onto him until they encountered General Fitzhugh Lee, who directed that Stuart be transported to Richmond once field surgeons stabilized him.

General Stuart was subsequently placed in the Richmond home of his brother-in-law. There, his condition worsened. By then, his doctors realized he would not survive. Jeb sensed the end was near. From his deathbed, he could hear the rumble of artillery in the distance. To his trusted adjutant, Major H. B. McClellan, he said, "Major, Fitz Lee may need you." Then he sighed and said with resignation, "But I must be preparing for another world."

Around noon the following day, President Davis came to Stuart's side, tenderly held his hand, and asked how he was feeling. Jeb responded, "Easy, but willing to die, if God and my country think I have fulfilled my destiny and done my duty."

As the afternoon progressed, Stuart's surgeon informed him that he had but a short time to live. Jeb said he would like to see his wife. At that very moment, Mrs. Stuart was making haste to reach her husband's side, but she would not arrive in time.

When one of his physicians began to monitor his pulse, the general said, "Doctor, I suppose I am going fast now. It will soon be over. But God's will be done. I hope I have fulfilled my destiny to my country and my duty to God." Noticing that Dr. Joshua Peterkin, an Episcopal minister, was at his side, Jeb requested that he sing "Rock of Ages." As Dr. Peterkin began, "Rock of Ages, cleft for me, / Let me hide myself in Thee," General Stuart joined in with his feeble voice.

Once the hymn ended, Dr. Peterkin and the other ministers attending Stuart offered prayers for his soul. The end was at hand when Jeb spoke one last time: "I am going fast now; I am resigned; God's will be done."

General James Ewell Brown Stuart, who had stared death in the face so many times, could fight no longer. With his passing, the South lost its "Cavalier of Dixie," and Robert E. Lee lost the eyes and ears of his army.

Artilleryman Edward Cooper

From the Firing Squad to the Firing Line

Cold Harbor, Virginia
Early June 1864

"General, I have one more shell left. Tell me, have I preserved the honor of Mary and Lucy?"

Few problems were of greater significance to the opposing armies during the Civil War than desertion. Although the Confederate soldier is revered as a model of courage and loyalty, more than 105,000 Southern men and boys were recorded as deserters over the course of the war. There were many reasons why Confederate warriors chose to leave the ranks without authorization—irregular pay, depression and disillusionment over the war effort, boredom. By and large, however, the most frequent excuse offered by Southern soldiers for abandoning their posts of duty was concern for their families back home. And so it was with Edward Cooper, a young husband and father assigned to man the artillery on the killing grounds of Virginia. But unlike many other deserters, Edward Cooper turned himself in to Confederate authorities after a brief visit with his family.

Snow covered the ground in December 1863 when a court-martial was convened by Brigadier General Armistead L. Long, Lee's chief of artillery, at Round Oak Church in Caroline County, Virginia. Scores of citizens swarmed the grounds as a long line of military prisoners was escorted into the makeshift courtroom. In the course of its business, the tribunal routinely disposed of a number of cases. Then the case of *Confederate States of America vs. Edward Cooper* was called.

Edward Cooper promptly walked from the prisoners' bench to the defendant's table. Upon being asked to tender a plea to the charge of desertion, he responded, "Not guilty." Before the judge advocate could begin his case against Cooper, the court inquired of the accused, "Who is your counsel?" Without hesitation, the prisoner replied, "I have no counsel." On the assumption that Cooper was going to represent himself, General Long instructed the prosecutor to proceed. The judge advocate then presented the evidence necessary to sustain the charge of desertion.

When the time came for Edward Cooper to present his case, he stoically informed the court, "I have no witnesses." Taken aback at his response and puzzled by his calm demeanor, General Long inquired, "Have you no defense? Is it true that you abandoned your comrades and deserted your colors without a reason therefor?" Refusing to give in to his emotions, the defendant said, "There is a reason, but it will not avail me before a military court." General Long immediately took issue: "Perhaps you are mistaken. You are charged with the highest crime known to military law, and it becomes your duty to make known the cause which influenced your action." Cooper's eyes filled with tears. His hands trembled as he handed a letter to General Long. He offered a simple response: "There, General, is what did it."

The presiding officer opened the letter and read it. Try as he might, the war-hardened artillery commander could not hold back tears. By and by, he passed the missive among the other officers on the panel, and each of the battlefield leaders "wept like children," according to General Long.

As soon as he regained his composure, Long read the letter aloud for the edification of all present: "My Dear Edward, I have always been proud of you, but since your connection with the Confederate army I have been prouder of you than ever before; but unless you come home at once we must die. Last night I was awakened by little Eddie's crying. I called to him and said: 'Eddie, what is the matter?' He replied: 'Oh, mamma, I am so hungry.' And Lucy, Edward, your darling Lucy, she never complains; but day by day she is growing thinner and thinner, and before God, Edward, unless you come home at once we will die. Your Mary."

Upon finishing, Long looked at Cooper and asked, "What did you do when you received this letter?"

A photograph of Brigadier General Armistead L. Long, who presided over Edward Cooper's court-martial and Cooper's death on the battlefield.
COURTESY OF LIBRARY OF CONGRESS

In a respectful tone, the prisoner replied, "I made application for a furlough; it was rejected." Cooper then informed the court that he had applied a second time and a third time, with the same result. Reflecting upon the receipt of the third rejection, he said, "That night as I wandered back and forth at the camp, thinking of my home with the wild, blue eyes of Lucy looking up at me and the burning words of Mary sinking in my brain, I was no longer the Confederate soldier, but the husband of Mary and the father of Lucy, and I would have passed through those lines that night had every gun in the battery been turned upon me."

Confident that his duty to his family was paramount, Edward Cooper had set out for home without the approval of his superiors. When she saw him in the distance, Mary had raced toward him. As the couple walked hand in hand toward the Cooper homestead, Mary said, "Oh Edward, I am so glad you have come; I am so glad you got your furlough." Joy turned to despair as Mary felt Edward's hand begin to tremble. "Edward, did you come home without furlough?" she asked. Before he could answer, Mary said resolutely, "Go back; let me and my children go down with sorrow to the grave, but for heaven's sake preserve the honor of our name."

Completing his story to the court-martial, Cooper said, "Here I am, gentlemen, not brought here by any military power, but by the command of Mary, to abide the sentence of your court."

As the officers deliberated Cooper's fate, each sympathized with the heartrending decision he had been forced to make. But having been trained in military law, they were duty bound to follow it. Their verdict was unanimous: Guilty.

Upon reviewing the proceedings of the Cooper trial, the commander of the Army of Northern Virginia tempered law and duty with compassion. "The finding of the court is approved," he wrote. "The prisoner is pardoned and will report to his company. R. E. Lee, General."

Edward Cooper was back in the heat of action in early June 1864 at the bloody battle of Cold Harbor, Virginia. At the height of that conflagration, General Long came face to face with the former deserter. The artillery chieftain recounted, "While shot and shell were falling like torrents from the mountain cloud, my attention was directed to the fact that one of our batteries was being silenced by the concentrated fire of the enemy. On reaching the spot I found that every gun in the battery had been dismantled except one, by the side of which stood a lone Confederate."

Gunpowder was smudged on his face and blood poured from a wound in his side, but Edward Cooper was yet manning the gun assigned to him. When he saw General Long, the dying soldier managed to raise his voice above the din: "General, I have one more shell left. Tell me, have I preserved the honor of Mary and Lucy?"

General Long raised his hat in affirmation. Saying no more, Cooper sent that final shell crashing into the Union lines. Then he collapsed in death beside his gun.

Dr. David Herbert Llewellyn, Assistant Surgeon

Every Man for Himself, Save One

Off Cherbourg, France
June 19, 1864

"I will not peril the wounded men."

By 1862, the United States Navy had blockaded the coastline of the Confederate states from Virginia to Texas. In order to counter the blockade, which threatened to cut off essential supplies for the Southern war effort, the Confederate government commissioned the purchase of numerous naval vessels, particularly blockade runners and cruisers. Of the dozen cruisers that flew the Confederate colors, the most famous were the *Alabama*, the *Florida*, and the *Shenandoah*. Each was constructed in Great Britain and purchased there by James D. Bulloch, an agent for the Confederate States of America.

In Liverpool in July 1862, Bulloch took delivery of the warship destined to become the *Alabama*. She came complete with a young English medical officer, Dr. David Herbert Llewellyn. Over the next two years as the *Alabama* sailed the high seas, the loyalty, courage, and skill of the ship's assistant surgeon became legend. But Dr. Llewellyn's finest hour came on June 19, 1864, when he went down with his ship, ironically almost within sight of his beloved homeland.

Born in 1837 in Wiltshire, England, into a family that valued education, David followed his two older brothers to Marlborough College. Sub-

A drawing showing the sinking of the CSS Alabama, *off Cherbourg, France. Dr. David Herbert Llewellyn, assistant surgeon aboard the* Alabama, *drowned during the naval battle.*
COURTESY OF *HARPER'S PICTORIAL HISTORY OF THE CIVIL WAR*

sequently, he was admitted to the Charing Cross Hospital Medical School, where he earned silver medals in surgery and chemistry. David was but twenty-two years old when he earned his license to practice medicine in 1859. Three years later, he decided to become a ship's surgeon at the very time the newly built vessel identified only as No. 290 (because it was the 290th vessel launched at the Laird Shipyards in Liverpool) needed a medical officer.

As the ship prepared to sail from Liverpool on her initial voyage, observers were in awe of her beauty. One eyewitness offered a description: "She was a perfect ship of her class; her model was of the most symmetry, and she sat the water with the lightness of a swan." There was also an aura of mystery surrounding No. 290. Officially, no one knew the initial destination or purpose of the steamer or the identity of her captain. But Dr. Llewellyn had heard gossip in the pubs and about the busy wharves of Liverpool. The new ship was to be a Confederate raider.

No sooner had she first sailed than No. 290 and her escort, the *Bahama*, anchored about a league off the English coast. There, all was revealed to the crew of the cruiser. Standing on a gun carriage, Captain Raphael Semmes of the Confederate States Navy read the commission from President Jefferson Davis appointing him the commander of the heavily armed warship. When he finished reading the official papers, Captain Semmes waved his hand, a signal gun fired, the halyard snapped, and the Confederate colors were unfurled to blow in the breeze. At the same time, the English flag was hauled down and No. 290 was officially christened the CSS *Alabama*.

Officers and sailors, their heads uncovered out of respect during the ceremony, broke out in a wild celebration as the band played "Dixie." Amid the exhilaration, Dr. David Llewellyn was faced with a decision. As a British national, he could not be impressed into service in the Confederate navy. If he chose, he could leave the *Alabama* at her first port of call, which was to be the Azores. After all, the ship already had a chief surgeon who was a Confederate officer. Nonetheless, David decided to remain aboard.

For twenty-two months, he provided outstanding medical care for the crew of twenty-four officers and 120 sailors as the Confederate warship cruised seventy-five thousand miles through the Atlantic, the Gulf of Mexico, the Indian Ocean, the Java Sea, and the South China Sea while raiding and capturing sixty-five Union ships. Despite the myriad diseases to which the sailors were exposed at foreign ports and the dangers inherent in sea warfare, not one man was lost during the grueling cruise. Much of the credit was due to Dr. David Llewellyn.

On June 10, 1864, the *Alabama* negotiated the Cape of the Hague on the coast of Normandy and sailed into her final port, Cherbourg, France. Captain Semmes, weakened by cold and fever, was bedridden and under the care of Dr. Llewellyn. Over the next several days, the ship lay at anchor in the harbor, awaiting permission to dock. News of the mighty warship's arrival quickly spread from Cherbourg throughout Europe. Visitors poured into the seaport to catch sight of the famous cruiser and meet her sailors, who were allowed to roam the city.

On June 12, the United States minister in Paris telegraphed news of the *Alabama*'s presence to Captain John A. Winslow, commander of the USS *Kearsarge*, which was at anchor three hundred miles away off the Dutch coast. Winslow, a native North Carolinian who had been a shipmate of Raphael Semmes during the Mexican War, was challenged to prevent the *Alabama* from escaping French waters.

In but two days, the *Kearsarge* was at anchor off the breakwater at Cherbourg. From the deck of each mighty ship, the crew surveyed the opposing man-of-war. In size and construction, the *Alabama* and the *Kearsarge* were equals. But in armament and firepower, the Union vessel was superior. More importantly, the *Kearsarge* was just two months out of dry dock, where her engines had been refurbished. On the other hand, the *Alabama* was a tired ship badly in need of repair. Nonetheless, Captain Semmes was determined to fight. A Confederate agent was dispatched with a note from Semmes that set the tone for the coming days: "I desire you to say to the U.S. consul that my intention is to fight the *Kearsarge* as soon as I can make the necessary arrangements. I beg she will not depart before I am ready to go out."

By Sunday, June 19, all was ready for the great showdown. Thousands of spectators, many having come by train from Paris, gathered on the roofs of Cherbourg's buildings on a bright, clear morning cooled by a gentle breeze. Aboard the *Alabama*, Dr. Llewellyn surveyed the crowd and observed that many hands waved tiny Confederate flags.

At nine forty-five, under the escort of the French frigate *Couronne* and a sizable flotilla of spectator craft, the Confederate raider hoisted anchor and sailed toward the English Channel. From the shore, the crowd cheered the *Alabama* and her crew. A band on one of the escort boats played "Dixie."

Once the Southern raider entered international waters, the French warship peeled away. As the *Alabama* steamed toward her adversary, Captain Semmes took his place atop the same gun where he had commissioned the ship. There, he made an impassioned war speech to the crew, saying, "The name of your ship has become a household word wherever civilization extends. Shall that name be tarnished by defeat?"

His excited warriors cried, "Never! Never!"

Though yet weak from his illness, Semmes was energized. "Remember that you are in the English Channel, the theatre of so much of the naval glory of our race," he continued. "The eyes of all Europe are at this moment upon you! The flag that floats over you is that of a young Republic that bids defiance to her enemies, whenever and wherever found. Show the world that you know how to uphold it! Go to your quarters!"

David Llewellyn hurried to the wardroom, where he set up an operating table in anticipation of the bloodshed soon to come.

Less than three-quarters of an hour later, the *Alabama* opened the battle when the ships were a mile apart. After closing the distance to a half-mile, Winslow answered his old mate with a salvo from the starboard battery of the *Kearsarge*. The great sea confrontation intensified as the ships traveled in parallel circles.

In short order, Dr. Llewellyn was engaged in a desperate struggle to save the lives of crewmen injured in the fight. From above came the deafening sounds of battle, and from the bleeding men all about the makeshift operating room came pitiful cries for help. The unrelenting rain of shot and shell was exacting a heavy toll on the *Alabama* and her crew. But when an eleven-inch shell tore into the cruiser's hull and seawater poured about his feet, David knew the vessel was in serious trouble.

With sailor after sailor falling on deck, Lieutenant Arthur Sinclair headed below to fetch some brandy from Dr. Llewellyn to provide comfort for the dying and wounded above. Noting the rising water in the wardroom, he addressed David by his nickname: "Why, Pills, you had better get yourself and the wounded out of this, or you'll be drowned." The surgeon shook his head and hardly looked up when he said, "I must wait for orders, you know." Almost as soon as the lieutenant vanished with the brandy, another shell hit the *Alabama*. This one smashed into the wardroom, destroying the operating table and killing the patient upon it. Somehow, Dr. Llewellyn was not injured.

About the same time, Captain Semmes received the damage report he had ordered. The news was grim: The engine room was flooded, and the *Alabama* was without power. In an instant, he shouted an order to Captain John M. Kell, his second in command: "Go below . . . and see how long the ship can float."

Rushing to confer with the chief engineer, Captain Kell passed through the wardroom, which was rapidly filling with water. Almost oblivious to the peril about him, Dr. Llewellyn was yet trying to render aid to his patients.

Kell returned to Semmes with a dismal answer: "Perhaps ten minutes."

Resigned to the fate of his ship, Semmes nevertheless resolved to save his men. He said to Kell, "Then, sir, cease firing, shorten sail, and haul down the colors. It will never do in this nineteenth century for us to go down with the decks covered with our gallant wounded."

Within seconds, the boatswain sounded the distress call: "All hands save yourself!"

When Dr. Llewellyn heard the order, he promptly assisted several injured survivors up to the main deck, where only two lifeboats—a dingy and a whaleboat—were seaworthy. Wounded sailors were loaded into the small boats. When an able-bodied seaman attempted to jump into the overloaded whaleboat, David pulled him back and said rather sternly, "See, I want to save my life as much as you do, but let the wounded men be saved."

From the boat, one of David's fellow officers pleaded, "Doctor, we can make room for you."

But David understood the boat could hold no more. He shook his head and said, "I will not peril the wounded men."

Moments later, the men in the two lifeboats watched in horror as Dr. David Herbert Llewellyn disappeared with the *Alabama* into the depths of the channel.

Captain Kell described his experience in the water: "It was a mass of living heads striving, struggling, and battling for life. On the wild waste of water there came no boats at first from the *Kearsarge* to our rescue. Had victory struck them dumb or helpless? Or had it frozen the milk of human kindness in their veins? The water was like ice, and after the excitement of battle it seemed doubly cold. I saw a float of empty shell boxes near me and called out to one of the men, an expert swimmer, to examine the float. He said: 'It is the doctor, sir, and he is dead!' Poor Llewellyn, almost within sight of home, the air blowing across the Channel from it into his dead face that had given up the struggle for life and liberty!"

Llewellyn's homeland would not forget the example and sacrifice of the young physician. A memorial window and tablet at Easton Royal Church in his beloved Wiltshire bear testimony to his character and courage. Likewise, a tablet was erected in the main hall of the medical school he attended. Physicians from all parts of the British Empire contributed to the memorial. Their overwhelming generosity made it possible to establish and endow the Llewellyn Scholarship and the Llewellyn Prize, which are yet awarded to deserving medical students.

Across the vast Atlantic, Southerners memorialized Dr. David Herbert Llewellyn by posthumously awarding him the Confederate Medal of Honor. After all, the young physician had given up the final seat in the last lifeboat and gone to his death in the English Channel with a secret no one else knew—he could not swim. And all this for a nation and a people not his own.

Lieutenant Isaac Lightner

Three Years Behind the Big Guns

Kennesaw Mountain, Georgia
June 27, 1864

"General, have I not won promotion today?"

As the end drew near for Ike Lightner on the miserably hot afternoon of June 27, 1864, in northwestern Georgia, the cause for which he was about to die was not the same as the one for which he had volunteered three years earlier.

Tensions were high across Lightner's native Missouri in May 1861 after a riot against invading Federal troops left twenty-eight people dead in the streets in St. Louis. In order to restore peace and defend the state capital at Jefferson City, the pro-Southern governor, Claiborne F. Jackson, issued a plea for volunteers. Among the first thirteen men to present themselves for duty was Ike Lightner, who made the long journey from his home in Lexington, a small town just east of Kansas City.

Ike was described at the time by an acquaintance as "very young, scarcely more than a boy." Within days, the "original thirteen," as Ike and the first volunteers came to be known, were joined by a sufficient quantity of men to form a company. As there was no one in the capital with the ability to man the three artillery pieces on hand, Ike and some of his comrades were assigned to artillery duty under the command of Captain Hiram Bledsoe.

Ike's service was of limited duration because a sizable Federal army soon forced Governor Jackson and his defenders to flee Jefferson City. As the pro-

A pen-and-ink drawing by Lieutenant Isaac Lightner
COURTESY OF *CONFEDERATE VETERAN*

Southern government regrouped in southwestern Missouri, the scope of Ike's mission changed dramatically. No longer was he fighting to preserve the peace in his state. Now, he was fighting for the independence of the South. Over the next four years, more than forty thousand other Missourians would join in that quest.

After demonstrating his courage in battle as a member of Captain Bledsoe's battery, Lightner was transferred to the Tenth Missouri Battery with the rank of second lieutenant. Throughout 1862 and 1863 and into the summer of 1864, he served in the Western theater, particularly in the grim, bloody combat in Tennessee and Georgia.

One of the lieutenant's young friends described him as "a gentleman by birth and instinct." About Ike's personality, he noted, "His disposition was of that bright and happy kind that always wins friends." A gifted artist, Ike often amazed his comrades by crafting pen-and-ink drawings in camp.

During the last week of June 1864, the inability of his army to make significant progress against Atlanta got the best of General William T. Sherman. His impatience caused him to plan a bold attack against General Joseph Johnston's army, which manned a seven-mile line of high ground two miles northwest of Marietta at Kennesaw Mountain. As Monday, June 27, dawned, Lieutenant Lightner stood by his field pieces on the slope of Kennesaw, ready to repel the Yankees on yet another field of battle. The cloudless day promised to be hot and deadly. One Confederate soldier chronicled the scene in the moments leading up to the battle: "The heavens seemed made of brass and the earth of iron, and as the sun began to mount toward the zenith, everything became quiet and no sound was heard save a peckerwood on a neighboring tree, tapping on its old trunk, trying to find a worm for his dinner."

The eerie silence came to an abrupt end at eight o'clock that morning, when hundreds of Union artillery pieces launched fiery projectiles into the Southern lines. Ike limbered up his command. Once the order was given, his guns joined in a unified Confederate response. Lieutenant Colonel Joseph Fullerton, a Yankee officer who witnessed the deafening exchange, observed, "Gun spoke to gun. Kennesaw smoked and blazed with fire, a volcano as grand as Etna."

Before the sun reached its noonday height, the temperature on the battlefield was a hundred degrees. In less than four hours, the fighting was over. The Southerners had dealt Sherman a serious setback. More than 3,000 Union soldiers had fallen in the assault. Two Yankee generals were dead. On the other hand, Johnston's Confederates had lost only 750.

But among the mortally wounded was Lieutenant Ike Lightner. In the heat of the fight, a cannonball had carried away both of his feet. As he was being carried from the field, he sensed that the day belonged to the Confederates. At length, he looked up to see the concerned face of his beloved commander, General Patrick Cleburne (see pages 222-27). Mustering a last bit of energy, the young lieutenant sported a weak smile and asked, "General, have I not won promotion today?"

In short order, Lieutenant Lightner succumbed to his terrible wounds far away from his home and family in western Missouri. When the wife of one of his fellow artillery officers was informed of Ike's death, she said, "I knew him well, and when my husband told me he was mortally wounded, I just laid down and wept. I felt that he was one man who ought to live always."

Private William Youree
Billy Reb

Peachtree Creek, Georgia
July 18, 1864

"I would rather stay with the boys."

Ever anxious to aid the Confederate cause, countless sick and injured soldiers took their places in the ranks without consideration for their personal health and well-being. When a battle loomed, these men and boys streamed from the hospitals, homes, and camps where they were being treated in order to join their comrades for a new trial under fire. Some of them never returned to their sickbeds because they became permanent casualties of the war. Private William Youree was one such soldier.

Young Billy Youree joined Company K of the Second Tennessee as a private when it took part in the horrific battle at Corinth, Mississippi, in the autumn of 1862. Dr. E. L. Drake, a member of the regiment, offered a description of Billy when he reported for duty: "He was a puny, sallow, undeveloped youth when he came to us at Corinth, seemingly too weak to handle a musket or endure a march."

Billy made up for his physical frailty through his determination, devotion to duty, and intense desire to be with his company when it went into battle. Although frequently ill, he never made excuses or asked for special consideration. Dr. Drake recalled, "He never missed a battle, I think, in

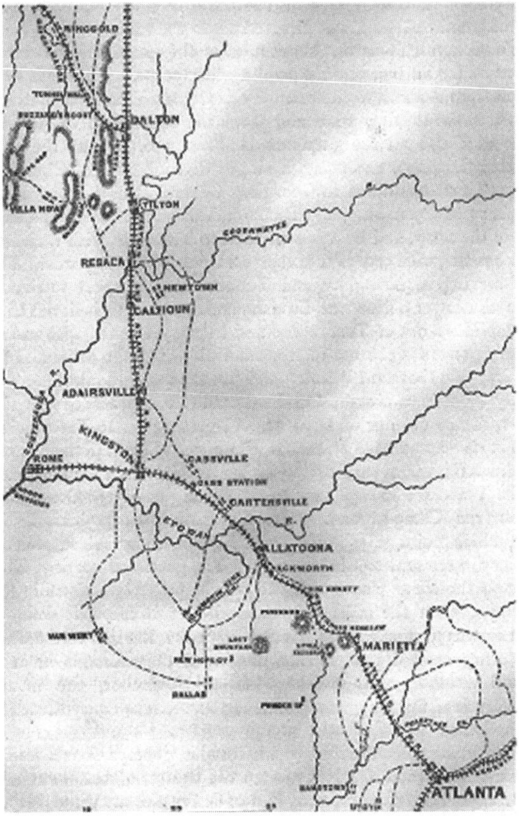

A map showing the campaign of Company K of the Second Tennessee—Private Billy Youree's last campaign.
LOSSING'S CIVIL WAR IN AMERICA

which we engaged." In camp, Billy's fellow soldiers admired his inner strength and moral character. "He had none of the vices of the camp," Dr. Drake said. "His Bible was his constant companion, and his morals pure; indeed, he shamed us all by his example of patient, uncomplaining fortitude under the most trying circumstances, though he was but a weak, pitiful-looking, undeveloped boy."

After participating in the Dalton Campaign in the early spring of 1864, the Second Tennessee moved deeper into Georgia, crossing the Chattahoochee River. The rigors of the march took a heavy toll on Billy Youree. After determining that Billy was unfit for duty, Dr. Drake ordered him to the hospital on July 17.

A day later, the regiment was preparing for battle at Peachtree Creek when Billy, still very ill, presented himself for duty. Dr. Drake chided him, but the youngster was determined. Before taking his place in the line, he made one simple statement: "I would rather stay with the boys."

In the course of the skirmish that followed, the Tennesseans were forced to retreat after the Yankees turned the Confederate left. As the gray-clad soldiers engaged in what Dr. Drake referred to as a "run for life," he happened upon Billy, who was trying to keep up. "I came across the poor fellow in much distress because he was unable to run," he recorded. Since there was no way to help the boy, Dr. Drake continued falling back. Though an enemy bullet soon brought the physician down, he managed to crawl back to the regimental camp.

When the fighting ended on July 18, Company K counted its casualties. Only one of its number had been killed. The very soldier whose fondest desire was to "stay with the boys" had been unable to do so that fateful day. Dr. Drake eulogized Private William Youree with these words: "It is not stature nor strength, but the spirit that makes the man."

Private Dewitt Smith Jobe

Action Rather Than Words

Near Triune, Tennessee
August 29, 1864

Muted silence

We shall never know the words that raced through the mind of twenty-four-year-old private Dewitt Smith Jobe as the end of his life neared in rural Tennessee on August 30, 1864. Even before the last breath of life was strangled from his body by his Yankee captors, the young Confederate scout was unable to speak because his adversaries had removed his tongue. But if the actions of the muted, blinded, and savagely tortured soldier in those final moments are suggestive of his silent parting words, then his death speech was one of defiance and loyalty to the cause of Southern independence.

Dee Jobe was born in Rutherford County, Tennessee, on June 4, 1840. On May 27, 1861, just one week before his twenty-first birthday, he made his way to adjacent Williamson County, where he enlisted as a private in the Twentieth Tennessee Volunteers. Just three years later, he would be brutally executed in a cornfield on a hot summer day in the very county where his Confederate service began.

Jobe spent his first six months of active duty in the defense of his native state. Then, on January 19, 1862, the Confederate division of Major General George B. Crittenden clashed with Federal soldiers commanded by Brigadier General George H. Thomas at Mill Springs, Kentucky. Private Jobe

Private Dewitt Smith Jobe
COURTESY OF *CONFEDERATE VETERAN*

was in the thick of that fight. When it was over, the vanquished Confederates were forced to abandon Kentucky to Union control. Jobe was left behind as a prisoner of war.

After being exchanged following seven months of confinement at Camp Chase, Ohio, Jobe returned to his regiment and again took part in combat on his native soil. As 1862 drew to a close, the warring armies squared off near Murfreesboro, Tennessee. As it turned out, the Battle of Stone's River—which took place from December 31, 1862, to January 2, 1863—was the last major engagement in which he participated.

Jobe's superiors saw something special in the young soldier. He was clever and resourceful, and he carried with him a wealth of information about Rutherford and Williamson Counties, both considered key in the fight for Tennessee. Knowing the Army of Tennessee was in dire need of scouts, General William Hardee requested that Private Jobe be detached from his regiment. In the spring of 1863, he was assigned to serve in Coleman's Scouts.

Commanded by Captain H. B. Shaw, known as "Captain Coleman,"

Coleman's Scouts was an elite Confederate intelligence unit deployed in middle Tennessee. Most members came from the regular army. Upon being assigned to the elite command, Dee Jobe was delighted to join forces with Sam Davis, a trusted old friend. Born less than eight miles apart, they had grown up together as playmates. Other scouts were familiar to Jobe, too. Among their number was his cousin Dee Smith and another close friend, Tom Joplin.

On occasion, an assignment required some of the scouts to ride together. But most often, they traveled alone. Their responsibility was great, for they were the eyes and ears of the regular army. Their missions were fraught with peril. Jobe and his compatriots were fully aware that each ride might be their last. Every time they took to the saddle, they were marked men.

No event of the war strengthened Jobe's resolve more than the hanging of twenty-one-year-old Sam Davis by the Yankees on November 27, 1863 (see pages 161-67). Deeply touched by the stories of Davis's courage on the gallows, Jobe vowed not to let the great sacrifice of his friend be in vain. Over the next nine months, he rode hard and fast.

About daybreak on Monday, August 29, 1864, Jobe was riding alone between Triune and Nashville in Williamson County. Union patrols were known to be in the area. He had been traveling all night, and he desperately needed food and rest. He knew he could find friends at the farmstead of William Moss, located several hundred yards off the main road leading to the state capital. After all, Moss's two sons had served with Jobe in the Twentieth Tennessee.

After welcoming the scout and providing him a hearty breakfast and important information, William Moss urged Jobe not to tarry because Yankees were on the prowl. Dee thanked his gracious host and rode off to locate a place where he might hide and get some sleep.

A mile into his ride, he came upon an expansive cornfield at Sam Watson's farm. A survey of the almost endless rows of tall stalks convinced Jobe that here was the perfect place to catch a nap. Federal patrols, he reasoned, would never find him. Little did he know that a Union officer's telescope was trained on him at that very moment.

Not long after he spread his blanket in the middle of the cornfield, the exhausted scout fell asleep. But upon being awakened by the rustling of stalks, he sat up and rubbed his eyes. He heard men in the distance. They spoke with Northern accents.

His first thought as a well-trained scout was to escape. But enemy soldiers appeared to be approaching from all directions. His capture was imminent. In an instant, Jobe gathered the sensitive papers entrusted to him and began tearing them up. As the Federals closed in, he stuffed the scraps into his mouth and tried to swallow them.

Like a swarm of bees, blue-clad troopers from the 115th Ohio descended upon the lone Confederate. As they wrestled him to the ground, some of the paper scraps fell from his mouth. While some of the Ohioans bound his hands behind his back, others scrambled to collect the torn pieces of paper. Notwithstanding their efforts, the soldiers could not put the message back together. Their ire growing by the second, they tried to pressure the helpless prisoner into revealing what the message said, where he had gotten it, and where and when he would next meet with his fellow scouts.

Not a word came from the mouth of the Confederate, who continued to swallow the paper yet in his mouth. Perhaps, thought the Yankees, the pressure should be less subtle. Someone affixed a bridle rein around his neck. The inquisitors drew it tighter and tighter each time Jobe refused to answer them.

Red-hot with anger, the Yankees punched Jobe in the face and body. Their brutality had no effect. The Rebel's silence was maddening. Even when they smashed rifle butts into his face and knocked out some of his teeth with a blow from a pistol, no information or pleas for mercy came from his bloody mouth.

Convinced that mere torture would not force the prisoner to talk, the Ohio troopers resorted to barbarity. But when they gouged out one of Jobe's eyes, he still fought them with his silence. Some of the cruelest of the Union soldiers then proceeded to carve out the other eye. Robbed of his sight, Dee Jobe finally spoke. But rather than providing answers to their questions, the barely conscious man mumbled epithets at his adversaries.

Galled, one of the Yankees pulled out his knife and cut off the scout's tongue. No more would he taunt his captors! Nonetheless, he could still save himself. They told the prisoner they would unbind him so he could write down the requested information. But Jobe shook his head in defiance. At their collective wits' end, the Yankees attached the Confederate to the rear of a horse and watched as the animal galloped up and down the rows of corn, dragging him to his death.

Private Dewitt Smith Jobe was subsequently laid to rest in his family's cemetery, just eight miles from the cornfield where he paid the ultimate price for his allegiance to the Confederate States of America.

Chaplain Emmeran Bliemel

Under the Din of Battle

Jonesboro, Georgia
August 31, 1864

Words known only to God

Confederate chaplains played a vital role in maintaining the morale of Southern fighting forces throughout the war. In camp, these military ministers preached, counseled, and attended to the spiritual and physical needs of the soldiers. In combat, the unarmed clergymen accompanied the troops they served onto the battlefield. Without regard to the extreme danger surrounding them, chaplains offered aid, comfort, and compassion to the wounded and dying in the heat of battle. Father Emmeran Bliemel, O.S.B., was one such man. When he fell on the battlefield at Jonesboro, Georgia, on August 31, 1864, Bliemel became the first Roman Catholic chaplain killed in action in an American war.

When Father Bliemel laid down his life for the Confederacy, he was thousands of miles away from the place where his life had begun thirty-two years earlier. Born in Bavaria on the feast day of Saint Michael, the patron of the sick and dying, young Bliemel was described by a lifelong friend and fellow priest as "a boy of grit and determination." In response to his burning desire to serve as a missionary to German Catholics in America, he enrolled as a candidate for the priesthood at the Benedictine Abbey of St. Vincent in Latrobe, Pennsylvania, in 1851. Five years later, his ordination was complete.

As tensions festered between North and South in the fall of 1860, Father Bliemel took up residence in Nashville, Tennessee, where he oversaw a small German Catholic parish. Six months into his ministry there, many of the men in Bliemel's congregation joined the Tenth Tennessee and marched off to war in defense of the South. Though much of the financial base of his church was thus lost, he labored to keep the parish alive. Matters went from bad to worse when Fort Donelson fell to Federal forces in February 1862. A month later, the Tennessee capital was captured by the Union army. Countless casualties from both sides began to pour into Nashville. Without regard to the color of their uniforms, Bliemel rendered aid to the injured soldiers filling the area hospitals.

Since Nashville was occupied by a large invading force, its citizens were subjected to military law, which limited their freedom of movement. But in the early months of the occupation, no one questioned Father Bliemel's activities, even though he did not attempt to mask his growing sympathy for the Southern cause. Granted, he had been educated in Pennsylvania and had spent the first years of his priesthood in the North. However, Bliemel was of the conviction that Southerners were a more tolerant people. As he saw it, "Union men, assisted by their various secret societies," were bent on persecuting Roman Catholics.

In October 1862, Major General William Rosecrans arrived in Nashville with thousands of additional Federal soldiers. Soon, a black market for contraband goods began to flourish in the city. Father Bliemel availed himself of that avenue of commerce to aid Confederate forces positioned south of Nashville. On December 11, Colonel William Truesdale, the military commander in the state capital, was informed that a man "genteely dressed and wearing specks" had purchased morphine for the Southern war effort. Father Bliemel was promptly arrested "for treasonable conduct." When questioned about the matter by General Rosecrans, the priest said, "The bundle which I brought here by this office today, I bought on the west side Cherry Street second door from the alley toward Cedar Street. It contained morphine. Bought nothing else there. . . . Have not other goods of that kind." Rosecrans then asked the priest about his allegiance. He responded, "Have never taken any part in this rebellion. Am a conservative Union man, would prefer the old Union as it was, but believe that the South has been deprived the rights which justified them in this rebellion."

After the interview, the Union general, a devout Roman Catholic whose brother was a priest, concluded it would be imprudent to jail Bliemel, who

A drawing of the battlefield of Jonesboro, Georgia, where Father Emmeran Bliemel was killed
LOSSING'S CIVIL WAR IN AMERICA

at worst was laboring to alleviate the pain and suffering wrought by war. The charges were dismissed after the priest received a stern lecture about smuggling.

Six months later, Father Bliemel was taken into custody again. This time, he was charged with writing and publishing inflammatory anti-Union articles under the pen name Charlie in the *Freemen's Journal*, a pro-Southern Catholic weekly printed in New York. Lacking evidence to sustain the charge, General Rosecrans released Bliemel with a warning about the priest's unabashed Confederate sympathies.

Concerned that his liberty was threatened in Nashville, Father Bliemel sought another avenue of ministry. Almost a year earlier, the Tenth Tennessee had elected him as its chaplain *in absentia*. Now was the time, he thought, to join the regiment as its spiritual adviser. After all, seven of its ten companies were filled with Irishmen from Nashville. His bishop was reluctant to part with the dedicated young priest, but at length Bliemel was authorized to assume his role in the Tenth Tennessee. The bespeckled cleric set out on horseback in September 1863 to find his regiment. During his arduous journey, he had to ride around the Union army and explain his intentions to countless Confederate patrols.

In late November, the regiment was delighted to greet its chaplain when Father Bliemel rode into camp near Dalton, Georgia, in the aftermath of the devastating Confederate defeat at Missionary Ridge. Colonel William Grace, the regimental commander, enthusiastically welcomed Bliemel but informed him that he could not be officially commissioned as chaplain until there was a lull in military activities. Nonetheless, the priest immediately went to work attending to the many needs of the soldiers.

Within a short time, the men in the regiment came to love "Father Emery," as they called him. A Kentucky soldier offered high praise for the minister: "His quiet demeanor, and frank, sweet face, suggested that self-reliant courage and manhood, that draws one to another. He just seemed to drop in with us and go uncomplaining along, helping this one to bear a burden, ministering to another who was sick, and ever keeping up with the infirmary corps. . . . But this young priest followed the line of duty as if he was used, all his life, to war's direct alarms. Pushing along with the litter-bearers he was the first on his knees over a wounded companion."

On January 16, 1864, Colonel Grace formally nominated Father Emery as chaplain of the Tenth Tennessee. His official commission was approved a month later.

According to Dr. Deering Roberts, one of Bliemel's messmates, there was never a time when the priest failed to respond when needed. Roberts recalled that Bliemel sprang into action "no matter in the hour of the day and night, how hot or cold, or whether weary, worn, or almost exhausted, to aid and assist, by word or deed, his fellow man." In order to give the soldiers a respite from thoughts of war, Father Emery often sat around the campfire entertaining them with jokes, stories, and homilies. "How crisp but never sharp his jokes; how bright but never painful his repartee; how choice and chaste the many anecdotes," Dr. Roberts noted. "How deep and profound the learning; how interesting and entrancing his relation of scenes in the Old Country; how kind, how true, earnest and devoted was he to those committed to his spiritual charge."

For nine months, Father Emery shared in the hardships of the Tenth Tennessee. At Resaca, Kennesaw Mountain, Atlanta, and many other killing fields, no one in the regiment displayed greater valor and attention to duty.

One of his Knoxville friends noted, "His life was really filled with danger, labor, and fatigue. But he never lost his courage, and his patience remained constant. Day and night, whether in the quiet of the camp or in the turmoil of the battlefield, he showed the same fatherly concern for all, always ready to dispense comfort and help everywhere."

On the last day of August 1863, the noon sun gleamed on the fixed bayonets of the soldiers of the Tenth Tennessee as they prepared for battle in Jonesboro, Georgia. The soldiers knew the stakes. If the town fell to the Yankees, then Atlanta was doomed. Anxiety was evident in their faces. Father Emery walked among them offering words of assurance and inspiration.

About midafternoon, the Confederate assault on the well-fortified enemy commenced. Storming through a cornfield toward the Yankees, the men of the Tenth Tennessee came face to face with a blistering fire from skirmishers. Then the Union artillery fired grape and canister into the onrushing Southerners. Huge holes were torn in the lines, causing the Confederates to falter on the field littered with casualties. On the front line, Father Emery scrambled from victim to victim in a desperate attempt to save a life or provide a peaceful passing. All about the chaplain, stretcher bearers were busy gathering wounded soldiers and carrying them to the rear.

Suddenly, the field pieces of the enemy began sending big shells into the mass confusion. Disregarding the explosions, Father Emery went about his duties. As he ministered to a fallen soldier lying on a stretcher, an officer fell nearby. Rushing to the side of the wounded man, the chaplain was shocked to see that it was Colonel Grace, whose wounds were obviously fatal. Feeling that his commander should not die on the battlefield, the priest screamed for assistance. Two soldiers attempted to carry the colonel away, but the severity of his wounds and the ongoing artillery barrage made further movement impossible.

As the melee continued, the last of the Confederate attackers took flight, but Father Emery maintained his vigil at the side of Colonel Grace, who had been laid in some soft grass. Life was ebbing from the officer when the chaplain gently cradled him in his arms. He turned his eyes toward heaven and offered a prayer for Colonel Grace, his words muffled by the thunder of artillery. As he prayed for mercy on his fallen comrade, a screaming cannonball carried away Father Emery's head.

Lieutenant Colonel David Berkley Lang

Wherever Duty Calls

Stephenson's Depot, Virginia
September 6, 1864

"Tell my wife I died on my post doing my duty."

Life was good for David B. Lang on the eve of the Civil War. He and his wife, Elizabeth, lived with their six children on a sprawling farm in Barbour County, Virginia (now West Virginia). A highly respected physician, David maintained a lucrative practice. Though he often traveled the mountain roads to tend to the health needs of his friends and neighbors, his trail always led back to the happiness of home. But his idyllic life changed forever once war clouds gathered over Virginia.

When delegates assembled at Virginia's Secession Convention in April 1861, Dr. Lang, an opponent of the institution of slavery, was among their number. His vote against secession was in the minority. In the weeks that followed, he watched as his state prepared for war. Soon, open hostilities came to the mountains of Virginia. David's brother volunteered for duty in the Union army. But for David, there was no question which side he would choose. Despite his views on slavery, his sympathies were with the South, and he bore a strong allegiance to his native state.

Once the war began in earnest, David was anxious to answer the call to duty, but he was initially undecided as to the manner in which he would

Lieutenant Colonel David Berkley Lang
Courtesy of *Confederate Veteran*

serve. In the early summer of 1861, he had not yet volunteered for Confederate service when he made frequent visits to the camp of Brigadier General Robert S. Garnett. There, Dr. Lang developed a warm friendship with the general and his lieutenants. He carried a double-barreled shotgun on each foray to the camp and often exchanged fire with the enemy, whose presence in the area increased on an almost daily basis.

During the second week of July, David was dismayed when the Confederates were forced to retreat from the mountainous region he called home. Colonel William L. Jackson, a kinsman of Stonewall Jackson, convinced Dr. Lang to remain home and operate as a Confederate scout. Because he was intimately familiar with the local terrain, the physician reckoned that he was called to that perilous duty.

It was in the autumn of 1861 that T. H. Neilson, a sixteen-year-old private in the Sixty-second Virginia, first witnessed the exploits of David Lang. He subsequently offered a detailed description of the Confederate scout, officer, and sometime spy: "In personal appearance as well as character Col. Lang was to me the most picturesque soldier of the war. He was six feet one inch, erect as an Indian, a frame well-knit and athletic, strong as an ox, smooth-shaven, regular features, square chin, piercing blue eyes, and a well-formed head surmounted by a heavy shock of hair that stood on end and was as red as a fox's tail."

No assignment was too bold for David Lang. His hairsbreadth escapes, the tricks he perpetrated on the enemy, and his brilliant successes as a scout became the talk of Confederate encampments in western Virginia. In late 1861, Brigadier General Edward Johnson, unwilling to rely on cavalry reports, chose Dr. Lang as his eyes and ears on the enemy. T. H. Neilson recalled, "Whenever Gen. Johnson wished to know their numbers, he would send out Lang, who, with two revolvers in his belt, his spyglass, and old field rifle, would take the trail, flank their pickets, and securing a position from which he could get a good view of their camp, would fire his revolvers rapidly, to make the 'Yanks' think that their pickets were being attacked, when they would beat the 'long roll,' tumble out, and form for battle. Lang would take his glass, estimate their number, and report on his return."

Dr. Lang was quick witted and an excellent marksman, both of which stood him in good stead as a scout. On one occasion, a company of a hundred Union soldiers picked up his trail in the snow. Upon discovering that he was being pursued by a sizable force, the doctor stopped on a ridge and waited until his adversaries came within a hundred yards. Taking deadly aim, he toppled an officer from his saddle. Dr. Lang reloaded as he raced down the ridge, then stopped and fired again. He repeated the process until the attackers gave up their pursuit after losing six of their number.

On another mission, the intrepid scout was instructed to ascertain the details of an enemy encampment. Satisfied that he was well hidden in a thicket, David was preparing a sketch of the camp when he was suddenly surrounded by Yankee soldiers. One of the Union troopers asked, "What are you doing there?" In a calm voice, Lang said, "O! I was only making a sketch of our camp." He nonchalantly folded the paper and put it in his pocket. When the Yankees denounced him as a spy and demanded he give up, he came out of his hiding place with his gun butt presented toward the Union captain, in the manner of a surrender. But when Dr. Lang drew close, he punched the captain in the stomach with the gun and raced away. Before the soldiers could gather their wits, he made good his escape.

After spending countless days and nights in and about enemy lines over an eighteen-month period, David Lang felt compelled to take to the battlefield. In early 1863, he was appointed major of the Sixty-second Virginia. From the rocky Pennsylvania landscape at Gettysburg to the fertile Shenandoah Valley of his native state, the thirty-two-year-old proved his worth as a field officer. His eldest son recalled, "It was his delight to command the skirmish line." As 1863 came to a close, the Confederate high command promoted Lang to lieutenant colonel.

On July 13, 1864, in one of his frequent letters home, Lang related to his wife the rigors of war. Since May 7, he had been under enemy fire every single day; he had marched over six hundred miles; and his spur had saved his foot by deflecting a Minié ball. But he remained steadfast. In another letter to his wife, he wrote, "If this unholy war should last until my youngest son is eighteen years old, I wish you would inspire such patriotism in each of them that they would shoulder their muskets in defense of their country."

On the morning of September 5, 1864, Lang was in command of the Sixty-second Virginia in the Shenandoah Valley when it was ordered to take part in an attack on Union forces at Stephenson's Depot, located between Winchester and Bunker Hill. When the time came for his regiment to move forward, he dismounted and led his men in the direction of the enemy. As the distance between the two armies decreased, the lieutenant colonel calmly urged his men to hold their fire, saying, "Boys, don't shoot till you can see the white of their eyes."

Then, at Lang's command, the Confederate guns blazed in unison. On the first volley, eighty Yankees fell. But the initial success of the Virginians faded as overwhelming numbers of Union soldiers filled the gap. Lang instructed his soldiers to fall back.

Once they regrouped, the Virginians stormed forward again, into the face of almost certain death. Lieutenant H. H. Stalnaker remembered the valor of Lieutenant Colonel Lang: "The balls were flying fast, and one of his comrades said, 'Colonel, you had better shelter behind the stone fence, or you might get hit,' but he replied, 'It is me they are shooting at.' "

In but a few moments, T. H. Neilson saw Lang place his hand on his side and fall. When nearby soldiers rushed to bear him out of harm's way, he said, "You had better leave me and take care of yourselves."

Dr. Lang was stabilized at a nearby house and transported to Winchester, where he clung to life until the next day. As the end neared, he said to those surrounding his deathbed, "Tell the boys that, if possible, I would like to see them, but for them to do their duty on all occasions."

Then, with his last breath, he muttered, "Tell my wife I died at my post doing my duty."

In one letter to his dear Elizabeth, David Lang had expressed his resolve this way: "I shall see Virginia free or be buried beneath her sod." That resolve was honored when he was laid to rest near the south gate of Winchester's famous Stonewall Cemetery in his beloved Virginia mountains.

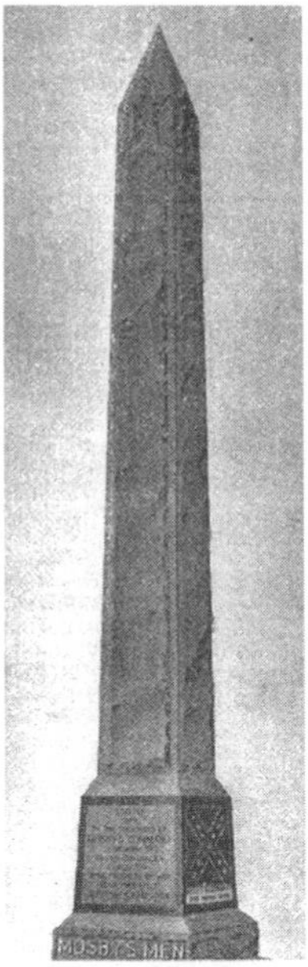

The monument erected in Front Royal, Virginia, in memory of Private William Thomas Overby and the other members of Colonel John S. Mosby's Rangers who were executed here
COURTESY OF *CONFEDERATE VETERAN*

Private William Thomas Overby

The Nathan Hale of the Confederacy

Front Royal, Virginia
September 23, 1864

"Mosby'll hang ten of you for every one of us."

In 1864, when Private William Thomas Overby joined Company D of Colonel John S. Mosby's Rangers just one month after his twenty-seventh birthday, he began a short, tragic association with perhaps the most effective and feared fighting unit in the Army of Northern Virginia. Its commander, an attorney in prewar Virginia, was mentioned in Robert E. Lee's official reports and orders more than any other officer. Mosby used Private Overby and his other raiders, who never totaled more than eight hundred, to terrorize Union forces in the northern and western portions of Virginia.

Born in Dunwoody, Virginia, in 1837, Overby moved to Georgia with his family two years later. In May 1861, he volunteered to fight for the South and was assigned to Company A of the Seventh Georgia. A severe wound at Second Manassas on August 31, 1862, temporarily disabled him. For the next eighteen months, he served as a nurse in military hospitals in

Virginia. By the spring of 1864, his recovery was sufficient to allow him the honor of taking to the saddle with the vaunted raiders of John S. Mosby.

Private Overby came to Mosby's band of regularly enlisted men at the very time the unit was set to achieve its enduring fame. In the late spring and summer of 1864, the Shenandoah Valley, controlled by the Confederacy since the outset of the war, became a prime target of the Union high command. Not only did the fertile valley serve as a breadbasket for the South, it also posed a military threat to Washington, D.C., because its axis was oriented toward the capital of the United States.

No sooner did the Union's massive Army of the Shenandoah arrive in the valley in August 1864 than Mosby put his rangers to work. Private Overby and his comrades seemed to strike the enemy everywhere. Time after time, the lightning-fast horse soldiers, each brandishing two revolvers rather than a sword, inflicted heavy damage on Federal wagon trains and troop details. These hit-and-run tactics were particularly annoying to Brevet General George Armstrong Custer, one of the chief Union operatives in the valley. On an almost daily basis from mid-August until mid-September, Custer was made to look the fool by Mosby and his men. Highly antagonized, Custer ordered his troops to hang all of Mosby's soldiers taken prisoner.

Irritated by the bold attacks on Federal forces, General U. S. Grant declared an all-out war in the valley through a harsh directive: "Eat out Virginia clear and clean as far as they go, so that crows flying over it for the balance of the season will have to carry their provender with them. . . . Destroy and carry off the crops, animals, Negroes, and all men under fifty years of age capable of bearing arms. In this way, you will get many of Mosby's men." Then, in an order giving official approval of Custer's harsh plan of action, Grant decreed, "When any of Mosby's men are caught, hang them without trial."

Once Custer and his troops took their torch-and-noose campaign to the valley, Overby and the other rangers bitterly nicknamed the tall, thin Union general "Attila the Hun." Despite the damage inflicted and the terror instilled in civilians by the Yankees' wave of mayhem, Custer's troops grew increasingly fearful of Mosby's Rangers. Many veteran Union soldiers said they preferred to charge into battle rather than patrol the domain of Mosby's men. Captain George Sanford of the First United States Cavalry noted, "No party of less than 50 men was safe a mile from camp. The loss in men, animals, and supplies was enormous."

When an injury temporarily took Mosby out of action, Custer decided to take advantage of his absence by ambushing the rangers on September 23, 1864. Captain Sam Chapman, one of Mosby's officers, spotted Custer's decoy—an ambulance train escorted by what appeared to be no more than two hundred cavalrymen—from his position on the wooded heights above Front Royal. With Private Overby and a hundred other experienced raiders ready to go, Chapman reasoned that he could surprise and capture the Union convoy.

Almost as soon as the two-column attack was launched, it became apparent that the rangers had poured into a trap. Hundreds upon hundreds of blue-jacketed Union troopers descended upon the scene and surrounded the raiders. During the ensuing melee, Private Overby was knocked from his mount. One of his friends, Tom Moss, attempted to throw the reins of a captured horse to him, but Overby found himself surrounded by enemy soldiers before he could mount. Most of the rangers escaped, but Overby was among six prisoners taken by Custer's troops.

As he and four of the other captives were being herded down the dusty road to Front Royal, news that Lieutenant Charles McMaster had been killed spread through the Yankee lines like wildfire. Although the facts surrounding McMaster's death are unclear to this day, the Union troops were told that he had been riddled with bullets after attempting to surrender to Chapman's attack force. Hot with anger and anxious to exact revenge, Custer's men hurried Overby and the four other prisoners to Front Royal, where they were summarily condemned to die. Marching slowly through the streets, a Yankee band played the death march. Two of the prisoners, Lucian Love and David L. Jones, were gunned down in a churchyard and abandoned to expire in their own blood. At almost the same time, a third captive, Thomas Anderson, was escorted to an elm tree, where he was executed by a firing squad.

Suddenly, two Union horsemen raised the level of terror gripping the town when they galloped through the streets dragging behind them a seventeen-year-old civilian, Henry Rhodes. To his captors, his crime was despicable: He wanted to be a Confederate soldier. Witnessing the horrible spectacle was Rhodes's mother, who pleaded for the life of her unconscious son. Ignoring her cries for mercy, the horsemen pulled Rhodes to an open field on the north side of Front Royal, where a volunteer emptied his pistol into the boy's face. The corpse was then dumped into a wheelbarrow and pushed to the front door of the grieving mother's house.

Now, only Private William Thomas Overby and a ranger named Carter were left. Minute by minute, the throng of highly agitated Yankee soldiers grew. The mob of bluecoats shouted epithets and screamed taunts as the two prisoners were shepherded to Petty's wagon yard. There, the captors promised to spare their lives if they would disclose the whereabouts of John S. Mosby. Carter, overwhelmed by fear, could do little more than weep as the military band played the dirge "Love Not, the One You Love May Die" over and over. But through it all, Overby kept his composure. According to eyewitness Dr. R. C. Buck, Overby "was standing with his hat and coat off, his wavy black hair floating in the breeze. I never saw a finer specimen of manhood. . . . He looked like a knight of old." A female observer recorded, "Well do I remember the picture, Overby, with head erect, defiant, and Carter overcome and weeping."

As the band continued playing its tune of death, General Custer, attired in a silk suit accented by a scarlet necktie, rode up. His long, golden hair flowing from under his hat, the general from Ohio munched on a branch of damsons he had picked en route to town. At that moment, Custer seemed oblivious to the warning he had received just days earlier from General Philip Sheridan, his immediate commander: "If the Rebs should ever lay you by the heels, they'll string you up directly." Indeed, the young, blue-eyed general was not about to rescind his order to hang Mosby's men.

Overby and Carter were hustled to a tree standing midway between Front Royal and the Shenandoah River. Union soldiers secured two ropes from sturdy limbs and quickly fashioned nooses in plain sight of the helpless captives. Again came the offer of leniency. For their lives to be spared, the men need only disclose the location of their leader. Private Overby stared coldly at the enemy troops, shook his head, and said, "We cannot tell that!" Another demand brought only a bold look of contempt from Overby. Their patience at an end, the mob's leaders ordered the prisoners' hands bound behind their backs. Soldiers flung the two men onto horses and placed the nooses around their necks. Startled by the commotion, the horses lurched forward, causing the nooses to tighten and burn the necks of the two Southerners.

There was yet time. Carter coughed and choked as he begged for an opportunity to bow his head in prayer. Overby stared ahead in stern defiance. One final offer came from the mob: "Tell us where Mosby is." Calmly but with great force, Private Overby exclaimed for all to hear, "Mosby'll hang ten of you for every one of us." Those words drew the ire of his captors. In a flash, the whips cracked, and Overby and Carter were left dangling.

Before the Union forces left Front Royal that black Friday, they hung a placard on the bloated corpse of Private William Thomas Overby. It read, "Such is the fate of all of Mosby's gang."

Not the least frightened by the warning but outraged by the executions, Colonel Mosby quickly returned to the saddle and set about making good on Private Overby's final words. On November 16, after ordering the execution of seven members of Custer's cavalry, he forwarded a threat to General Sheridan: "Hereafter any prisoners falling into my hands will be treated with the kindness due to their condition, unless some new act of barbarity shall compel me reluctantly to adopt a course of policy repulsive to humanity."

Cognizant of Private Overby's prediction and Mosby's ability and intention to carry it out, Sheridan promptly put an end to the executions. Even now, some historians maintain that it was the warfare raged by Private William Thomas Overby and the other raiders commanded by Mosby that prevented the Union army from successfully concluding the Civil War in the summer or fall of 1864.

Major General Stephen Dodson Ramseur

From Birth to Death— In the Company of Friends

Cedar Creek, Virginia
October 20, 1864

"Tell General Hoke that I died a Christian and have done my duty."

Two of the youngest division commanders in the Confederate army were born just four days apart in the same town in the Piedmont region of North Carolina. Major General Robert Frederick Hoke was born in Lincolnton, the second-oldest town in western North Carolina, on May 27, 1837. Four days later, Stephen Dodson Ramseur was born only blocks away. The two developed a lifelong friendship that came to a tragic end when Ramseur died at the age of twenty-seven from battlefield wounds sustained at Cedar Creek, Virginia. Though Ramseur was surrounded by blue-jacketed friends in his final moments, some of his last thoughts were for his boyhood chum and fellow major general.

As children, Ramseur and Hoke were frequent companions. They played about the streets of the old county seat named for Revolutionary War general Benjamin Lincoln; they swam and fished in the nearby river and creeks; they learned horsemanship; they became excellent marksmen by hunting in nearby fields and forests; and they studied mathematics, classics, grammar,

Above:
Major General Stephen Dodson Ramseur
Courtesy of The North Carolina State Archives

Right:
Stephen Dodson Ramseur, pictured when he was a cadet at West Point
Courtesy of Daniel W. Barefoot

and ancient languages at the outstanding preparatory school in their hometown. As teenagers, they went their separate ways to complete their educations. Dodson, as Ramseur was known to family and friends, received an appointment to the United States Military Academy, where he was part of the last full class before the Civil War. On June 14, 1860, he graduated fourteenth in a class of forty-one. Among his closest friends at West Point were Northerners he would not see again until they offered him solace on his deathbed four years later.

Ramseur's service as an artillery lieutenant in the United States Army was short lived. North Carolina had not yet seceded in the spring of 1861, but Dodson was convinced that war between the North and the South was inevitable. After resigning his commission in the first week of April, he headed toward Montgomery, Alabama—then the Confederate capital—where he intended to join the army as a captain of artillery. But in the meantime, Governor John W. Ellis of North Carolina tendered an attractive offer to Ramseur. By early May, the young West Pointer was in Raleigh as captain of the sixty-two-man Ellis Light Artillery.

On May 20, a sea of people congregated on the grounds of the Capitol at Union Square in the heart of Raleigh. Among the crowd were Captain Ramseur and his artillerymen. Inside the building, the statesmen were debating an ordinance of secession for North Carolina. Suddenly, a white handkerchief was waved from a second-story window. Ramseur drew his men to attention and directed them to fire a hundred-cannon salute. The young captain thus claimed the honor of giving the order to hail North Carolina's entry into the Confederacy.

After serving as an artillery major for much of the first twelve months of the war, Dodson was promoted to colonel and assigned to the infantry as commander of the Forty-ninth North Carolina in April 1862. Less than three months later at Malvern Hill, Virginia, a well-directed Union ball plowed into Dodson's upper right arm. After a lengthy furlough, he reported for duty in early November and returned to the battlefields of Virginia with a withered, paralyzed right arm. He also returned as a brigadier general. In recognition of Ramseur's reputation as one of the most skillful and hardest-hitting young officers in the Army of Northern Virginia, Robert E. Lee had recommended the promotion on October 27.

At Chancellorsville in early May 1863, General Ramseur once again proved his mettle by leading his four North Carolina regiments in a fearless charge that penetrated the Federal lines.

One of the brightest days of his military career occurred a year later at Spotsylvania Court House, where he spearheaded the fierce Confederate counterattack that led to the crucial Southern victory. As a result of his stellar performance, he was summoned to the headquarters of Robert E. Lee, where the commander of the Army of Northern Virginia offered his personal gratitude—the highest compliment that could be afforded a Confederate officer. One day after Ramseur's twenty-seventh birthday, Lee promoted him to major general, making him the youngest West Pointer to attain that rank in the Southern army.

On the cool night of October 18, 1864, Major General Ramseur and Major General John B. Gordon (who would subsequently serve as governor of Georgia and a United States senator) sat on a bluff and watched a line of ten thousand Confederate soldiers snake its way along the banks of the Shenandoah River in anticipation of a clash at Cedar Creek in northwestern Virginia. The two generals chatted about the impending battle and matters back at home. As the last of his division passed, Dodson stood up, looked down at Gordon, and parted with words of excitement: "Well, General, I shall get my furlough today." Just two nights earlier, Ramseur had received from the Confederate Signal Corps a rather cryptic message reading, "The crisis is over and all is well." He knew exactly what it meant: His wife, Ellen, had given birth to their first child. But whether the baby was a son or a daughter, he did not know, and he was anxious to return to North Carolina to find out.

But first, there was a battle to fight. As Dodson prepared for action in the predawn hours of Wednesday, October 19, he pinned a flower to the lapel of his gray frock coat in honor of his newborn child.

Early-morning success by Ramseur and his comrades convinced Lieutenant General Jubal Early that the day would belong to the Confederates. But by midafternoon, General Philip Sheridan arrived on the scene to rally the Federals in a savage counterattack. In less than two hours, the Confederates were in serious trouble. Major General Joseph B. Kershaw's troops were on the retreat. Only Ramseur's division and a small remnant of Kershaw's men were left to face the hard-charging Yankees, who were pouring in on three sides.

Dodson reasoned that if he could hold the line until darkness enveloped the battlefield, the Confederates could avoid a disastrous defeat.

Ramseur had displayed magnificent leadership and uncommon bravery on numerous battlegrounds all over Virginia, but according to Jubal Early, "never did those qualities shine more conspicuously than on the afternoon of the 19th." Unable to hold his sword in his right hand, Ramseur thrust it high with his left as he galloped up and down his lines, urging his men to hold. A bullet toppled his horse, and Dodson was injured as he fell. He quickly shook off the pain, regained his wits, secured another horse, and rode only a short distance before the second animal was killed. A third mount was brought forward by a courier. Just as the general attempted to climb into the saddle, a Yankee sharpshooter sent a ball that passed through both of Dodson's lungs and lodged in his left arm.

Members of the general's staff directed that their fallen commander be carried to the rear, where he was placed in an ambulance wagon. As the driver headed up the Valley Pike, his progress was impeded by the many wagons in the massive Confederate retreat. During the delay, a Union cavalry detail approached Ramseur's ambulance. One of the horse soldiers demanded to know who was being transported. The slow-thinking driver replied, "The General says I must not tell."

In a flash, the ambulance, under the escort of Federal cavalrymen, was moving at a fast pace toward Belle Grove Mansion, the headquarters of General Philip Sheridan. Upon its arrival, Dodson was carried to a front room on the first floor of the expansive house. There, the chief medical officer of the Union army and a captured Confederate surgeon labored side by side in a desperate attempt to save the general's life. They soon concurred that the wound was fatal.

Throughout the night, Ramseur lingered in excruciating pain. Surrounding him in his final hours was a bevy of Union officers, a number of them old friends from West Point, including General George Armstrong Custer and General Wesley Merritt. Also at his bedside was his friend Henry DuPont, a Union officer and the grandson of the founder of the famous chemical company. Dodson had lived across the hall from DuPont at the academy.

During his conscious moments, Ramseur spoke to those attending him about his family and friends in North Carolina. He expressed the wish that he could see his wife and their child before he died. As the end neared, he dictated a message to his old friend Robert F. Hoke, the youngest man to hold the rank of major general in the Confederate army: "Tell General Hoke that I died a Christian and have done my duty."

At 10:27 on the cold, gray morning of October 20, Major General Stephen Dodson Ramseur lost his final battle just one week short of his first wedding anniversary. He died without knowing that his child was a daughter named Nellie. His body was transported by a Federal honor detail to the lines outside Richmond, where Major General Hoke received it under a flag of truce. Dodson was interred in a church cemetery bordering the Lincolnton streets where he and Hoke had played as children. His wife and the daughter he never saw were subsequently buried on either side of him.

Major General Patrick Ronayne Cleburne

The Wearing o' the Gray

Franklin, Tennessee
November 30, 1864

"If we were to die, let us die like men!"

Half a million foreign-born soldiers took part in the American Civil War. A large majority of them fought for the North, yet perhaps the most famous of all the emigrant combatants was Patrick Ronayne Cleburne, a Confederate major general. Born on St. Patrick's Day in County Cork, Ireland, in 1828, Cleburne ultimately achieved the highest rank of any officer of foreign birth in the Southern army. When he laid down his life in the bloodbath at Franklin, Tennessee, on November 30, 1864, he was known as "the Stonewall Jackson of the West."

Cleburne's father was a highly respected physician in Ireland, and Patrick sought to follow in his footsteps. However, his deficiencies in French, Latin, and Greek caused him to fail his medical-school entrance examinations. Highly embarrassed, he enlisted as a private in the Forty-first Regiment of the British army in 1846. Three years later, an inheritance enabled Cleburne, then a corporal, to purchase his military discharge. He and his siblings promptly sought their fortunes in the United States.

Several months after the Cleburne family arrived in New Orleans, twenty-one-year-old Patrick settled in Helena, Arkansas, where he became the manager of a drugstore. Citizens in the frontier community found favor with the polite Irishman, an active participant in the local debate society, dances,

Major General Patrick Ronayne Cleburne
COURTESY OF LIBRARY OF CONGRESS

the Masons, and the Episcopal Church. His attractive personality and keen mind led his friends to encourage him to embark upon a legal career.

In 1855, in the midst of Cleburne's legal studies, a terrible yellow-fever epidemic ravaged Helena. Every able-bodied citizen fled the disease-ridden town, save three physicians and three volunteers. Among the volunteers were Patrick Cleburne and Thomas C. Hindman, a local attorney and future Confederate general. Without regard for his own health, Cleburne tended the sick and buried the dead. News of his example led the residents of Helena to return to town and do their part in the emergency.

That same year, Cleburne became a naturalized citizen of the United States. The following January, he was admitted to the Arkansas bar. His reputation in the state continued to grow.

Amid the turmoil leading up to the Civil War, Cleburne was a victim of an assassination attempt in the summer of 1856. But the fearlessness he exhibited in the incident became his hallmark. The citizens of Helena were watching from behind doors when the gunfire began. Thomas Hindman,

Cleburne's friend and fellow attorney, fell in the street when the assassins struck. Cleburne was wounded in the back as he ran to assist Hindman. Struggling to remain on his feet, he made his way to the entrance of the building into which the assailants had run. Taking deadly aim, he proclaimed that he would kill the scoundrel who had shot him. As soon as the culprit dropped in death, Cleburne collapsed in a pool of blood. For a week, the same physicians with whom Cleburne had labored during the yellow-fever emergency treated the hero as he lingered at death's door. Once the crisis was over, he offered this response when the doctors asked him why he had not fled from the attack: "I had either to defend myself or run, and I was trained in a school where running formed no part of the accomplishments." Throughout the Civil War, Cleburne would time and again honor those words.

In 1860, a local military company called the Yell Rifles was organized, and Cleburne was elected its captain. When Arkansas seceded on May 8, 1861, the company and its commander were in Little Rock. Less than a week after his state joined the Confederacy, Cleburne was named colonel of the First Arkansas Infantry. At the time, he made a prophetic statement to a friend: "I know nothing of the future, but I suppose I will have a conspicuous share in the events approaching."

His British military service stood him in good stead. When a division was formed for General William Hardee in March 1862, the command of one of its brigades was assigned to Cleburne. A month later at the Battle of Shiloh, the new brigadier general turned in a stellar performance in an engagement that cost him 1,013 of his 2,700 men. Hardee offered words of praise for Cleburne: "No repulse discouraged him; but after many bloody struggles he assembled the remnant of his brigade and was conspicuous for his gallantry to the end of the battle."

Less than five months later, Cleburne led the vanguard of the Confederate invasion of Kentucky. He deserved much of the credit for the decisive Confederate victory that followed at Richmond, Kentucky, in late August. But in that battle, the general sustained a serious injury, the first of a number of combat wounds. On the second and last day of the clash at Richmond, a Minié ball crashed into his left check, damaged his mouth, and destroyed several teeth. Unable to speak, the general was out of action for three weeks. In the meantime, the Confederate Congress adopted a resolution of thanks for Cleburne's gallantry at Richmond. In his official report of the battle, General Edmund Kirby-Smith referred to Cleburne as "one of the most gallant, zealous, and intelligent officers of my whole army."

Back in action in early October, Cleburne was at the head of his brigade in a clash at Perryville, Kentucky, when he was again injured. Disregarding the painful wound near his ankle, he remained on the field as his charges successfully pierced the center of the enemy line. In the struggle, the general's horse was shot from under him. After the battle, Major General Hardee again praised Cleburne, saying he had performed "with his usual courage and judgment, was wounded, but remained in command until the close of the day."

In December 1862, General Braxton Bragg, the North Carolina-born general then in command of the Army of Tennessee, lauded Cleburne as "exceedingly gallant, but sufficiently prudent" and reported that he had "the admiration of his command as a soldier and a gentleman." Accordingly, Cleburne was promoted to major general on December 20, making him the highest-ranking foreign-born officer in the Confederate army.

In short order, Cleburne's new division acquired a reputation as the hardest-hitting unit in the Western theater. Throughout 1863, the general courageously led his brigades on numerous battlefields such as Stone's River, Chickamauga, and Missionary Ridge. When the Confederate left and center broke at Chattanooga, Cleburne held firm on the north. His subsequent protection of the rear of the massive retreating Southern army at Ringold Gap on November 27 drew another resolution of thanks from the Confederate Congress.

Had not Cleburne been mired in a pair of controversies during 1864, many historians believe he would have risen to lieutenant general, perhaps full general. Many generals in the Army of Tennessee, including Cleburne, openly voiced their opposition to General Bragg that year. Their denunciation of their commander was not well received in the Confederate capital, where President Jefferson Davis remained one of Bragg's best friends and staunchest supporters. Even more troublesome for Cleburne's military career was his support of the notion that depleted Southern divisions could be replenished with slaves armed by the Confederate government. He prepared a paper on the subject, and thirteen fellow officers affixed their endorsements. Although the document was never officially tendered to Richmond, President Davis saw a copy of it and directed that it be suppressed.

Notwithstanding the rancor within the Confederate high command,

Cleburne enhanced his military reputation during the fight for Atlanta and the subsequent retreat during the summer of 1864.

Late that fall, General John B. Hood's thirty-nine-thousand-man Confederate army invaded Tennessee in a futile attempt to bring the state under Southern control. Cleburne's division was a vital component of the expeditionary force. On the morning of November 30, as the army clad in gray and butternut marched toward a showdown with the heavily fortified Union army at Franklin, Cleburne paused at a picturesque little Episcopal church beside the road leading from Spring Hill. As his horse pranced on the soft grass of the church lawn, the general offered prophetic words: "It is almost worth dying for, to be buried in such a beautiful spot."

Once he neared the enemy stronghold, the general's mood grew somber. From his vantage point on Winstead Hill, the Federal entrenchments on the southern edge of Franklin, two miles distant, were visible. Putting his field glasses aside, Cleburne took up his pencil and made an entry in his daybook: "They are very formidable."

Awaiting orders, he and a staffer enjoyed a game of checkers until a courier from General Hood arrived. When Cleburne reported to his commander, a council of war was already under way. Several of Hood's subordinates were arguing against an attack, owing to the strength and complexity of the enemy works. But Hood persisted: "I prefer to fight them here. We will make them fight." Although Cleburne disagreed with Hood, he said nothing because the two had quarreled the day before. Turning to Cleburne, Hood directed, "Form your division on the right of the pike. . . . Give orders to your men not to fire a gun until you run the Yankee skirmish line from the first line of works . . . then charge the enemy's works. Franklin is the key to Nashville, and Nashville is the key to independence."

Cleburne rode off in disbelief. En route to his troops, he stopped at Merrills Hill to once again survey the Union position. There, he muttered despondently, "They have three lines of works. And they are all completed."

When he appeared before his division for the last time to prepare them for battle, one of his admiring soldiers made a mental picture of his commander: "Cleburne, at the time of his death, was about thirty-seven years of age. He was above the medium height, about five feet eleven inches, and though without striking personal advantages, would have arrested attention from a close observer as a man of mark. His hair, originally black, became gray under the care and fatigue of campaigning. His eyes, a clear steel-gray in color, were cold and abstracted usually, but beamed genially in seasons of social intercourse, and blazed fiercely in moments of excitement. . . . His manners were distant and reserved to strangers, but frank and winning among friends. He was as modest as a woman, but not wanting in that fine ambition which ennobles men."

One of the brigadiers, Daniel C. Govan, noticed Cleburne's gloomy countenance as the battle loomed: "General Cleburne seemed to be more despondent than I ever saw him." Ever bound to duty, however, Cleburne rode among his men on Pepper, his horse, offering inspiration and encouragement.

The men's bayonets were fixed and gleaming in the sun when Cleburne shouted the order at four o'clock that afternoon: "Right shoulder shift; forward; double quick, march!" He then fearlessly led the division in an assault against overwhelming odds, though one Federal soldier saw it another way: "It looked to me as though the whole South had come up there and were determined to walk right over us." Henry Stone, a Union staff officer, concurred: "With that wild rebel yell which once heard is never forgotten, the great human wave swept along and seemed to engulf the little force that so sturdily awaited it."

For a while, it appeared that the Confederates would carry the day in some of the bloodiest hand-to-hand combat of the war. At the Union breastworks, soldiers in both armies fell in great heaps. As they parted for the last time in battle, Dan Govan shouted to his commander, "Well, general, there will not be many of us that will get back to Arkansas." Cleburne, who had already had two horses killed in the battle, prepared to storm ahead on foot. He bid his brigadier farewell by saying, "Well, Govan, if we are to die, let us die like men!"

Extending his sword and waving his cap, Cleburne disappeared "in the smoke and din of battle," according to Govan. He soon fell, one of the six Confederate generals who perished at Franklin. When his comrades found him at dawn the following day, his lifeless body had been stripped of its watch, daybook, boots, and sword. He was buried in a temporary grave in the Episcopal churchyard he had admired the previous day.

Throughout his life, Patrick Cleburne had often said, "An honest heart and a strong heart should never succumb." But at Franklin, Tennessee, he honored his prewar promise to his adopted homeland: "I am with the South in life or death, in victory or defeat."

Colonel Mike Farrell

The Fighting Irishman

Franklin, Tennessee
December 1864

"John, you're not going to let Colonel Lowry beat me for brigadier general, are you?"

Irish Catholics fought and died in significant numbers for the first time in American military history during the Civil War. Their bravery and fighting ability became legend as they participated on both sides on countless battlefields. Without question, the most famous Irish-born warrior to give his life for the Confederacy was Major General Patrick Cleburne (see pages 222-27). But there were many others. Colonel Mike Farrell, a full-blooded Irishman, displayed the same tenacity, attention to duty, and zeal that won enduring fame for General Cleburne. And Mike Farrell, like Cleburne, fought his last battle on the bloody landscape at Franklin, Tennessee.

Born in New York to Irish immigrants, Mike Farrell was assigned to duty at the Jefferson Barracks in St. Louis prior to the Civil War. After his discharge from the United States Army, he took up residence in Mississippi, where he worked as a brick mason in the construction of the bridge over the Yalubusha River for the Mississippi and Tennessee Railroad.

Described as strikingly handsome, Farrell stood six feet tall and was blessed with an athletic build. He possessed dark blue eyes and straight black hair. His Irish brogue never left him.

A photograph of McGavock Mansion, where Colonel Mike Farrell was treated after he fell in the Battle of Franklin
COURTESY OF *CONFEDERATE VETERAN*

Soon after Mississippi became the second state to secede in January 1861, the need for experienced drill masters became acute, as thousands of volunteers stepped forward to fill the ranks. Mike Farrell was delighted when he was asked to train the men of the company organized in Grenada County in north-central Mississippi. His skill as a drill master drew attention throughout the region. As a consequence, Farrell's services were in great demand as Mississippi prepared for war.

After readying many Southern men for the fast-approaching conflict, Mike Farrell was rewarded with the command of one of the best companies he had trained. Not long after he took part in the bloody engagement at Shiloh, Tennessee, in April 1862, the volunteer forces of Mississippi were reorganized. Farrell was unanimously elected colonel of the Fifteenth Mississippi that same spring.

Among the qualities that enabled Farrell to excel as an officer was his competitive spirit. It came to the fore when his regiment went into winter quarters after the first Union campaign against Vicksburg in late 1862. In that encampment, an intense rivalry grew between the Third Kentucky and the Fifteenth Mississippi. Most observers regarded Colonel Farrell's troops as the best-drilled soldiers in the Western theater, but the Kentuckians were anxious to dispute the honor. Their colonel challenged Farrell and his Mississippians to a drill competition during a lull in the fighting. Farrell was only too happy to agree to the contest.

After weeks and weeks of training, the time was at hand for the friendly dispute to be settled. Impartial West Point-trained officers were selected to judge the grand competition, which took place on a warm, sunny day in February 1863 in a pasture on the outskirts of Canton, Mississippi. Local ladies were in attendance. With them, they brought a special prize promised to the winner—a beautiful silk flag. In addition to the thousands of citizens who had traveled from far and wide to observe the competition, all the soldiers in the encampment took their places on the ridge above the field.

Each regiment was given ninety minutes to display its precision and polish. When the Kentucky soldiers paraded onto the field, the spectators watched them in wonderment as they went through their paces in resplendent new uniforms. Riding over the field, the judges made notes as the soldiers performed their assigned program. Then it was time for Colonel Farrell to lead his men forward. Their uniforms were no match for their competitors'. But in terms of the stated contest, the Mississippians stood head and shoulders above their challengers. After both regiments completed their presentations, the judges withdrew from the field to arrive at their decision.

The leading belle of Canton rode to the center of the field on a fine Kentucky thoroughbred. In her hand, she carried a flagstaff bearing the coveted prize. Riding at her side was a Confederate officer who carried with him the verdict. Excitement mounted as the crowd began to cheer. The competing regiments were at attention as the soldiers nervously awaited the decision. Suddenly, the two riders galloped in the direction of Mike Farrell, who sat atop his trusted horse, Bullet. Captain John L. Collins, one of the Mississippi warriors, described what happened next: "Receiving the flag from the lady's hand, the military salute was exchanged. Immediately at the command of Colonel Mike, Bullet about faced, as proud as a peacock, and the Colonel drew his sword and gave the military recognition due his regiment."

Nowhere was Farrell's competitive spirit more in evidence than on the battlefield. In combat, he combined a fierce spirit with cleverness and courage. For example, at the Battle of Peachtree Creek in July 1864, Farrell unwittingly rode into an advance Federal picket hidden in the Georgia woodlands. His adversary halted him and demanded his surrender. In response, the colonel drew his sword. Once again, he was warned that he would be shot if he did not halt. Farrell promptly sheathed his weapon and proclaimed that, under military custom, he should surrender his sword to his captor. The Yankee soldier concurred. As he dismounted, Farrell pulled forth the sword and put his hand in the middle of the blade. But instead of handing it over, he slammed it into the head of the unsuspecting Northerner. In short order, the vanguard of the Fifteenth Mississippi rushed forward and took 139 prisoners.

Colonel Farrell was in the middle of his third year as a regimental commander when he took to the field in the horrendous battle at Franklin, Tennessee, on the last day of November 1864. As his soldiers and the other troops in the brigade of General John Adams charged the enemy breastworks, they encountered a deep railroad cut they had to cross. General Adams, himself born of Irish parents, grew concerned that his two regiments on the right might lap each other as they struggled to make the crossing. He promptly dispatched his aide-de-camp, John L. Collins, to instruct Farrell to ease his men to the right.

Collins galloped to the Fifteenth Mississippi, where he found Farrell "taking that gallant band of Mississippi sons into the fight with sword in hand and his back to the enemy, as though he was out on the drill grounds." Collins further noted that "his regiment, under such pressure, with arms trailing and wavering more or less, was well under every word of their brave New Yorker fighting for the Southern cause."

As Collins rode closer to Farrell, who was back-stepping at a brisk pace, he distinctly heard the inspiring commands spoken with a heavy Irish accent: "Steady, men! Steady, men!" When Collins relayed General Adams's order, Farrell exclaimed, "John, I am doing the best I can, you see."

The soldiers of the Fifteenth Mississippi successfully maneuvered over the gap and rushed headlong toward a hedge protecting the heavily fortified Federal lines of Major General John M. Schofield. During the attack, Farrell and many of his men fell in bloody heaps. The badly wounded colonel was carried to nearby McGavock Mansion, where many of the casualties were being treated.

Two weeks after the battle, Captain John Collins was granted permission to visit Farrell at the stately home. Before entering the second-floor room, he dreaded the sorrow he was sure to find there. Nurses had advised him that Colonel Farrell, despite his physical vitality, could not survive.

Farrell raised his right hand to warmly clasp that of Collins. Both his legs were missing, but he sported a beaming smile and offered cheerful greetings. After engaging in a brief but warm reunion, Collins was preparing to take leave of his fallen comrade when Farrell once again exhibited the feisty spirit that was his trademark: "John, you're not going to let Colonel Lowry beat me for brigadier general, are you?"

Trying hard to keep his emotions in check, the captain offered these words of parting: "Colonel, you know that it is not within my province to control such a matter. I only wish it were, for you justly deserve promotion, which you know I would cheerfully grant."

With that, the two officers bade each other a fond farewell.

Not long thereafter, the Irish eyes of Colonel Mike Farrell closed and smiled no more.

Captain John Yates Beall, Confederate States Navy

Master of Intrigue

Fort Columbus, New York
February 24, 1865

"I die in the service and defense of my country! I have nothing more to say."

Many of the Southern casualties of the Civil War who were "lucky" enough to survive their wounds were disabled and thus unfit for further combat duty. Rather than remain on the home front for the duration of the war, some of these "discharges" sought other avenues of service for the Confederate cause. Among the most famous of the disabled die-hard warriors was Captain John Yates Beall.

Born on January 1, 1835, in Jefferson County, Virginia, into a family that traced its noble lineage to England and Scotland, Beall grew up surrounded by privilege and affluence. At the death of his father, John was twenty-one years old and a graduate of the University of Virginia. Management of the vast Beall estate, known as Walnut Grove, immediately devolved to him, and he was so occupied when his native state joined the Confederacy.

Although an ardent supporter of the Union, Beall promptly answered the call of Virginia when he perceived that the rights of his state were being threatened by Washington. Turning his back on the life of luxury, the rich

Captain John Yates Beall
COURTESY OF *CONFEDERATE VETERAN*

young planter volunteered for service in the Second Virginia. Among the soldiers of the famous Stonewall Brigade that took part in the legendary stand at Manassas on July 21, 1861, was John Yates Beall, then a twenty-six-year-old private.

Less than three months later, Beall was the commander of an entire company of General Turner Ashby's cavalry. On October 16, 1861, a severe gunshot wound to the chest toppled him from the saddle as he was leading a charge in the Shenandoah. So severe was the wound that a Confederate medical board discharged him from military service.

Though it was apparent his recovery would never be complete, Beall was anxious to return to action. He rejoined Stonewall Jackson in the great Valley Campaign in the spring of 1862, but the rigors of the expedition were more than he could take. He returned home, where he began formulating plans to aid the Confederacy. Beall reckoned that if he could not fight for the South on land, he could do so on water.

From Virginia, he traveled to Iowa and then to Canada, where he gathered information for a plan to wage war on Union shipping interests on the

Great Lakes and Chesapeake Bay. Just after his twenty-eighth birthday, he returned home to mature his scheme. His physical appearance at the time was described thus: "He had a strong, clearly cut English face. . . . The tightly compressed lips indicated great firmness, while the expression of the eye gave earnest of the benignity and moral purity which were leading traits in his character. . . . There was always, however, in his face a slight shade of sadness: of late years, since the war, this expression had deepened until it became more palpable, more fixed and habitual."

Despite his physical infirmities and rather unhappy countenance, Beall was filled with fire when he reported to Confederate officials in Richmond in February 1863. "Exposure, hardship, suffering, the drain of an unhealed wound; anxiety, hope deferred, have done the work of time on the body; they have not quenched my spirit, nor impaired the tenacity of my will," he noted.

Beall's plot to wage war in Union-controlled waters was well received in the Confederate capital. Accordingly, he was appointed acting master in the Confederate States Navy. Thereafter, he was known as Captain Beall.

With just two small vessels—the *Swan* and the *Raven*, so named for their colors—Captain Beall was authorized to engage in privateering in Chesapeake Bay. Over a six-month period beginning in April 1863, he wreaked such havoc on Federal shipping that a sizable armada of Union gunboats was deployed to eliminate the menace.

In early November, Beall and his crew were captured and imprisoned in Fort McHenry as pirates. In order to gain the captain's release, Confederate officials threatened reprisals against Yankee prisoners incarcerated in Southern facilities. Beall was duly exchanged in May 1864.

Anxious to resume his operations against the enemy, he journeyed north of the American border again, where he conferred with Jacob Thompson, commander of Confederate secret operations in Canada. Beall received approval for an intricate plan to disrupt Northern trade on the Great Lakes. To put the scheme into action, he was authorized to secretly obtain a well-armed vessel with which to sweep the lakes from Chicago to Detroit to Buffalo of all enemy traffic. One crucial target was the USS *Michigan*, which protected the Union prison at Johnson's Island, Ohio. Once the *Michigan* was either eliminated or neutralized, the thousands of Confederates imprisoned at Camp Chase could be freed with relative ease. Once they were armed, they would march through the states along the Canadian border.

Such a campaign, it was believed, would result in Northern demands for peace.

Initially, all went well for Captain Beall and the men assigned to his command. On September 19, 1864, he successfully commandeered two ships on Lake Erie and sailed toward Johnson's Island. Meanwhile, another Confederate operative, Major Charles H. Cole, was arrested before he could successfully drug the officers of the *Michigan*. Unaware that Cole had been foiled, Beall pressed on until the enemy ship was in sight. Suddenly, fourteen of his seventeen crewmen announced that they would not participate any further in the operation. With no alternative, Beall set sail for Canada. Little did he know that the mutiny spared him certain capture or death.

As disappointing as the failure at Johnson's Island was, it did not deter Captain Beall. Operating in the Buffalo area, he made repeated unsuccessful attempts to derail trains so as to enable the Confederate prisoners on board to escape.

On December 16, 1864, Beall was returning to Canada by train over the Niagara suspension bridge in the company of a Confederate lad who had escaped from a Federal prison. Their identities were not discovered until Beall attempted to wake the sleeping boy. When two policemen intervened and confronted Beall, the startled boy unwittingly gave him away.

News of the capture of Captain John Yates Beall brought jubilation throughout the North. Beall spent this thirtieth birthday in the jail at the New York City police headquarters. On January 5, he was transferred to the military prison at Fort Lafayette on the harbor. Two weeks later, a military tribunal comprised of six Union officers appointed by Major General John A. Dix arraigned Beall on charges of violating the laws of war as a guerrilla, pirate, and spy.

Dix ignored the desperate pleas by Daniel B. Lucas, Beall's lifelong friend from Jefferson County, Virginia, that he be allowed to represent the accused and present evidence on his behalf. To assist Beall in his defense, James T. Brady, one of the preeminent attorneys in New York City, stepped forward. Brady was eloquent in his arguments to the court. The seizure of ships on Lake Erie and the attempts to rescue Confederate prisoners from trains, he said, were legitimate acts of war by a commissioned officer of the Confederate States Navy. From the outset of the trial, however, it was apparent that the Union military was intent on convicting Beall. A guilty verdict was rendered on February 8, and the sentence of death by hanging was scheduled to be carried out ten days later.

The condemned man was transported under heavy guard to nearby Fort Columbus, where he was thrown into a dimly lit dungeon. Efforts to save his life resulted in a six-day reprieve. One account holds that Beall's friends and legal team convinced Abraham Lincoln to spare his life. But when two of the president's cabinet members, Edwin Stanton and William Seward, learned of the proposed leniency, they were adamant that Beall be executed, and Lincoln acceded to their wishes. Some historians have suggested that John Wilkes Booth, Beall's close friend and an ardent Confederate sympathizer, subsequently assassinated Lincoln in retaliation for his decision to hang the Southern officer.

In his last days, Beall was allowed to have at his side several close friends, including James A. McClure and Albert Ritchie, both of Baltimore. Also providing comfort were numerous local ministers and the chaplain of the Seventh New York.

February 24, the day of execution, broke fresh and bright. Reflecting on his friend's last morning, Daniel B. Lucas noted, "He had dressed himself . . . with unusual neatness. His linen was white and clean, and his black silk cravat was gracefully tied beneath a rolling collar. He wore a new pair of dog-skin gloves of saffron color." McClure and Ritchie were with Beall in his cell as the appointed time approached. Lucas recorded that "as the hour waned, McClure looked at his watch. Beall noticed the movement, smiled, and inquired the hour. It was twelve o'clock. The execution, by the order, was to take place between twelve and two."

Beall, deprived of sleep the previous night by an excruciating toothache, was allowed a last meal, which he shared with McClure and the Yankee chaplain. Then came a brief period of spiritual meditation, after which prison officials began the preparations to carry out the death order. Beall made but one simple request: "All I ask is that there be no unnecessary consumption of time in the execution, for, after all, it will be to me but a muscular effort."

McClure and Ritchie were reunited with their friend as he was led from his cell. McClure extended his hand to shake Beall's, but the prisoner only smiled: "I cannot shake hands; I am pinioned." Before the march to the gallows commenced, Beall remarked to his friends, "Good-bye, boys; I die in the hope of a resurrection, and in the defense of my country."

Soon, the scaffold came into view. Before ascending the platform, Beall quipped to the chaplain of the Seventh New York, "As some author has said, we may be as near God on the scaffold as elsewhere."

Once on the stage of doom, the prisoner sat in the chair directly under the noose. Daniel B. Lucas described Beall as the end neared: "Just the extremities of his fingers protruded from the blue military cloth cape thrown over his shoulders, which entirely concealed the manacles of his wrists. . . . Upon his head was placed the fatal cap, the blackness of which heightened by contrast the whiteness of the martyr-face beneath it. This face, naturally colorless, was blanched by long and solitary confinement. It was smooth, white, and almost transparently clear. The eyes, whose dullness and suffusion always betray weeping, nervous agitation, or a sleepless night, were as clear, bright, and calm as an infant's."

When the post adjutant began reading the charges against him, Beall rose in respect, fully expecting only a brief recitation, in deference to his request. Instead, as Lucas put it, "the whole prolix and unsoldierly pronunciamento of General Dix" was to be proclaimed. Perceiving this, Beall again took his seat, his back to the adjutant, his face turned toward the South. Upon hearing the recitation that he was "a citizen of the insurgent state of Virginia," his eyes flashed pride and defiance. When declared to be a pirate because he attempted to rescue three thousand Confederate comrades, he shook his head in denial. On and on went the seemingly endless litany, until the executioner finally screamed out, "Cut it short! Cut it short! The captain wishes to be swung off quick!"

The reading finally came to an end, and the chaplain stepped forward to offer a benediction. As the noose was being fitted around Captain Beall's neck, the provost marshal offered him an opportunity to make his final statement. Beall spoke in a calm but firm voice: "I protest against the execution of this sentence. It is a murder! I die in the service and defense of my country! I have nothing more to say."

Behind Beall's back, a sword was lifted to signal the executioner to finish his grim task. In an instant, the noose tightened, and the grand Confederate schemer breathed no more.

Captain Robert Cobb Kennedy
Burning and Hanging in New York

Fort Lafayette, New York
March 25, 1865

"Turn my face to the South; crack your whip; I'm ready!"

Volumes have been written about General William T. Sherman's fiery "March to the Sea," a bitter, sometimes ruthless campaign that commenced in November 1864. Far less attention has been paid to the Confederate attempt to burn New York City, a scheme instituted at the very time Sherman's bummers began blazing a sixty-mile-wide swath through the heart of Georgia. Of the eight Confederate operatives who took part in the daring raid on America's largest city, only one, Captain Robert Cobb Kennedy, was executed. Kennedy died on the gallows at Fort Lafayette, New York, just two weeks before Lee's surrender at Appomattox, making him the last Confederate soldier executed by the Union during the war.

In the decade before the Civil War, Kennedy left his home near Shreveport, Louisiana, to enroll at the United States Military Academy. He graduated in 1856. Once hostilities between North and South commenced, he offered his military training and knowledge to his home state as a junior officer of the First Louisiana. One of his comrades, Lieutenant T. E. Fell, described Kennedy as “a perfect dare-devil” and observed that “no situation, however perilous, seemed to daunt his courage.”

At a clash near Decatur, Alabama, in 1864, Union forces captured Captain Kennedy. Almost from the outset of his incarceration at Johnson’s Island on Lake Erie, Kennedy sought ways to escape. After failing at several attempts, he spent long, grueling nights digging a tunnel under the parapets of the compound. Guards were unable to detect his escape. Using one of the prison boats, Kennedy safely made it to shore. From there, he set out for the relative safety of Canada, which was politically neutral. He moved on foot through the rural countryside under cover of darkness until reaching the border just north of Buffalo.

Kennedy subsequently joined forces with a group of fifty Southern soldiers who had come to Canada after escaping various military prisons in the North. These soldiers were led by John Yates Beall (see pages 233-38), one of several Confederate agents dispatched to Canada by President Jefferson Davis. They were to mastermind raids on the northern frontier of the United States to keep upwards of twenty thousand Federal troops from being deployed to the South.

Captain Kennedy had been free less than six weeks when he took part in the bold Confederate scheme to burn New York City. The plan was devised by the Confederate Secret Service in retribution for Union atrocities committed during the Atlanta Campaign.

In late October 1864, Kennedy arrived in New York as a member of a select eight-man team commanded by Lieutenant Colonel Robert M. Martin, a Kentuckian. Dressed in civilian clothing, the Southern agents met in a downtown newspaper office with the city’s leading Copperheads (Peace Democrats) on October 28. There, Kennedy and his Confederate compatriots agreed to set a series of fires throughout the city on November 8 so as to aid the Copperheads in their planned Election Day uprisings in New York and other Northern cities.

Not long after the secret meeting, the Copperheads backed away from the plot for fear that it had been uncovered by Union agents. Undaunted, Captain Kennedy and his comrades resolved to set fires in hotels in the city of over eight hundred thousand people. An elderly chemist working out of a basement on the west side of Washington Place was employed by the Confederates to prepare twelve dozen bottles of “Greek Fire,” an incendiary combination of naphtha, sulfur, and quicklime designed to burst into

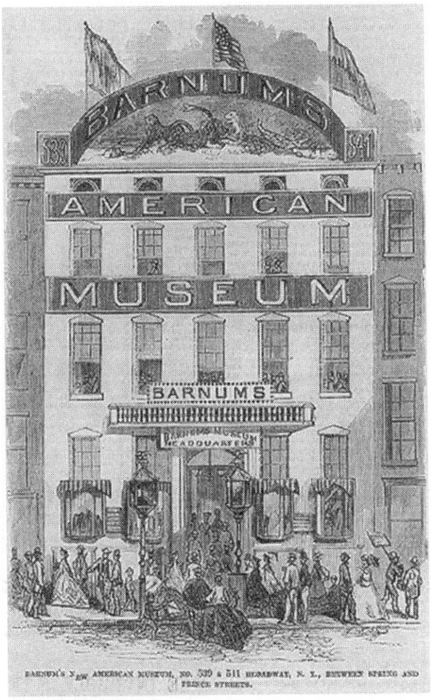

A drawing of Barnum's Museum, one of the buildings in New York City that Captain Robert Cobb Kennedy set fire
Courtesy of Library of Congress

flame when exposed to air. Named for the ancient Greeks who invented it, the mixture had been used throughout history with great effect.

As the night selected for the attack neared, each of the agents booked rooms at several designated hotels, all of them along Broadway. According to the plan, their operations would begin at eight o'clock on the evening of Friday, November 25. Kennedy and his accomplices chose an early hour so the guests of the hotels could escape. When the Confederates took leave of each other on the eve of the raid, Kennedy remarked to one of his colleagues, "We'll make a spoon or spoil the horn."

At six o'clock on the appointed evening, Kennedy and five of his comrades showed up at the assigned place to pick up their Greek Fire. Each man took ten bottles and departed for the buildings assigned to him.

As the church spires of the city tolled eight bells, the agents put their plan into action. After Kennedy touched off fires in his hotels, he hurried over to Barnum's Museum, where some twenty-five hundred people were assembled. There, he heard alarms sounding all over the city. Kennedy reasoned that it would "be fun to start a scare" inside the massive building.

Thus, he broke a bottle of Greek Fire on a step in the fifth-floor staircase. John W. Headley, another of the operatives, later recalled the results of Kennedy's visit: "The greatest panic was at Barnum's Museum. People were coming out and down the ladders from the second and third floor windows and the manager was crying out for help to get his animals out. It looked like people were getting hurt running over each other in the stampede, and still I could not help some astonishment for I did not suppose there was a fire in the museum."

Headley happened upon Kennedy on the streets of the burning city. "I closed behind him and slapped him on the shoulder," he recalled. "He squatted and began to draw his pistol, but I laughed and he knew me." Kennedy exclaimed, "I ought to shoot you for giving me such a scare!"

No one was killed during the night of bedlam, and structural damage to the hotels was minimal. Lieutenant Colonel Martin speculated that the chemist had skimped on the essential ingredients for Greek Fire. In reality, the fires were limited in scope because the Confederate agents failed to open windows to ensure the necessary oxygen. But New Yorkers were outraged all the same. *Frank Leslie's Illustrated Newspaper* termed the incident "the most diabolical attempt at arson and murder of which there is any record in the history of our country." In response to the attack, Major General John A. Dix, the Union commander of the Department of the East, quickly issued an order to hang the Confederate raiders if captured.

Kennedy and his colleagues boarded a train on the evening of November 26 and slipped quietly back into Canada. After spending two weeks in Toronto, Kennedy, described by one of his fellow Confederates as "the boldest of men," was ready to embark upon another perilous mission. He and several comrades crossed back into New York, where they unsuccessfully attempted to rescue seven Confederate generals being transferred from one prison to another by rail. Once again, the Southern operatives made their way into Canada. But this time, Kennedy was a marked man. As Lieutenant T. E. Fell noted, "Few officers of inferior rank figured more conspicuously during the late war than Robert Cobb Kennedy." A Federal detective was on his trail. Over the next several months, the detective secretly monitored Kennedy's every movement in Toronto.

Commander John Yates Beall was captured by Federals in December 1864. With Beall's execution looming two months later, Kennedy decided to return to the Confederate lines in his home state. After reentering the United States, he and a fellow New York raider, Lieutenant John Ashbrook, boarded a Detroit-bound train at St. Clair Station, Michigan. Ironically, during the attack on New York City, Ashbrook had set fire to the LaFarge House, which stood adjacent to the Winter Garden Theatre. At the very moment the hotel blazed, the role of Marc Antony was being portrayed on the Winter Garden stage by Southern actor John Wilkes Booth.

In order to protect their cover, Kennedy and Ashbrook took seats at opposite ends of the passenger car. An hour into the trip, two Federal detectives approached Kennedy with guns drawn. Noting the danger, Ashbrook leaped from the train and escaped. But Kennedy was not so lucky. After desperately trying to fight off the detectives, he was subdued, placed in irons, and taken prisoner. Once he was formally charged as one of the culprits in the New York raid, the heavily shackled Confederate agent was transported to the city he had tried to burn. En route, he attempted to jump from the moving train. When his captors added further restraints, Kennedy held up his bound arms, defiantly boasted that the irons were "ornaments," and told the civilian passengers he was proud to wear them.

In New York City, military justice was swift and lethal. Kennedy was presented before a tribunal chaired by General Dix, whose headquarters was located in one of the hotels set afire the previous November. Kennedy told the judges that the fire at the Barnum Museum was "simply a reckless joke" and that "there was no fiendishness about it." His remarks failed to impress them. Dix subsequently announced the decision of the court: "The attempt to set fire to the city of New York is one of the greatest atrocities of the age. There is nothing in the annals of barbarism which evinces greater vindictiveness. . . . Robert C. Kennedy will be hanged from the neck till he is dead at Fort Lafayette, New York Harbor, on Saturday, the 25th of March."

Kennedy spent the final days of his life in the prison of the fort named for the French hero of the American Revolution. Decried by Southern prisoners as "that American Bastille," Fort Lafayette offered Kennedy no opportunity for escape.

On March 25, just hours before he was led to the gallows, Kennedy put a photo of himself and a lock of his hair into an envelope for delivery to his loved ones. Once on the hanging platform, the Louisianian was offered an opportunity to make a final statement. He boldly began to sing his death song: "Trust to luck, trust to luck, stare Fate in the face; / Your heart will be easy if it's in the right place. / Though Luck may betray, though Fate may destroy; / Be faithful to Duty, and she'll give you joy. / O, had I a score of lives, I would give / One and all to my Southland; I'm hers, die or live. / Though life is sweet, though earth is dear, / To die for my country brings heaven more near."

When Kennedy finished his tune, the executioner approached him with the black death hood. In a final act of defiance, he refused to have his head covered. To the crowd assembled to witness the spectacle, he shouted, "I'll show you that a Southern soldier can die facing you fellows. If I had a dozen lives, I'd give them all for the same cause. Turn my face to the South; crack your whip; I'm ready!"

The noose was tightened and the order given. Kennedy's neck snapped. He was buried at nearby Fort Hamilton in a marked grave reading, "R. C. Kennedy, Rebel spy, executed March, 1865."

Colonel William Johnson Pegram

Tempting Fate

Five Forks, Virginia
April 1, 1865

"I have done my duty and now I turn to my Saviour."

Some of the most tragic deaths in the Civil War occurred in the days leading up to and just after Lee's surrender at Appomattox. Of the thousands upon thousands of Union and Confederate soldiers who died during the four years of warfare, the lives most wasted were those lost when there was little doubt about the outcome. Colonel William Johnson Pegram was one such Virginian who willingly gave up his life in a vain attempt to postpone the inevitable doom of the Southern army.

A member of one of Richmond's most distinguished families, Willie Pegram did not hesitate to leave the University of Virginia at the age of nineteen in the spring of 1861 to rally to the defense of the South. In his hometown, which was soon to become the capital of the Confederacy, Willie enlisted as a private in the artillery. His older brother, John, a graduate of West Point, soon followed his example.

Over the first twelve months of the war, Willie displayed outstanding gallantry while manning the big guns in battle. On June 27, 1862, he rendered a masterful performance at Mechanicsville during the Seven Days' Campaign. His efforts helped keep the Union army of General George

A drawing depicting the last moments of Willie Pegram
COURTESY OF *CONFEDERATE VETERAN*

McClellan at bay from Willie's beloved Richmond.

As a reward, Confederate officials promoted him to major and presented him with the command of five batteries in the late summer of 1862. The vaunted battalion that bore his name earned distinction in the great battles that followed over the next year—Cedar Run, Second Manassas, Chantilly, Chancellorsville, and Gettysburg. Meanwhile, its youthful commander acquired the soubriquet "Lee's Boy Artillerist."

On the battlefield, Willie was anything but a boy. He so impressed officials in the Confederate capital that he was recommended for appointment as a brigadier of the infantry. But Robert E. Lee, unwilling to lose his artillery genius, objected. Insisting that Pegram "could not be spared from the artillery," the commander of the Army of Northern Virginia promoted him to colonel of artillery, which was deemed to be a higher rank than brigadier general of infantry.

When Willie's name was posted for promotion, his brother was already a brigadier general. Ever modest about the prospects of high command, Willie wrote his mother, "You must not think that I am conceited, and that I rely on my own ability, if I get this position and take it. . . . I hope sincerely that before I am promoted to that grade, if it is to be done, brother will be made major general; for otherwise, I shall not believe that they ever promote according to merit. . . . Do not be disappointed if General Lee refuses to have me promoted. He will do whatever is for the good of the service. . . . Besides, I believe that God rules in small affairs as in great. He orders all things for the best."

Throughout 1864, Colonel Pegram used his artillery effectively in his native state as Lee battled Grant to keep Confederate hopes alive. At the Wilderness, Spotsylvania, Petersburg, Benfield, Reams Station, Burgess Mill, and many other places, his field pieces offered thunderous blasts into enemy lines.

In January 1865, Willie returned home for the wedding of his brother, Brigadier General John Pegram, and Miss Hetty Cary at St. Paul's Church in Richmond. Considered the social event of the year in the Confederate capital, the wedding was the zenith of the brothers' happiness.

Three weeks later, both Pegrams were involved in the heavy fighting at Hatcher's Run, Virginia. John Pegram was killed in the battle, and soon thereafter Willie again attended a service for his brother at St. Paul's. Colonel Pegram noted to a comrade, "Words cannot express the grief this blow has brought upon us all. We can only thank God that He did not take him from this world until he had learned to look above it."

In the wake of John's death, friends confided in Willie that Confederate forces might soon have to withdraw from Virginia. His spirit of defiance yet strong, the young colonel declared, "I would rather die than see Virginia given up, even for three months; but we'll follow the battle-flag anywhere."

On April Fool's Day 1865, the ground was bursting with new plant life at Five Forks, Virginia. But on that day, the spring flowers would offer no promise for the Confederacy. Instead, they would serve as the deathbed for Willie Pegram.

During the previous two days, he had spent long hours in the saddle monitoring and engaging the enemy where necessary. Upon his arrival at Five Forks on the morning of April 1, he was cold, wet, famished, and exhausted. No food was readily available other than a handful of parched corn, which he shared with a fellow soldier. Before the battle began in earnest, Willie lay down for a brief nap. His slumber was interrupted in midafternoon by the sounds of musketry.

His gunners went to work, their commander riding up and down the lines. Blue-jacketed troops were within a hundred feet as Willie cheered his men. His youthful voice, hardened by war, rang out, "Fire your canister low, men!" That was the colonel's last order. He suddenly toppled from the saddle. Captain George McCabe, one of his closest friends, described the scene: "Small wonder that he was first to fall. The infantry were lying down, by order, firing over a low 'curtain' which they had hastily thrown up; he was sitting on his white horse in the front line of battle, cheering and encouraging his men."

When he fell, Willie sensed that his wound was fatal. To the comrades kneeling at his side, he mustered a farewell to his family: "Tell my mother and sisters that I commend them to God's protection. It will be a great blow to them at home to lose me so soon after 'brother;' but for myself, I am ready. I have done my duty, and now I turn to my Saviour."

Once Colonel Pegram went down, the Union attackers overwhelmed the Confederates at Five Forks and turned the right flank of Robert E. Lee's army. Willie Pegram was subsequently laid to rest at the side of his brother in a plot overlooking the James River in Richmond's famous Hollywood Cemetery. Just days later, Lee surrendered the Army of Northern Virginia at Appomattox, less than a hundred miles from Willie's freshly dug grave, which was covered with the flowers of spring.

Edmund Ruffin, Fire-Eater

The First and Last Shots of the War

Amelia County, Virginia
June 17, 1865

"And now with my latest writing and utterance, and with what will be near my last breath, I here repeat and would willingly proclaim my unmitigated hatred to Yankee rule."

In a conflict that involved millions of soldiers, it is ironic that the first and last symbolic shots of the Civil War were fired by the same man, who was by and large a civilian. Edmund Ruffin, an early champion of Southern nationalism, manned one of the big guns that belched the first shots at Fort Sumter on Friday, April 12, 1861. Over the ensuing four years, physical infirmities and wartime exigencies forced the firebrand to endure the ebb and flow of Confederate fortunes at his estate in his native Virginia. When the ultimate fate of the war effort became evident, the seventy-one-year-old fired one last shot, which came to represent the death knell of the cause of Southern independence.

Many years before he took his life in the aftermath of the debacle of the Army of Northern Virginia, Ruffin gained enduring fame as an innovative agricultural reformer and geologist. Born in 1794 into a prominent Tidewater family in Prince George County, he attended the College of William and Mary in the second decade of the nineteenth century. By 1818, Ruffin

Edmund Ruffin
COURTESY OF *HARPER'S PICTORIAL HISTORY OF THE CIVIL WAR*

was deeply involved in farming operations on James River property inherited from his father.

Upon discovering that the soil on the estate was unresponsive to traditional farming practices, he began the first of many successful experiments that ultimately added millions of dollars to the value of farmland in eastern Virginia. Ruffin's revolutionary work in fertilizers, drainage, plowing techniques, and crop rotation was widely disseminated throughout America by various agricultural publications. From 1833 to 1842, he edited the much-acclaimed *Farmers' Register*. Highly respected by his peers, he was four times elected president of the Virginia State Agricultural Society. As Ruffin's fame spread, James H. Hammond, the governor of South Carolina, appointed him as the agricultural surveyor of the Palmetto State.

In the mid-1850s, Ruffin decided to retire from the active management of his burgeoning Virginia estate and turn his attention to political affairs on a state, regional, and national basis. To that point in his life, he had disdained active participation in politics, save for a brief stint in the Virginia

Senate in the 1820s. Throughout much of his early career, Ruffin had been considered a moderate among Virginia's landed gentry. During the Nat Turner uprising in 1831, it was Edmund Ruffin who had stepped forward to defend the black man wrongfully charged with complicity in the slave revolt.

By the middle of the nineteenth century, Ruffin was of the opinion that slavery must be maintained in order to sustain the economic viability of the South. As the abolition movement grew in popularity in the North and other parts of the United States, he became convinced that the states of the South must leave the Union in order to salvage the institution of slavery.

Lacking the silver tongue of other famed secessionists, Ruffin used his pen to draw attention to the approaching conflict between North and South. His articles and pamphlets, widely circulated throughout Dixie, proclaimed that the South could survive only through becoming a new, independent nation. To further advocate his cause, he traveled by train and ship to conventions and meetings throughout the South. Distinguished by his long, flowing white hair, the Virginia fire-eater became a fixture at gatherings where the fate of the region was discussed.

During the first five years of his crusade, it seemed that his message was not taking hold. But Ruffin was relentless in his campaign for an independent Southern nation. He was present at the hanging of John Brown at Charles Town, Virginia, on December 2, 1859. Following the execution, Ruffin collected the pikes seized from Brown and his fellow conspirators and shipped them to the governors of the slave states. Accompanying the pikes was Ruffin's directive that the weapons be exhibited as a "sample of the favors designed for us by our Northern Brethren."

As regional tensions intensified in 1860, Edmund Ruffin's stature grew. He was the honored guest of secessionist groups in many parts of the South. But in his native Virginia, he mustered little support for his agenda, much to his dismay. In March 1861, on the eve of the inauguration of Abraham Lincoln as president of the United States, Ruffin took leave of Virginia, vowing not to return until his state left the Union. While the fate of the United States hung in the balance, three states invited Ruffin to attend their secession conventions. Nowhere was he more welcomed than in South Carolina, where he was regarded as a hero. In Charleston, Ruffin was named a member of the Palmetto Guard.

On the morning of April 12, 1861, the Palmetto Guard was stationed on Cummings Point, just south of Fort Sumter, when, according to Ruffin, he was accorded the honor of firing the first battery against the Union-held fort. Contemporary reports support Ruffin's claim that he fired the shot that opened the curtain on the Civil War. Modern historians have proven skeptical of Ruffin's boast, but there seems little doubt that his barrage was one of the first.

Three months later, Ruffin made another appearance with the Palmetto Guard. On that occasion, he was back in his native state at Manassas. During the stunning Confederate victory there on July 21, 1861, the fire-eater was bestowed a great honor. As the Union soldiers beat a hasty retreat, Ruffin delighted in firing the artillery that blocked their escape across the Cub Run Bridge.

But age and a lack of military training were not on the side of Edmund Ruffin. Reluctantly, he returned to his home, where he was forced to endure the conflict as an observer. The Federal campaigns against Richmond robbed Ruffin of much of his personal wealth and caused him to take refuge at Redmour, a tiny farm thirty-five miles west of the capital. Despite enormous personal losses, he maintained his passion for the Confederate cause until Lee tendered the sword of surrender at the McLean House at Appomattox on April 9, 1865, just three days short of the fourth anniversary of the famous shot fired on Fort Sumter.

Ruffin's dream suddenly turned into a nightmare. His health was poor; his family had been decimated by the war; his personal fortune had vanished; his cause was lost. For two months, he brooded over what was to him a hopeless situation. Finally, on June 17, 1865, Edmund Ruffin picked up his pen to make one final entry in his diary. Robbed of everything that was near and dear, he evinced a defiant spirit until the bitter end: "I here declare my unmitigated hatred to Yankee rule—to all political, social and business connection with the Yankees and to the Yankee race. Would that I could impress these sentiments, in their full force, on every living Southerner and bequeath them to every one yet to be born! May such sentiments be held universally in the outraged and downtrodden South, though in silence and stillness, until the now far-distant day shall arrive for just retribution for Yankee usurpation, oppression and atrocious outrages, and for deliverance and vengeance for the now ruined subjugated and enslaved Southern states! . . . And now with my latest writing and utterance, and with what will be near my last breath, I here repeat and would willingly proclaim my unmitigated hatred to Yankee rule—to all political, social, and business connections with Yankees, and the perfidious, malignant and vile Yankee race."

Having had his final say in the matter, the man who claimed to have fired the first shot of the Civil War put down his pen. He picked up his silver-plated pistol, placed it against his head, and fired what has been termed "the last shot of the Civil War."

Captain George Washington Summers and Sergeant Isaac Newton Koontz

Injustice in the Name of Justice

Rude's Hill Virginia
June 27, 1865

"Would to God that I had died upon the battlefield in defense of my dear native South."
Captain George Washington Summers

"They are now ready to shoot me."
Sergeant Isaac Newton Koontz

By and large, Civil War combat ended with Lee's surrender to Grant at Appomattox, Virginia, on April 9, 1865. But sporadic engagements between Union and Confederate troops took place for more than a month in the Eastern theater and for even longer at places west of the Mississippi. To make matters worse, as war-weary Rebel soldiers limped home from their final encampments or made their way to receive their paroles, their encounters with victorious Yankee soldiers added names to the death roll of the four-year struggle. George Washington Summers and Isaac Newton Koontz, both members of the Seventh Virginia Cavalry, were the victims of one such incident in the fourth week of May 1865.

In the early morning of May 22, a quartet of young men, all veterans of Company D of the Seventh Virginia Cavalry, set out from their homes in Page County, Virginia, for Woodstock to obtain their paroles. In the group

A monument near New Market, Virginia, which was erected to memorialize the executions of Captain George Washington Summers and Sergeant Isaac Newton Koontz
Courtesy of *Confederate Veteran*

were twenty-two-year-old captain George W. Summers, Sergeant Isaac N. Koontz, Jacob Dallas Koontz (a cousin of the sergeant), and Andrew Jackson Kite. After a tedious climb over Massanutten Mountain, the four Confederate veterans made their way into the Shenandoah Valley, where they ran into a detail of Union troops. Under guard in the Federal caravan was the former wartime governor of Virginia, John Letcher. The two groups passed without incident. But a few minutes later, trouble ensued when the foursome came upon six Yankee stragglers from Company H of the Twenty-second New York Cavalry. After a heated exchange, Captain Summers and his compatriots drew their pistols and demanded that the horse soldiers surrender their mounts. All of the Federals save one lieutenant acquiesced. Instead, he produced his pistol and pulled the trigger at the exact moment one of the Virginians attempted to fire his gun. Neither weapon discharged. The lieutenant then relented, and the cavalrymen surrendered to the Southerners.

The Confederates pondered the gravity of their illegal acts as they made their way back to their homes in the Luray Valley with the stolen horses. After relating the story to his father, Captain Summers expressed his sincere regret. The elder Summers promptly dressed down his son, then went about trying to set matters right. He noted, "When I learned the facts, I told my son that some evil would grow out of the affair. Effort was made to adjust the matter, and several good citizens were induced to go to the camp near Rude's Hill."

Mr. Summers, Captain Summers, the Koontz cousins, Kite, and numerous local citizens reached the encampment of the 192nd Ohio Volunteer Infantry on the morning following the incident. There, they were courteously received by the post commander, Colonel Francis W. Butterfield. After the visitors carefully explained the purpose of their mission, Colonel Butterfield was agreeable to a swift resolution of the affair. According to Mr. Summers, Butterfield "remarked that return of the property would be adjustment of the whole matter, and that the horses and other things could be sent or the boys might bring them over and they should not be molested."

With great dispatch, the property—including $1.50 taken from one of the New Yorkers—was returned. Though he failed to note the proceedings in the regimental order book, Colonel Butterfield prepared receipts for the four transgressors. Both sides were apparently satisfied that justice had been served. The Virginians journeyed back to their homes. Mr. Summers later recollected, "It was thought that this would be an end of the unfortunate affair, but I still think the matter would have rested there but for a circumstance that occurred in the neighborhood."

The matter to which Mr. Summers referred took place on the last Sunday of June 1865. While Captain Summers and his three comrades were attending church, one of their neighbors, William Tharp, became embroiled in an argument with another parishioner about an event during the war. When one of the former horse thieves interceded, the outraged Tharp screamed, "You had better return those horses stolen from the Yankees!" Mr. Summers described what followed: "During this controversy my son and two other boys said nothing. Tharp said he would go to the Yankee camp and get revenge, and he went from the meetinghouse to the camp at Rude's Hill."

Early the next morning, June 27, Lieutenant Colonel Cyrus Hussey, acting regimental commander while Colonel Butterfield was on leave, issued Order No. 3 and instructed Captain Lycurgus D. Lusk, the commanding officer of Company H of the Twenty-second New York Cavalry, to execute it. Specifically, Luck was directed to "proceed to Luray Valley . . . and there arrest and execute severally and all without delay whatsoever, the . . . men who had been guilty of attacking U.S. groups and stealing horses since the surrender." Summers, the Koontz boys, and Kite were listed in the order, their names underlined in red.

Later that Monday morning, Lusk and his troopers surrounded the Summers homestead and arrested the Confederate captain, over the protests of his father. In a desperate attempt to ameliorate the volatile situation, Mr. Summers invited Captain Lusk and one of his junior officers to breakfast with his family. At the table, the Yankee officers, sitting next to their prisoner, listened to the father's impassioned address. According to Mr. Summers, the soldiers "informed me that I could get some of the best citizens and go over the next day; that it might aid in securing his release." The Yankees then departed with their captive without informing Mr. Summers that they also bore General Order No. 1. Under its dictates, the four men were to be summarily executed without benefit of trial.

Sergeant Koontz was likewise arrested, but his cousin and Andrew Kite somehow evaded their pursuers. As he prepared to leave with his captors, Koontz hurriedly penned a note to his fiancée. It read in part, "I write to inform you that I was arrested this morning at Uncle Daniel Koontz's in bed. . . . I expect to be carried to Mt. Jackson, where I suppose they will give me an honorable trial. . . . I am conscious of having acted the part of a gentleman in returning the horses. I have the consolation of knowing I have faced death on a hundred battle fields, and should it be my sad lot to suffer death, I shall endeavor to die a brave man and gentleman."

Once Captain Lusk and his men transported the two prisoners over Massanutten Mountain, the detail came to a sudden halt, and there the commanding officer informed Summers and Koontz of their plight. Despite their protests that they had atoned for their transgressions, the prisoners were positioned for execution. A last-minute plea by Captain Summers that he and Koontz be taken to the Union camp brought a temporary reprieve.

Onward the death caravan proceeded. When it reached the foot of Rude's

Hill, just a few hundred yards from the Federal bivouac, a group of infantrymen halted the procession. The news was grim: The prisoners were to be executed on the spot. Captain Summers begged for the Federal soldiers to wait for the arrival of his father and the delegation who were coming to speak for him and Koontz.

When it became apparent that the end was at hand, Summers and Koontz scrawled final messages to their loved ones. Koontz wrote Emma, his intended, "They are now ready to shoot me. Oh Emma, dearest in the world to me, how can I leave you, but I must." To his father and his siblings, Summers wrote, "Would to God that I had died upon the battlefield in defense of my dear native South. But it has been otherwise ordered. I submit to my fate." As the Union executioners took their positions, Summers dictated a last message to his folks: "I bid you all farewell in this world, hoping to meet you all in a better and happier world. I have been bandaged and tied to be shot, but have sent for Pastor Henkel. . . . I wish to be buried beside my dear mother."

His unsuspecting father—an unavowed Union man throughout the war—and the supporting delegation arrived at Rude's Hill around eleven the following morning. Mr. Summers later described what he saw: "I found my dear, dear George and his comrade on the cold earth with stones for their pillows. He was my only son."

An obelisk near New Market marks the exact spot where Captain George W. Summers and Sergeant Isaac N. Koontz were shot to death in the name of justice.

Captain Champ Ferguson

The Master of Mayhem

Nashville, Tennessee
October 20, 1865

"I repeat that I die a Rebel out and out."

In the annals of Confederate military history, no officer was as ruthless and bloodthirsty as Champ Ferguson. By the end of the war, Ferguson killed at least 120 men, many of them in one-on-one guerrilla attacks. For his unparalleled wave of killing in the Cumberland Mountains in Tennessee and eastern Kentucky, the unrepentant Rebel died by the rope in Nashville in the fall of 1865.

Born in the Cumberlands on November 19, 1821, Champ Ferguson was the oldest of ten children. As a young adult, he became a horse trader and hunter who was widely regarded as a gambler, a drinker, and a rowdy. In the early days of the war, he moved with his wife and children to Sparta, Tennessee. Most local folks presumed that he would side with the Union, as had his mother and nine siblings. But Champ went the other way.

Why he chose to take up arms for the South remains a subject of debate. One story holds that he refused to enter the conflict until the day a detail of Yankee soldiers passed his house. On the porch stood his three-year-old son, waving a Confederate flag. One of the Federal horsemen shot and killed the little boy. Outraged by the wanton murder, Champ reputedly warned that his baby's death would cost a hundred Yankee lives. Another account holds that eleven men, all Union sympathizers, arrived at the Ferguson home one day early in the war while Champ was away. In his absence, they forced his wife and twelve-year-old daughter to remove their clothes and walk down the street.

Notwithstanding the personal outrages suffered by Champ and his family, there was a more practical reason why he joined the Confederate army. Prior to the war, he had been jailed for the murder of a constable in Jamestown, Tennessee. "When the war broke out," he subsequently explained, "I was induced to join the army on the promise that all prosecution in the case would be abandoned. This is how I came to take up arms."

Once he became a Confederate soldier, Champ Ferguson rarely offered quarter to the enemy. Whether serving as a partisan ranger, as a guerrilla, as a captain of his independent cavalry company, as a scout for John Hunt Morgan, or as an officer for General Joseph Wheeler, the Tennessean killed wantonly and defended his actions as self-defense. He once said, "We were having a sort of miscellaneous war up there, through Fentress County, Tennessee, and Clinton County, Kentucky, and all through that region. Every man was in danger of his life; if I hadn't killed my neighbor he would have killed me. Each of us had twenty to fifty proscribed enemies, and it was regarded as legitimate to kill them, at any place, under any circumstances, even if they were wounded on a sick-bed."

On more than one occasion, Champ took care of his enemies with preemptive strikes. On November 1, 1861, he and two comrades visited the home of William Frogg. Although both Ferguson and Frogg were natives of Clinton County, Kentucky, they were at odds over the war. At the front door, Champ demanded to see his adversary, but Esther Frogg explained that her husband was sick in bed and could not have visitors. Ignoring her, Champ walked in alone. He found Frogg, a member of the Twelfth Kentucky (Union) home on medical furlough, in a bed near the crib that held the couple's infant. In an attempt to keep Champ from approaching him, Frogg warned that he had measles. Champ responded, "I reckon you caught measles at Camp Dick Robinson." To Ferguson and his fellow Confederate raiders in the Cumberlands, Camp Robinson, where Southerners were trained to fight for the Union, was a repugnant place. Champ then took aim and killed Frogg in his bed. In response to queries as to why he had committed the act, Champ related rumors that Frogg had been planning to kill him.

Captain Champ Ferguson is pictured on the right in this photograph.
Courtesy of *Confederate Veteran*

He said rather bluntly, "I told the boys that I would settle the matter by going direct to Frogg's house and killing him."

Champ spent his early months of military service in the Confederate guerrilla outfit of a fellow mountaineer, Scott Bledsoe. In short order, he came to command his own partisan band. During the first half of 1862, there was little organized military activity in Tennessee. Murder, robbery, and violence were the order of the day in the Cumberlands, where families and friends were divided by politics and military loyalties. Indeed, before Champ's brother James was killed while fighting for the Union army, the two siblings were out to get each other.

Anxious to rid the area of the enemy and its supporters, Champ and his raiders rounded up Union loyalists. These prisoners rarely returned home. Some were shot to death. Others died of knife wounds to the heart. Champ Ferguson was never shy about using his prized bowie knife.

Mercy was not in the vocabulary of Champ Ferguson. On the day he and his raiders confronted Reuben Wood at his Clinton County home, the old man pleaded for his life. Champ screamed in response, "Don't you beg, and don't you dodge!" Wood died two days later from wounds inflicted by Champ. When he was subsequently called upon to account for the death, Champ said, "Reuben Wood and I were always good friends before the war, but after that he was connected with the same company in which my brother, Jim, was operating. I knew that he intended killing me if he ever got a chance. They both hunted me down, and drove me fairly to desperation. . . . On the day he was killed, we met him in the road and he commenced on me, and I believe he intended to shoot me. . . . If I had not shot Reuben Wood, I would not likely have been here, for he would have shot me. I never expressed a regret for committing the act, and never will. He was in open war against me."

On the rare occasion that he spared a Union man, Champ later expressed regret for his leniency. After freeing one captive, he remarked, "I have a good notion to go back and hunt that man. I am afraid I have done wrong, for he is the very best shot in this part of the country; and if he does turn bushwhacker, he will kill a man at every shot."

While serving as a scout for Colonel Morgan in April 1862, Champ was ordered, much to his chagrin, to refrain from harming prisoners. At length, he promised that he would not physically mistreat regular officers taken in battle. After all, he had no score to settle with them, though he felt they were "wrong, and oughtn't to come down here and fight our people."

After his house was burned by enemy raiders in the summer of 1864, Champ joined the army of General Joe Wheeler as it moved north into Virginia. There, he participated in the Confederate victory at Saltville on October 2. Almost as soon as the engagement was over, he was accused of killing prisoners and wounded men on the battlefield. For the Federals, the incident became known as the Saltville Massacre.

Among the visitors at the Confederate hospital at nearby Emory early the next morning were Champ and one of his lieutenants, Rains Philpot. Champ was outraged that Lieutenant Elza C. Smith of the Thirteenth Kentucky (Union) had killed Oliver P. Hamilton, a Confederate who had tried to surrender. As he searched for the wounded enemy officer, Captain Ferguson was heard to say, "I have a begrudge against Smith. We'll find him." Indeed they did. After making his way to the ward where wounded

Federal prisoners were being treated, Champ shot and killed the bedridden Smith.

Champ was not without his counterparts in the Cumberlands. Tinker Dave Beaty and his comrades terrorized and tortured Confederate sympathizers much as Ferguson did Union sympathizers. Ferguson and Beaty survived several personal showdowns. “Well, there are meaner men than Tinker Dave,” Champ once said. “He fought me bravely and gave me some heavy licks, but I always gave him as good as he sent.”

Despite concerted efforts by the Union high command to capture or kill Champ, he remained free until May 26, 1865, when he turned himself in at his hometown, fully expecting to receive a parole, as had his fellow partisans who had surrendered. To his dismay, he was arrested and imprisoned in Nashville.

Federal authorities had decided to make an example of Champ Ferguson. Ignoring similar cruelties perpetrated by pro-Unionists in the Cumberlands, Northern journalists had a field day when they came to Tennessee to cover the trial. Their papers condemned Champ as “a monstrous criminal” and lauded Tinker Dave Beaty as “the celebrated Union scout.”

From July 11 to September 26, 1865, the military tribunal hearing the case against Champ Ferguson called witness after witness, many of them unreliable. When the prosecution rested, the defendant produced a few character witnesses, including the revered Confederate general Joe Wheeler, all to no effect. Lieutenant B. L. Ridley, a Confederate veteran, summarized Champ’s legal quandry: “His nature had instilled in him the strongest incentive of wreaking vengeance for a wrong. His method was indiscreet, his warfare contemptible; but in palliation, how was it compared to the open murder of starving out our women and children, burning our houses, and pillaging our homes?” There was little surprise on October 10 when general orders were issued upholding Champ’s conviction and decreeing his death by hanging.

The grim spectacle of the gallows took place in Nashville ten days later. Standing silently near the deadly rope, Champ listened intently as Colonel J. N. Shaftner of the Nineteenth Michigan read his litany of offenses: how he had slashed the throats of wounded soldiers; how he had killed citizens as well as soldiers; how he had murdered a father with his daughter clinging to him; how he said as he killed one of his victims, “That’s ninety-seven of the Yankees gone, and I'll go and kill three more to make it an even hundred." As Shaftner continued the recitation, Champ quipped, "I could tell it better than that." The colonel responded curtly, "No doubt you could, for you saw it."

Champ's wife and sixteen-year-old daughter watched in tears as Shaftner turned to the prisoner and said, "Well, Champ, you hear what these say, and I am about to carry them out and execute you. I hope you bear me no malice for the discharge of my duty."

Champ responded, "Not the least—none in the world."

Colonel Shaftner asked, "Do you want to say anything? Have you a request to make?"

Champ expressed the wish that he be buried in a graveyard near his house. Then he looked at his executioner and said, "I wish you would wipe my face before I go." After Colonel Shaftner obliged him, Champ uttered his final statement: "I was a Southern man at the start. I am yet, and will die a Rebel. I believe I was right in all I did. I repeat that I die a Rebel out and out, and my last request is that my body be removed to White County, Tennessee, and be buried in good Rebel soil."

The order was given, and Champ Ferguson dangled at the end of the rope, thus putting to an end a long chapter of death in the Cumberlands.

Bibliography

Allan, William. *History of the Campaign of Gen. T. J. (Stonewall) Jackson in the Shenandoah Valley of Virginia*. 1880. Reprint, Dayton, Ohio: Morningside Bookshop, 1974.

Anderson, Bern. *By Sea and by River: The Naval History of the Civil War*. 1962. Reprint, New York: Da Capo Press, 1989.

Appleton, W. S. *The Family of Armistead of Virginia*. Boston: Press of David Clapp & Son, 1899.

Ashe, Samuel A. "The Charge at Gettysburg." *North Carolina Booklet* 1, no. 11 (1902).

———. *History of North Carolina*. 2 vols. Raleigh, N.C.: Edwards and Broughton, 1925.

Ashe, Samuel A., Stephen B. Weeks, and Charles L. Van Noppen, eds. *Biographical History of North Carolina*. 8 vols. Greensboro, N.C.: Charles L. Van Noppen, 1905-17.

Bakeless, John. *Spies of the Confederacy*. Philadelphia and New York: J. B. Lippincott Co., 1970.

Barefoot, Daniel W. *General Robert F. Hoke: Lee's Modest Warrior*. Winston-Salem, N.C.: John F. Blair, Publisher, 1996.

Bauer, K. Jack. *The Mexican War, 1846-1848*. Norwalk, Conn.: Easton Press, 1990.

Bearss, Ed, and Chris Calkins. *Battle of Five Forks*. Lynchburg, Va.: H. E. Howard, 1985.

Bennett, W. W. *The Great Revival in the Southern Armies*. Harrisonburg, Va.: Sprinkle Publications, 1989.

Bigelow, John. *The Peach Orchard: Gettysburg, July 2, 1863*. Minneapolis: Kimball-Storer, 1910.

Bond, W. R. *Pickett or Pettigrew?* 1888. Reprint, Gaithersburg, Md.: Butternut Press, 1984.

Booksher, William R., and David K. Snider. *Glory at a Gallop: Tales of the Confederate Cavalry.* Washington, D.C.: Brassey's, 1993.

Brandt, Nat. *The Man Who Tried to Burn New York.* Syracuse, N.Y.: Syracuse University Press, 1996.

Bridges, Hal. *Lee's Maverick General: Daniel Harvey Hill.* New York: McGraw-Hill, 1961.

Buck, Irving A. *Cleburne and His Command.* Dayton, Ohio: Morningside Bookshop, 1982.

Bushong, Millard K. *General Turner Ashby and Stonewall's Valley Campaign.* Verona, Va.: McClure Printing Co., 1980.

Cannon, Devereaux D. *The Flags of the Confederacy: An Illustrated History.* Wilmington, N.C.: Broadfoot Publishing Co., 1988.

Carmichael, Peter S. *Lee's Young Artillerist: William R. J. Pegram.* Charlottesville: University of Virginia Press, 1995.

Castel, Albert E. *Decision in the West: The Atlanta Campaign of 1864.* Lawrence: University of Kansas Press, 1992.

Clark, Walter, ed. *Histories of the Several Regiments and Battalions from North Carolina in the Great War, 1861-1865.* Raleigh: State of North Carolina, 1901.

Clemmer, Gregg S. *Valor in Gray: The Recipients of the Confederate Medal of Honor.* Staunton, Va.: Hearthside Publishing Co., 1998.

Connell, Moody K. *Rebel Scouts: The Last Ride Home.* Privately published, 1995.

Cooke, John Esten. *Stonewall Jackson: A Military Biography.* New York: D. Appleton and Co., 1886.

Cozzens, Peter. *No Better Place to Die: The Battle of Stones River.* Champaign-Urbana: University of Illinois Press, 1990.

———. *This Terrible Sound: The Battle of Chickamauga.* Champaign-Urbana: University of Illinois Press, 1996.

Craven, Avery O. *Edmund Ruffin, Southerner: A Study in Secession.* Baton Rouge: Louisiana State University Press, 1966.

Cunningham, S. A., ed. *Confederate Veteran Magazine.* 40 vols. 1893-1932. Reprint, Wilmington, N.C.: Broadfoot Publishing Co., 1987-88.

Current, Richard, ed. *Encyclopedia of the Confederacy.* 4 vols. New York: Simon & Schuster, 1993.

Dabney, R. L. *Life and Campaigns of Lieut.-Gen. Thomas J. Jackson.* Harrisonburg, Va.: Sprinkle Publications, 1983.

Davis, Archie K. *Boy Colonel of the Confederacy: The Life and Times of Henry King Burgwyn, Jr.* Chapel Hill: University of North Carolina Press, 1985.

Davis, Burke. *Jeb Stuart: The Last Cavalier.* New York: Rinehart, 1957.

Davis, William, ed. *The Confederate General.* 6 vols. Harrisburg, Pa.: National Historical Society, 1991.

Davis, William C. *The Orphan Brigade.* Baton Rouge: Louisiana State University Press, 1983.

Dekay, James T. *The Rebel Raiders: The Astonishing History of the Confederacy's Secret Navy.* New York: Ballantine Books, 2002.

Detzer, David. *Donnybrook: The Battle of Bull Run, 1861.* New York: Harcourt, 2004.

Dickert, D. Augustus. *History of Kershaw's Brigade.* Wilmington, N.C.: Broadfoot Publishing Co., 1990.

Douglas, Henry Kyd. *I Rode with Stonewall.* Chapel Hill: University of North Carolina Press, 1968.

Downey, Fairfax. *Clash of Cavalry: The Battle of Brandy Station.* New York: David McKay Co., 1959.

Drake, James V. *Life of General Robert Hatton.* Nashville, Tenn., 1867.

Early, Jubal Anderson. *Jubal Early's Memoirs: Autobiographical Sketch and Narrative of the War Between the States.* Baltimore, Md.: Nautical and Aviation Publishing Co. of America, 1989.

Faust, Patricia, ed. *Historical Times Illustrated Encyclopedia of the Civil War.* New York: Harper & Row, 1986.

Foote, Shelby. *The Civil War: A Narrative.* 3 vols. New York: Random House, 1958.

Freeman, Douglas Southall. *Lee's Lieutenants.* 3 vols. New York: Charles Scribner's Sons, 1942-43.

———. *R. E. Lee.* 4 vols. New York: Charles Scribner's Sons, 1934.

Gabner, Virginia Armistead. *The Armistead Family, 1610-1910.* Richmond, Va.: Whittier & Shepperson Printers, 1910.

Gallagher, Gary E., ed. *The First Day at Gettysburg.* Kent, Ohio: Kent State University, 1992.

Gallagher, Gary W. *Stephen Dodson Ramseur: Lee's Gallant General.* Chapel Hill: University of North Carolina Press, 1985.

Gragg, Rod. *Covered with Glory: The 26th North Carolina Infantry at*

Gettysburg. New York: HarperCollins, 2000.

Hale, Laura Virginia. *Four Valiant Years in the Lower Shenandoah Valley*. Strasburg, Va.: Shenandoah Publishing, 1973.

Harrison, Kathy George, and John W. Busey. *Nothing But Glory: Pickett's Division at Gettysburg*. Gettysburg, Pa.: Thomas Publications, 1993.

Hassler, William W. *Colonel John Pelham: Lee's Boy Artillerist*. Chapel Hill: University of North Carolina Press, 1960.

Hirshson, Stanley. *Grenville M. Dodge*. Bloomington: Indiana University Press, 1967.

Iobst, Richard W., and Louis H. Manarin. *The Bloody Sixth: The Sixth North Carolina Regiment, Confederate States of America*. Gaithersburg, Md.: Butternut Press, 1987.

Jones, J. William. *Christ in the Camp*. Harrisonburg, Va.: Sprinkle Publications, 1986.

Jones, Terry. *Lee's Tigers: The Louisiana Infantry in the Army of Northern Virginia*. Baton Rouge: Louisiana State University Press, 1987.

Jones, Virgil Carrington. *Gray Ghosts and Rebel Raiders*. New York: Henry Holt and Co., 1956.

______. *Ranger Mosby*. Chapel Hill: University of North Carolina Press, 1944.

Jordan, Weymouth T., Jr., et al. *North Carolina Troops, 1861-1865*. 15 vols. Raleigh: North Carolina Division of Archives and History, 1966-2003.

Kinchen, Oscar A. *Confederate Operations in Canada and the North*. North Quincy, Mass.: Christopher Publishing House, 1970.

Krick, Robert K. *Lee's Colonels*. Dayton, Ohio: Morningside House, 1991.

Lewis, Thomas A. *The Guns of Cedar Creek*. New York: Harper & Row, 1988.

Longacre, Edward G. *Pickett: Leader of the Charge*. Shippensburg, Pa.: White Mane Publishing, 1995.

Lonn, Ella. *Foreigners in the Confederacy*. Chapel Hill: University of North Carolina Press, 1940.

McDonough, James L., and Thomas Connelly. *Five Tragic Hours: The Battle of Franklin*. Knoxville: University of Tennessee Press, 1983.

McKee, James W. "William Barksdale: The Intrepid Mississippian." Ph.D. diss., Mississippi State University, 1966.

Mitchell, Betty. *Edmund Ruffin*. Bloomington: University of Indiana Press, 1981.

Mitchell, Reid. *Civil War Soldiers: Their Expectations and Their Experiences.* New York: Viking, 1988.

Moore, Frank, ed. *Rebellion Record.* 12 vols. New York: G. P. Putnam, 1862-69.

Motts, Wayne E. *Trust in God and Fear Nothing: Gen. Lewis A. Armistead, CSA.* Gettysburg, Pa.: Farnsworth House Military Impressions, 1994.

Official Records of the Union and Confederate Navies in the War of the Rebellion. 30 vols. Washington, D.C.: Government Printing Office, 1894-1922.

O'Reilly, Francis Augustin. *The Fredericksburg Campaign: Winter War on the Rappahannock.* Baton Rouge: Louisiana State University Press, 2002.

Pfanz, Harry. *Culp's Hill and Cemetery Hill.* Chapel Hill: University of North Carolina Press, 1993.

Porter, David D. *Naval History of the Civil War.* Secaucus, N.J.: Castle, 1984.

Powell, William S., ed. *Dictionary of North Carolina Biography.* 6 vols. Chapel Hill: University of North Carolina Press, 1974-1996.

Rable, George. *Fredericksburg! Fredericksburg!* Chapel Hill: University of North Carolina Press, 2002.

Ramage, James A. *Gray Ghost: The Life of Colonel John Singleton Mosby.* Lexington: University of Kentucky Press, 1999.

Reardon, Carol. *Pickett's Charge in History and Memory.* Chapel Hill: University of North Carolina Press, 1997.

Robertson, James I. *Stonewall Jackson: The Man, the Soldier, the Legend.* New York: Macmillan, 1997.

Rollins, Richard. *Pickett's Charge: Eyewitness Accounts.* Redondo Beach, Calif.: Rank and File Publications, 1994.

Scarborough, William K., ed. *The Diary of Edmund Ruffin.* 3 vols. Baton Rouge: Louisiana State University Press, 1972-1989.

Scharf, J. Thomas. *History of the Confederate States Navy from Its Organization to the Surrender of Its Last Vessel.* 1887. Reprint, New York: Fairfax Press, 1977.

Sears, Stephen W. *Gettysburg.* Boston: Houghton Mifflin, 2003.

Sensing, Thurman. *Champ Ferguson: Confederate Guerilla.* Nashville, Tenn.: Vanderbilt University Press, 1985.

Siepel, Kevin H. *The Life and Times of John Singleton Mosby.* New York: St. Martin's Press, 1983.

Sifakis, Stewart. *Who Was Who in the Civil War.* New York: Facts on File, 1988.

Smith, Troy. *Good Rebel Soil: The Champ Ferguson Story.* Lincoln, Nebr.: Writers Club Press, 2002.

Spencer, Warren F. *Raphael Semmes: The Philosophical Mariner.* Tuscaloosa: University of Alabama Press, 1997.

Stern, Philip Van Doren. *An End to Valor: The Last Days of the Civil War.* Boston: Houghton Mifflin, 1958.

———. *Secret Missions of the Civil War.* 1959. Reprint, New York: Gramercy, 1990.

Stewart, George R. *Pickett's Charge.* Boston: Houghton Mifflin, 1959.

Stiles, Robert. *Four Years under Marse Robert.* 1904. Reprint, Dayton, Ohio: Morningside Bookshop, 1977.

Supplement to the Official Records of the Union and Confederate Armies. 100 vols. Wilmington, N.C.: Broadfoot Publishing Co., 1994-1999.

Symonds, Craig L. *Stonewall of the West: Patrick Cleburne and the Civil War.* Lawrence: University of Kansas Press, 1997.

Tanner, Robert G. *Stonewall in the Valley.* New York: Doubleday, 1976.

Thomas, Emory M. *Bold Dragoon: The Life of J. E. B. Stuart.* New York: HarperCollins, 1986.

———. *The Confederate Nation, 1861-1865.* New York: Harper & Row, 1979.

Thomason, John W., Jr. *Jeb Stuart.* New York: Scribner's, 1930.

Troiani, Don, and Brian C. Pohanka. *Don Troiani's Civil War.* Mechanicsburg, Pa.: Stackpole Books, 1995.

Trudeau, Noah André. *Bloody Roads South: The Wilderness to Cold Harbor, May-June, 1864.* New York: Little Brown & Co., 1989.

———. *Gettysburg: A Testing of Courage.* New York: HarperCollins, 2002.

Tucker, Glenn. *Chickamauga: Bloody Battle in the West.* 1961. Reprint, Dayton, Ohio: Morningside Bookshop, 1976.

———. *Front Rank.* Raleigh: North Carolina Confederate Centennial Commission, 1965.

———. *High Tide at Gettysburg.* Indianapolis, Ind.: Bobbs-Merrill Co., 1958.

Vandiver, Frank E. *Mighty Stonewall.* New York: McGraw-Hill, 1957.

Walther, Eric H. *The Fire-eaters.* Baton Rouge: Louisiana State University Press, 1992.

War of the Rebellion: A Compilation of the Official Records of the Union and Confederate Armies. 70 vols. Washington, D.C.: Government Printing Office, 1880-1901.

Warner, Ezra. *Generals in Gray: Lives of the Confederate Commanders.* Baton Rouge: Louisiana State University Press, 1959.

Waugh, John C. *The Class of 1846 from West Point to Appomattox: Stonewall Jackson, George McClellan and Their Brothers.* New York: Warner Books, 1994.

Welch, Jack D. *Medical Histories of Confederate Generals.* Kent, Ohio: Kent State University Press, 1995.

Wert, Jeffrey D. *From Winchester to Cedar Creek: The Shenandoah Campaign of 1864.* Carlisle, Pa.: South Mountain Press, 1987.

———. *Gettysburg, Day Three.* New York: Simon & Schuster, 2001.

———. *Mosby's Rangers.* New York: Simon & Schuster, 1991.

Wilson, Clyde N. *Carolina Cavalier: The Life and Mind of James Johnston Pettigrew.* Athens: University of Georgia Press, 1990.

Index